A TRIP THROUGH TIME AND BEAUTY . . .

The lush tropical gardens of SÃO PAULO . . . The Moorish fantasies in the jewels and carvings of QUITO . . . The ancient Incan temples of PERU . . . The sparkling beaches of COZUMEL and ZIHUATANEJO . . . The thrill and excitement of the bullfights . . . The charm and gaiety of the fiestas . . . Luxurious hotels and restaurants near towering mountains and primitive jungles . . .

This Total Travel Planner tells you everything you need to know. Compiled by local experts who have checked every detail for accuracy and completeness. From the splendors of the cities to the thousand natural wonders of the land,

**THE REAL MEXICO AND SOUTH AMERICA**
takes you there—in style!

# The Real Mexico and South America

PAN AM'S TOTAL TRAVEL PLANNER

Published by arrangement with Simplified Travel, Inc.

A NATIONAL GENERAL COMPANY

THE REAL MEXICO AND SOUTH AMERICA

*A Bantam Book / published by arrangement with Simplified Travel, Inc.*

*Bantam edition published June 1973*



*Published simultaneously in the United States and Canada*

---

*Bantam Books are published by Bantam Books, Inc., a National General Company. Its trade-mark, consisting of the words "Bantam Books" and the portrayal of a bantam, is registered in the United States Patent Office and in other countries. Marca Registrada. Bantam Books, Inc. 666 Fifth Avenue, New York, N.Y. 10019.*

---

PRINTED IN THE UNITED STATES OF AMERICA

# Table of Contents

## ACKNOWLEDGMENTS

At the outset we would like to acknowledge the superb cooperation we have had from Pan Am's Offices throughout Latin America. Without their extensive local knowledge, this guide could not have been done. Their reports show how effectively they can provide more help for the visitor during his stay.

This guide represents the combined effort of over 150 reporters from the countries it covers. To all of them a vote of thanks for a job well done.

Above all thanks to Ann Aslan, Project Director; Dee Dakers and Sandy Jacobson, Assistant Project Directors; Brendan Nolan, Wallace Jackson, Gabrielle Townsend and Pat Kornberg, Editors; Patrick Smith, Art Director; Lorraine Johnson, Designer; and Terry Sullivan, Typographer.

We also wish to thank the following for their invaluable talents: writers Pauline Lee, Ron Daniels, Judith Kohane, Betty Thomson, Gilbert O'Brien, Peter Townsend and Errol Simmons.

Researchers, Loralie Collinson, Barbara Crofts, Oswald de Sybel, Derrick Gillingham, Louise Mills and Jane Sears.

Illustrators Adrian George, Peter Brooks, Len Bedford, Leigh Taylor, Mick Wellington and Lorraine Johnson.

Editorial Director: Kit van Tulleken.

As an airline gains experience it learns more than just the mechanics of running an airline and catering for its passengers. It learns a lot about the places to which it flies. Pan Am was one of the first intercontinental airlines and flies more people further and, frequently, faster to more places on earth than any other airline. It is the world's most experienced airline. And part of this experience is a comprehensive knowledge of cultures, climates and conditions in distant countries.

Pan Am's *The Real Mexico and South America* is one of the ways Pan Am shares this knowledge with its passengers. In each guide you will find the results of Pan Am's research, plus the observations of leading travel writers compiled into easy-to-read fact-filled travelogues that get down to the fundamentals of travel. And if you intend to travel as a tourist you will also find a complete list of the most interesting sights the country has to offer.

This guide is just one of the guidebooks in the series. With any Pan Am guide in your pocket you will feel free to relax and enjoy the things that make international travel today's most exciting pastime.

## HOW THE GUIDE WORKS

In this book there are complete travelers' guides to Mexico and South American countries. Each one has been covered in great detail. Broadly speaking, the information is grouped into four categories. First, there is a section on general geographical and cultural information. Secondly, comes a wealth of detail concerning local laws, transportation, airport facilities, accommodations and specific tips for helping you get around. Thirdly, all the low-down on entertainment, dining out, nightlife and shopping, plus a few hints on unusual and interesting things to see and do. In the fourth section you will find all you need to know about sightseeing trips and how to arrange them.

But there are one or two things worth bearing in mind. The world is constantly changing. Prices in restaurants and hotels, and the cost of public services go up and down. This means that Pan Am Publications' offices are the focal points for a constant stream of information. At the time of going to press you can rest assured that every effort was made to ensure this Pan Am guide contained the latest information. But things do change and the publishers think it only fair to disclaim absolute responsibility for accuracy.

**The Weather:** All the quoted climatic statistics are accurate, but freak weather can upset the best calculations.

**Currency:** Official currency exchange rates are again accurate at the time of going to press, but these can fluctuate dramatically. You are advised always to check exchange rates and currency laws with your local bank before you take off.

**Hotels:** Every hotel mentioned in the Guide is known to the Pan Am Publications' staff. But the publishers cannot guarantee that when you get there the price will be as quoted, or that the service will still warrant its inclusion in the book. Throughout the Guide hotels have been classified according to the price in dollars for single and double rooms, wherever possible with bath. The following abbreviations are used: CP (Continental Plan)—room and breakfast; AP (American Plan)—full board; MAP (Modified American Plan)—half pension.

**TRAVELERS' LAW**

A brief introduction to US and International traveling laws and US Customs and Excise Regulations.

**Papers Please:** A valid US Passport is a must. To get one you will need a baptismal certificate, your expired passport, a birth certificate or a notarized affidavit of your birth vouched for by a relative or someone who has known you for a long time. Take any one of these and apply *in person* to the Passport Division of the Department of State, or the Passport Agencies of the Department of State in Miami, Philadelphia, San Diego, New Orleans, Los Angeles, San Francisco, Seattle, Honolulu, Chicago, Washington DC, Boston and New York; in other cities apply to the Clerk of a Federal Court or at selected Post Offices. You will also need two identical photographs (front view head and shoulders, 2¼" x 3" on a white background; get several copies, you may need them for visas) and a check or money order for $12 (no cash). A single passport can cover your whole family and it will remain valid for a five-year period. Remember, when traveling, always carry your passport with you—**never pack it in your baggage.** Do not surrender it except to authorized immigration authorities and, when required to do so, to hotel receptionists.

Many countries also require your passport to carry a visa stamp before you may enter. These stamps are issued for a small fee by the Embassies and Consulates for the countries concerned. When your itinerary is settled check with your Pan Am office or travel agent to find out which visas you require. In each chapter of this book you will find a list of the vaccination certificates you will need. Under the World Health Organization Regulations many countries require visitors to have been vaccinated against smallpox, cholera and yellow fever. The respective validity of these certificates is as follows: smallpox, three years; cholera six months; yellow fever 10 years. Typhus and typhoid-paratyphoid innoculations are not required under WHO Regulations but in some countries they are advisable. If you are in any doubt about vaccination procedures, call Pan Am. They have all the forms and can direct you to an approved doctor or clinic. Have all your necessary documentation in order long before you leave.

**Papers Please—Other Nationalities:** The ground rules for international traveling are the same for all nationalities although the procedures for application, validity and cost of passports and visas, varies from country to country. The World Health Organization Regulations apply irrespective of nationality. Find out what papers you require by calling your nearest Pan Am office.

**What Your Travel Agent Can Do:** Your travel agent will book your flight and hotel and make arrangements for any additional rail, sea or bus travel. He is also helpful for information, itineraries, reservations, vaccinations and other queries.

**Bringing It All Back Home:** The duty-free allowances you may take into each country are dealt with in the country listings. First a word about what you will be able to bring back into the States.

One of the great joys of traveling is shopping en route. The US Customs Authorities are pretty lenient with travelers from abroad provided the goods they have brought are:

- Self-evidently for the travelers' own use, or gifts
- The goods are declared on arrival in the US
- The goods were not ordered before original departure date from the US

You are allowed to bring in goods purchased abroad up to $100 in value, provided your stay outside the US exceeds 48 hours. If you are arriving from the US Virgin Islands, Guam or American Samoa, you may bring in goods worth up to $200. Such items must accompany you on the flights and it is a good idea to keep receipts to prove the value of your purchases. You may, however, also send gifts by post to the US, although the value of such gifts must not exceed $10 each.

Original works of art and antiques (articles over 100 years old) may be brought into the US duty free, provided they are accompanied by a document which supports their authenticity. You may bring in an unlimited quantity of cigarettes 1 quart of wine or spirits and 100 cigars. Coming from the US Virgin Islands, Guam or American Samoa, you may bring in 1 gallon of wines or spirits.

If you have taken a quick business trip outside the US and are ineligible for the above duty exemptions, then you qualify for the "ten dollar rule". In this case you may bring in goods to the value of $10—a maximum of 50 cigarettes; 10 cigars or a half pound of tobacco.

**General US Excise Regulations:** Meats, fruits, vegetables, plants and plant products will be impounded and destroyed by the US Customs unless they are accompanied by an import license from a US Government Agency. Similar restrictions apply to the furs and pelts of "endangered species" such as leopard skins. Dogs must have proof of a rabies vaccination at least one month before their arrival in the States, unless they have come directly from: Australia, The Bahamas, Bermuda, Denmark, Eire, Fiji, Iceland, Jamaica, New Zealand, Norway, Sweden or Great Britain. Healthy cats are usually admitted without vaccination certificates unless arriving from a rabies-endemic country.

The importation or purchase abroad of anything originating in North Korea, North Vietnam, Rhodesia or Cuba, is prohibited without a US Treasury license—don't bother to try to get one, it is almost impossible for tourists. You are, however, now permitted to enter the US with goods made in Communist China.

## HEALTH, WEALTH AND HAPPY TRAVELING

There was a time when traveling in hot countries was a health hazard. Now, provided you adhere strictly to your own personal hygiene rules, there is very little harm you can come to, no matter where you travel. Minor stomach upsets are the most common cause for complaint, more often than not caused by a change in diet and drinking water. If you want to play safe, drink bottled water (available everywhere) and avoid split fruit. And do take care in the sun—start your sun tanning by easy stages and do not forget you can catch sunburn very quickly in the tropics, even when the sky is overcast.

**Intermedic** at 777 Third Avenue, New York, NY 10017, is an organization formed to enable its traveling members to obtain immediate help from highly qualfied, English-speaking physicians. Members are assured that fees will not exceed $8 for the first office visit, $10 for the first house (or hotel) call, or $15 for an emergency night time call. Intermedic provides a directory of 340 participating physicians in 174 cities in 80 countries overseas, with their day and night telephone numbers. The directory also has pages to be filled in with member's medical history. Membership to Intermedic is sold directly from its headquarters and through travel agents. Annual dues are $5 for a single member and $9 for a family membership.

**Wealth:** The best way to carry money when traveling is in travelers' checks. They can be cashed almost anywhere in the world at almost anytime. But do not forget to tear out the counterfoil and keep it separate from the checks themselves. This enables you to claim in the event of loss. It is also useful to carry a few single dollar bills, which saves breaking big notes for exchange into currencies you do not really need—especially useful during stopovers. It is also helpful to arrive at your destination with some small change in the local currency for tipping. When planning your travel finances you could consider a **Pan Am Credit Plan.** Not only can you pay for your air tickets over two years, but you can use a **Pan Am Take Off Card** to charge excess baggage fees, meals, hotel accommodations, sightseeing tours, car rentals, and purchases in duty-free shops. Over two years the annual interest rate is 18% on the first $500 and 12% on the balance; a quick way over the horizon well worth considering.

**Meet your Pan Am Travel Agent:** If you are planning an extensive tour it will pay you to discuss it with a Pan Am appointed travel agent. Not only will he make sure you get the very best travel bargains for your money, but he will sort out all the arrangements for you. Remember a travel agent's services cost you nothing and apart from financial considerations he will save you a lot of time. Give him a call.

**Photography and Filming:** In each chapter of this book you will find a paragraph entitled 'Photography'—it gives you a quick rundown on available photographic services and any local restrictions like shooting of religious services or the royal family. Bear in mind if you are taking an expensive camera, it is important to carry the original purchase invoice. This will save you trouble at Customs checkpoints. There are few places in the world where 35mm and 2¼ color film is not available, but prices vary and you may be able to get only 64 ASA. If you want really fast film or infra-red, take it with you, but note there are some countries that restrict the import of film to just a few rolls.

**A Salient Point:** Photography will revive the best memories of your trip—but if you are visiting remote spots do not expect people to react naturally in front of a camera. Where the locals are used to photographers you may suddenly find only the backs of heads in your viewfinders until you have forfeited the obligatory coin or cigarette. You may also come across people who do not want to have their photograph taken. In such cases it is wise to desist. Remember too that what might look like a charming rural bridge to you may be a military installation. Another warning: increasingly electronic devices are being used for baggage checks and can lead, in rare cases, to damage of exposed but undeveloped film. It is safest to carry such film in your hand baggage.

**Climatic Changes:** Flying in a matter of hours from one climate to another sounds traumatic. But much of the sting has been taken out of it. Cold climes cater for visitors with central heating, and air conditioning has reached the most distant corners of the tropical countries. As a general rule the closer you get to the equator (which passes through Indonesia and Ecuador) the hotter and more humid the climate becomes. But altitude is also a significant factor—the temperature dropping 5° for every 5,000 feet of altitude. That, for example, is what accounts for the idyllic climate in the mountains of the Lebanon. If you have the right sort of clothes for the climate you are approaching you will have nothing to worry about—read the paragraph entitled *What to Pack* in the next chapter.

**Be Sure to Insure:** Insurance of personal effects is well worth a few dollars on your expenditure. If there is a feeling worse than having your baggage stolen it is not being able to file an insurance claim for it. And again we stress the value of medical insurance if you have a health problem.

**Driving Overseas:** There are countries in the world where only the adventurous are advised to drive themselves. It may be that the laws of a country do not offer adequate protection to a visitor in the event of a mishap. But there are many more places ideally suited to a leisurely motoring tour. In any case, before you travel contact your local American Automobile Association which will issue you with an International Driver's License valid for just about every country in the world. They will also put you in touch with an affiliated motoring organization in the country you are planning to visit, usually a reciprocal service without extra charge. If you intend to rent or even buy a car abroad your **Pan Am Reservations Office** can handle the entire transaction for you.

Alternatively, for international auto rentals contact Avis, 1860 Broadway, New York, NY (tel: 212—765-4820); Hertz, 660 Madison Avenue, New York, NY (tel: 212—PL2-2000); or National, Minneapolis, Minn. (call collect tel: 800—328-4567).

**Electricity Across the Water:** Travelers can avail themselves of a wide range of specially designed lightweight electrical appliances—shavers, travel irons, hair dryers and baby bottle heaters to name a few. Most of them come with adapter plugs to fit the different types of sockets. But be warned: they do not necessarily have a transformer to reduce the local voltage to the American domestic power supply. In fact, most of the world has followed the States in providing a 120 volt/60 cycle alternating current supply. Some places adhere to the European system, however, with a 200-400 volt/50 cycle supply (some remote corners still offer an old fashioned 'direct current' power supply, but most places offer AC). These high voltage power outlets will burn out an American appliance without a transformer. If you really want to carry electrical appliances with you, your nearest electrical dealer will fix you up with a lightweight all-purpose transformer that will cope with just about any eccentricity in power supplies. If a foreign hotel prohibits the use of electrical appliances, it is probably in your own interest not to try. Electric shaver owners should note that a 50 cycle characteristic will make a shaver run more slowly than in the States even with a transformer—but this will not damage your shaver motor.

## GETTING READY FOR TAKE OFF

As your departure date gets closer you will find a thousand and one things that need doing, from arranging for the cat to be looked after, to stopping the milk. Here are a few reminders to help you on your way to a smooth getaway.

**Shades and Pills:** If you wear glasses and you are heading for sunshine or snow, make sure you have a pair of prescription sun-glasses. Be sure to also carry a spare pair of your regular glasses. It could save you heartache later on. If you take a prescribed contraceptive pill, either buy a stock to last the duration of your trip or make sure your brand is available where you are going. Have a doctor write a clear list of any other prescriptions you might need to have made up en route.

**Weighing-In:** IATA agreements dictate that the international free baggage allowance is as follows: First class, 66lbs (30 kilos); Economy Class, 44 lbs (20 kilos). Any baggage in excess of these limits will be charged at 1% of the First Class Fare for the flight concerned per kilo (2.2 lbs) over the limit. In addition to this you can also carry a reasonable amount of hand baggage, provided no pieces exceed 8″ x 14″ x 21″ in size. You will find there is very little problem staying inside these limits if you plan carefully what you really need for the trip.

**What to Pack:** This is a difficult one. Wherever you are going men should be able to get away with one dark suit and a sports-coat, and ladies with a couple of cocktail dresses. Where shirts and blouses are concerned be careful about artificial fibers; some can be uncomfortable in heat. But washable non-iron clothes are always a boon when you are away from home. However hot your destination, be sure to pack at least one sweater (or cardigan) you might need it in the evenings or if you head for the hills. If you are jetting into inclement weather a thick topcoat is a must as is a stout pair of waterproof shoes. And do not forget sandals for hot countries. A small, collapsible umbrella is a useful item anywhere in the world, but jewelry is likely to be a worry. Wherever you go, do not forget your swimsuit. Keep the bathroom scales handy while you pack, and do not forget to include your suitcase as part of the weigh-in. These days smart baggage does not have to be heavy and the lighter the suitcase, the more you can afford to put in it.

**Dressing for the Flight:** All Pan Am Clippers have a cabin temperature regulated to a comfortable 70°-75°. Wear loose clothing and a pair of lightweight shoes. On hand in the aircraft you will find a wide range of male and female cosmetics and electric shavers for the men. However, it is a good idea to have a toothbrush in your handbag or attache case, and needle and thread; a nailfile and a pair of small scissors could go in as well.

**Checking In:** Officially, passengers checking-in after the quoted check-in time cannot be guaranteed a seat on the flight. You should plan to arrive at the airport at least one hour before take-off—two hours if you are going from the air terminal.

**Cooling Your Heels:** Naturally, travelers arriving in a strange country are eager to explore. But you will only cause yourself upsets if you try doing too much too soon. International jet travel is by no means exhausting, but it is tiring in a way that can 'catch up with you' if you do not take your time. All travelers are strongly advised to unwind after a long flight with a hot bath and a catnap. That way you will wake up fresh and in

## USEFUL PHRASES

| | | | |
|---|---|---|---|
| Today | Hoy | One | uno |
| Yesterday | Ayer | Two | dos |
| Tomorrow | Mañana | Three | tres |
| Monday | lunes | Four | cuatro |
| Tuesday | martes | Five | cinco |
| Wednesday | miércoles | Six | seis |
| Thursday | jueves | Seven | siete |
| Friday | viernes | Eight | ocho |
| Saturday | sábado | Nine | nueve |
| Sunday | domingo | Ten | diez |
| Yes | Sí | Where? | ¿Dónde? |
| No | No | How? | ¿Cómo? |
| Please | Por favor | How much/ many? | ¿Cuánto/ cuántos? |
| Thank you | Gracias | When? | ¿Cuándo? |
| That's all right | Está bien | Do you speak English? | ¿Habla usted inglés? |
| Good morning | Buenos días | I don't speak Spanish | No hablo español |
| afternoon | Buenas tardes | Could you speak more slowly? | ¿Puede usted hablar más despacio? |
| evening | Buenas noches | | |
| night | Buenas noches | | |
| Good bye | Adiós | | |
| See you later | Hasta luego | I don't understand | No comprendo |
| How are you? | Cómo está usted? | Can you direct me to . . . | ¿Puede usted indicarme la dirección a . . . ? |
| Very well. And you? | Muy bien. Y usted? | | |

better shape to begin a tour of the places, described in this Pan Am Guide.

**Group Travel:** Preplanned group travel is a great form of economy. On an Escorted Tour an experienced host travels with a group of 15 to 40 people and everything from transport to hotels is taken care of. With **Pan Am's World Hosted Tours** a host meets you at each city and is always around if you need him, but will not interfere if you want to be independent.

## LET'S HEAR FROM YOU

Despite the constant checking and revision work that goes into this guide, on the part of many hundreds of people all over Europe, Pan Am would welcome your personal comments. Where in your opinion have you found the guide to be helpful, and where have you found it not to be so? And where in your experience you have found it to be correct or erroneous. For every 10th letter of suggestions received, Pan Am will mail a free Pan Am Publication. Address your comments to:

Simplified Travel, Inc.
c/o Pan American Airways
Pan Am Building—48th Floor
200 Park Avenue
New York, New York 10017
USA

# CURRENCY CONVERSION CHART

| | United States $ | | | | United Kingdom £ | | | |
|---|---|---|---|---|---|---|---|---|
| | 5c | 10c | 50c | $1 | 5p | 10p | 50p | £1 |
| **Argentina** pesos•centavos | .49 | .98 | 4.90 | 9.81 | 1.17 | 2.34 | 11.70 | 23.40 |
| **Bolivia** pesos•centavos | .58 | 1.17 | 5.88 | 11.77 | NOT AVAILABLE | | | |
| **Brazil** cruzeiros•centavos | .29 | .59 | 2.95 | 5.90 | .71 | 1.42 | 7.14 | 14.29 |
| **British Honduras** dollars•cents | .10 | .20 | 1.00 | 2.00 | .23 | .47 | 2.35 | 4.70 |
| **Chile** escudos•centesimos | 1.4 | 2.8 | 14.00 | 28.00 | NOT AVAILABLE | | | |
| **Colombia** pesos•centavos | 1.9 | 2.18 | 10.90 | 21.80 | 2.56 | 5.13 | 25.67 | 51.35 |
| **Costa Rica** colones•centimos | .32 | .65 | 3.27 | 6.55 | 1.1 | 2.2 | 10.10 | 20.20 |
| **Ecuador** sucres•centavos | 1.30 | 2.60 | 13.00 | 26.00 | 3.02 | 6.04 | 30.22 | 60.45 |
| **El Salvador** colons•centavos | .12 | .25 | 1.25 | 2.50 | .29 | .59 | 2.95 | 5.90 |
| **French Guinea** francs•centimes | .25 | .50 | 2.50 | 5.00 | .59 | 1.18 | 5.91 | 11.82 |
| **Guyana** dollars•cents | .12 | .25 | 1.25 | 2.50 | .26 | .52 | 2.60 | 5.21 |
| **Guatemala** quetzals•centavos | .05 | .10 | .50 | 1.00 | .12 | .24 | 1.20 | 2.40 |
| **Honduras** lempira•centavos | .10 | .20 | 1.00 | 2.00 | .58 | 1.17 | 2.35 | 4.70 |
| **Mexico** pesos•centavos | .06 | .12 | 6.25 | 12.50 | .14 | .29 | 14.60 | 29.20 |
| **Nicaragua** cordoba•centavos | .35 | .07 | 3.5 | 7.00 | .82 | 1.64 | 8.23 | 16.45 |
| **Panama** balboa•centesimos | .05 | .10 | .50 | 1.00 | .11 | .23 | 1.17 | 2.35 |
| **Paraguay** guaranis•centimos | 6.17 | 12.34 | 61.72 | 123.45 | 14.65 | 29.30 | 146 | 293 |
| **Peru** sols•centavos | 2.18 | 4.36 | 21.80 | 43.60 | .05 | .10 | .52 | 1.05 |
| **Surinam** florins•cents | .10 | .20 | 1.04 | 2.08 | .21 | .42 | 2.1 | 4.3 |
| **Uraguay** pesos•centesimos | 42 | 84 | 417 | 834 | 80 | 159 | 794 | 1587 |
| **Venezuela** bolivars•centimos | .21 | .43 | 2.18 | 4.37 | .05 | .10 | 5.15 | 10.30 |

# Comparative Table of Clothing Sizes

All over the world there are different ways of sizing things up. If in doubt, it is always best to try on a garment before purchase.

## Men's Clothing

| | | | | | | | | |
|---|---|---|---|---|---|---|---|---|
| Great Britain | 34 | 35 | 36 | 37 | 38 | 39 | 40 | 42 |
| United States | 34 | 35 | 36 | 37 | 38 | 39 | 40 | 42 |
| Continental | 34 | 36 | 38 | 40 | 42 | 44 | 46 | 48 |

Shirts

| | | | | | | | | | | |
|---|---|---|---|---|---|---|---|---|---|---|
| Great Britain | 14 | 14¼ | 14½ | 15 | 15¼ | 15¾ | 16 | 16½ | 17 | 17¼ |
| United States | 14 | 14¼ | 14½ | 15 | 15¼ | 15¾ | 16 | 16½ | 17 | 17¼ |
| Continental | 35 | 36 | 37 | 38 | 39 | 40 | 41 | 42 | 43 | 44 |

Shoes

| | | | | | | | | | |
|---|---|---|---|---|---|---|---|---|---|
| Great Britain | 6 | 7 | 7½ | 8 | 9 | 10 | 10½ | 11½ | 12 |
| United States | 6½ | 7½ | 8 | 8½ | 9½ | 10½ | 11 | 12 | 12½ |
| Continental | 39 | 40 | 41 | 42 | 43 | 44 | 45 | 46 | 47 |

Socks—Sizes are international

Hats

| | | | | | | | |
|---|---|---|---|---|---|---|---|
| Great Britain | 6¾ | 6⅞ | 7 | 7⅛ | 7¼ | 7⅜ | 7½ |
| United States | 6⅞ | 7 | 7⅛ | 7¼ | 7⅜ | 7½ | 7⅝ |
| Continental | 55 | 56 | 57 | 58 | 59 | 60 | 61 |

## Women's Clothing

Dresses

| | | | | | | |
|---|---|---|---|---|---|---|
| Great Britain | 10 | 12 | 14 | 16 | 18 | 20 |
| United States | 8 | 10 | 12 | 14 | 16 | 18 |
| Continental | 38 | 40 | 42 | 44 | 46 | 48 |

Cardigans, Sweaters, Blouses

| | | | | | | |
|---|---|---|---|---|---|---|
| Great Britain | 32 | 34 | 36 | 38 | 40 | 42 |
| United States | 10 | 12 | 14 | 16 | 18 | 20 |
| Continental | 38 | 40 | 42 | 44 | 46 | 48 |

Shoes

| | | | | | | | | | |
|---|---|---|---|---|---|---|---|---|---|
| Great Britain | 3 | 3½ | 4 | 4½ | 5 | 5½ | 6 | 6½ | 7 |
| United States | 4½ | 5 | 5½ | 6 | 6½ | 7 | 7½ | 8 | 8½ |
| Continental | 35½ | 36 | 36½ | 37 | 37½ | 38 | 38½ | 39 | 39½ |

Stockings

| | | | | | |
|---|---|---|---|---|---|
| Great Britain | 8½ | 9 | 9½ | 10 | 10½ |
| United States | 8½ | 9 | 9½ | 10 | 10½ |
| Continental | 1 | 2 | 3 | 4 | 5 |

## Liquid Measures

(1 gallon = 3.785 liters
1 imperial = 1.2 US gallons or 4.5 liters.)

| Liters | 1 | 2 | 3 | 4 | 5 | 6 |
|---|---|---|---|---|---|---|
| US Gal | 0.264 | 0.53 | 0.79 | 1.06 | 1.32 | 1.58 |

| Liters | 7 | 8 | 9 | 10 | 50 | 100 |
|---|---|---|---|---|---|---|
| US Gal | 1.85 | 2.11 | 2.38 | 2.64 | 13.20 | 26.40 |

## Weight

(1 pound = 0.454 kilogram)

| Kilograms | 1 | 2 | 3 | 4 | 5 | 6 | 7 | 8 |
|---|---|---|---|---|---|---|---|---|
| Pounds | 2.2046 | 4.4 | 6.6 | 8.8 | 11.0 | 13.2 | 15.33 | 17.64 |

## Lengths and Distances

(1 foot = 0.3048 meter; 1 meter = 39 inches)
(1 mile = 1.609 kilometers. Roughly speaking 1 kilometer = ⅔ mile)

| Meters | 1 | 2 | 3 | 4 | 5 | 6 |
|---|---|---|---|---|---|---|
| Feet | 3.3 | 6.6 | 9.8 | 13.1 | 16.4 | 19.7 |
| Meters | 7 | 8 | 9 | 10 | 50 | |
| Feet | 23.0 | 26.2 | 29.5 | 32.8 | 164.0 | |
| Kilometers | 1 | 2 | 3 | 4 | 5 | 6 |
| Miles | 0.62 | 1.24 | 1.86 | 2.48 | 3.11 | 3.73 |
| Kilometers | 7 | 8 | 9 | 10 | 20 | |
| Miles | 4.35 | 4.97 | 5.58 | 6.20 | 12.40 | |

## Temperature

| Centigrade | 40 | 39 | 38 | 37 | 36 | 35 |
|---|---|---|---|---|---|---|
| Fahrenheit | 104.0 | 102.2 | 100.4 | 98.6 | 96.8 | 95.0 |
| Centigrade | 34 | 33 | 32 | 31 | 30 | 29 |
| Fahrenheit | 93.2 | 91.4 | 89.6 | 87.8 | 86.0 | 84.2 |
| Centigrade | 28 | 27 | 26 | 25 | 24 | 23 |
| Fahrenheit | 82.4 | 80.6 | 78.8 | 77.0 | 75.2 | 73.4 |
| Centigrade | 22 | 21 | 20 | 19 | 18 | 17 |
| Fahrenheit | 71.6 | 69.8 | 68.0 | 66.2 | 64.4 | 62.6 |
| Centigrade | 16 | 15 | 14 | 13 | 12 | 11 |
| Fahrenheit | 60.8 | 59.0 | 57.2 | 55.4 | 53.6 | 51.8 |
| Centigrade | 10 | 9 | 8 | 7 | 6 | 5 |
| Fahrenheit | 50.0 | 48.2 | 46.4 | 44.6 | 42.8 | 41.0 |
| Centigrade | 4 | 3 | 2 | 1 | 0 | −1 |
| Fahrenheit | 39.2 | 37.4 | 35.6 | 33.8 | 32.0 | 30.2 |
| Centigrade | −2 | −3 | −4 | −5 | | |
| Fahrenheit | 28.4 | 26.6 | 24.8 | 23.0 | | |

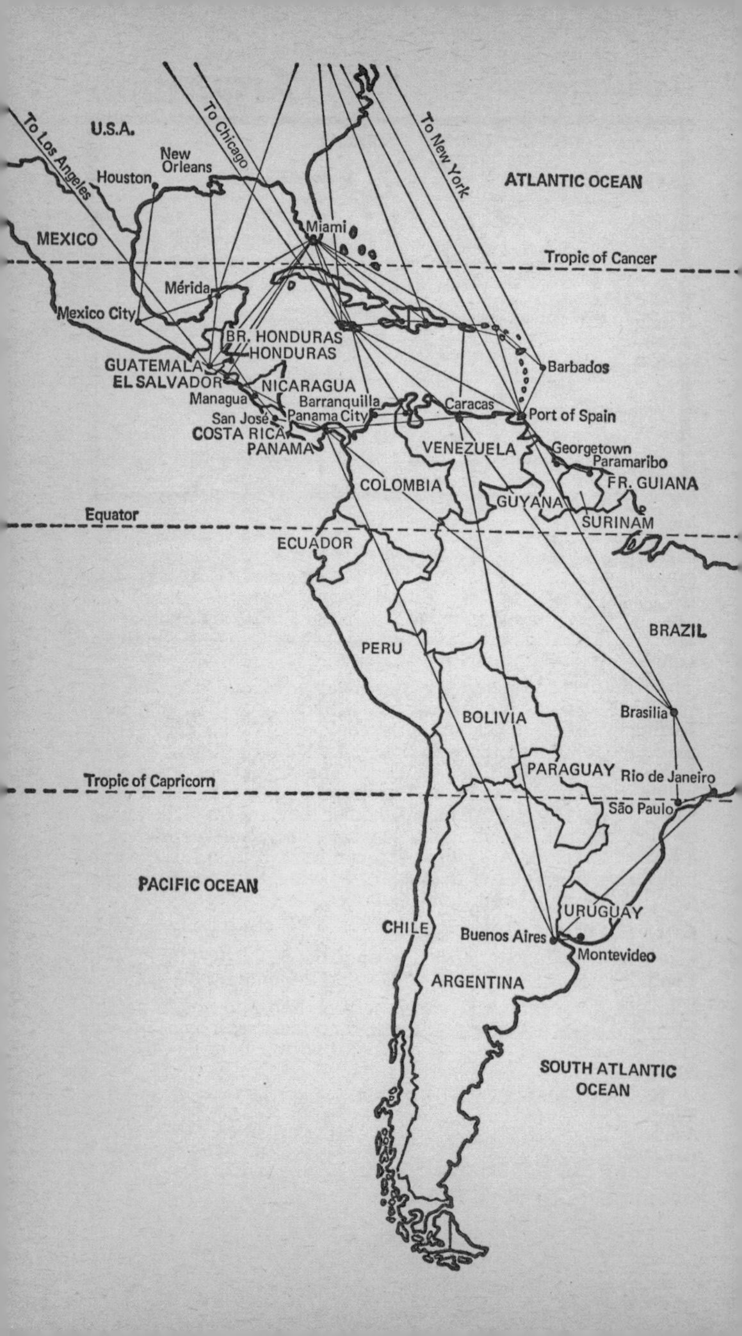
U.S.A.
To Los Angeles
To Chicago
To New York
Houston
New Orleans
ATLANTIC OCEAN
MEXICO
Miami
Tropic of Cancer
Mérida
Mexico City
BR. HONDURAS
HONDURAS
GUATEMALA
EL SALVADOR
NICARAGUA
Managua
Barranquilla
Caracas
Barbados
Port of Spain
San José
Panama City
COSTA RICA
PANAMA
VENEZUELA
Georgetown
Paramaribo
FR. GUIANA
COLOMBIA
GUYANA
SURINAM
Equator
ECUADOR
BRAZIL
PERU
BOLIVIA
Brasilia
PARAGUAY
Rio de Janeiro
Tropic of Capricorn
São Paulo
PACIFIC OCEAN
URUGUAY
CHILE
Buenos Aires
Montevideo
ARGENTINA
SOUTH ATLANTIC OCEAN

# Argentina

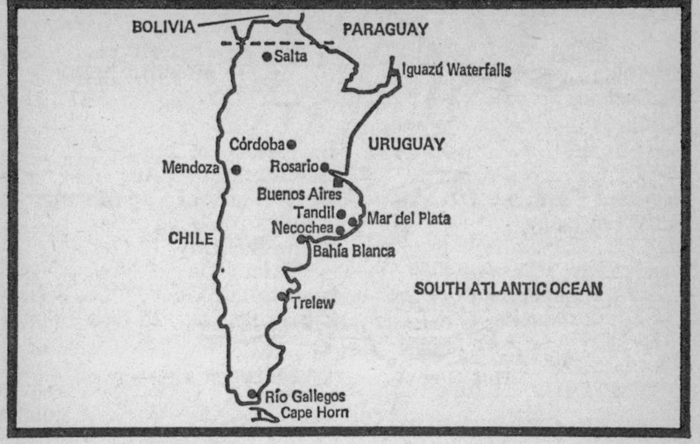


## WHAT'S SPECIAL

A country as huge as this is more like a continent. It is as varied and as different region to region as the whole of North America. Any land made up of tropical jungle with waterfalls, vast "prairie" plains, the Pampa, wild mountains that once were Inca country, through a little "Switzerland" to the ice of the Antarctic, cannot fail to show you something new.

The essence of Argentina is the richness of the land and the people. This really is cattle country—there are over 100,000,000. In Buenos Aires, the capital, the people are as sophisticated and as cosmopolitan as those in Paris, London or Rome. Life in Buenos Aires is lived in high style. The Argentines are a very united people, a mixture of European immigrants and Indian stock. They all speak Spanish. Whether they are from the jungle or the mountain ice and snow, they have one common interest—a love of sport. In Argentina, you can hunt, fish, sail, ski, climb mountains, see a glacier that is still growing, explore the jungle, just sit in the sun, swim from sandy beaches or ride.

## COUNTRY BRIEFING

**Size:** 1,072,749 square miles **Population:** 24,040,200
**Capital:** Buenos Aires **Capital Population:** 8,594,800

**Climate:** There are vast changes from north to south but in Buenos Aires it is temperate. There is no rainy season so you can visit Argentina all the year round. But the best months are October-April.

**WEATHER IN BUENOS AIRES**—Lat S34°35′—Alt 89 ft

| Temp | Jan | Feb | Mar | Apr | May | Jun | Jul | Aug | Sep | Oct | Nov | Dec |
|---|---|---|---|---|---|---|---|---|---|---|---|---|
| Ave Low | 63° | 63° | 60° | 53° | 47° | 41° | 42° | 43° | 46° | 50° | 56° | 61° |
| Ave High | 85° | 83° | 79° | 72° | 64° | 57° | 57° | 60° | 64° | 69° | 76° | 82° |
| Days of No Rain | 24 | 22 | 24 | 22 | 24 | 23 | 23 | 22 | 22 | 22 | 21 | 23 |

**Government:** A Federal Republic.

**Language:** Spanish. English, French and German spoken.

**Religion:** Roman Catholic; churches of all denominations.

**Currency:** The Peso; 100 centavos = 1 peso

| | 20c | 50c | 1 peso | 5 peso | 10 peso | 50 peso | 100 peso | 500 peso |
|---|---|---|---|---|---|---|---|---|
| US(Dollars.Cents) | .02 | .05 | .10 | .51 | 1.02 | 5.10 | 10.19 | 50.97 |
| UK(Pounds.Pence) | — | .02 | .04 | .21 | .42 | 2.13 | 4.27 | 21.36 |

**Public Holidays:**

New Year's Day
Día de los Reyes, 6 Jan
Pre-Lent Carnival, 5/6 Mar
Holy Thursday
Good Friday
Labor Day, 1 May
National Anniversary of the Cabildo Abierto 1810, 25 May
Flag Day, 20 June
Corpus Christi, 21 June
Independence Day, 9 July
Assumption, 15 Aug
Anniversary of San Martín's Death, 17 Aug
Columbus Day, 12 Oct
All Saints' Day, 1 Nov
Immaculate Conception, 8 Dec
Christmas Day, 25 Dec

## HOW TO GET THERE

Fly Pan Am direct to Buenos Aires, Ezeiza Airport, from New York (some days via Rio de Janeiro or Caracas) Miami via Caracas; San Francisco via Los Angeles; Guatemala City and Panama City; and from Montevideo. Flying time from New York is 10¾ hours; Rio de Janeiro, 3 hours; Caracas, 6½ hours; Miami, 9½ hours; San Francisco, 14½ hours; Los Angeles, 13¼ hours; Guatemala City, 8¾ hours; Panamá City, 6¾ hours; Montevideo, ¾ hour.

## REQUIREMENTS FOR ENTRY AND CUSTOMS REGULATIONS

Passport. Visas not necessary for citizens of the US and UK, and a number of other countries. Smallpox vaccination certificate; cholera vaccination advisable; other vaccinations if arriving from an infected area. No limit on foreign currency taken in. Most countries will not exchange Argentinian pesos. Currency may be changed at National Bank (open 24 hours a day) provided you have receipts showing original currency exchange was made at a bank or authorized exchange agency.

Authorization is given for tourists' guns, cameras, radios etc., but these should be declared. They can be cleared for the visitor by the airline or travel agent in advance. Duty-free allowance: 2 liters spirits (inclusive of wine); 50 cigars; 400 cigarettes; perfume for personal use only. Any gifts up to a value of US$150. These allowances halved for passengers under 18. These regulations do not apply to tourists arriving from neighboring countries. No restrictions on belongings taken out up to US$300. Gold must be declared.

## AIRPORT INFORMATION

Ezeiza International Airport, Buenos Aires, is 26 miles from the city center. Buses meet every arrival. Fare is 10 pesos—no allowance for children. No taxis. Fare in private car is 40 pesos.

The local bus service will not accept luggage. There is no arrival tax. Departure tax to countries outside South America is 16 pesos; to other South American countries, 8 pesos; domestic flights, 5 pesos. No duty-free shop at the airport. Hotel reservations can be made through the private car operator (*Tienda León*) at the Airport.

## ACCOMMODATIONS

There is no central hotel reservation service and no off-season rate. If you are staying for a long visit you can rent a service apartment. The best way to do this is through a local newspaper. Hotels in Buenos Aires:

**Single from US$20 (196 pesos); double from US$24 (235 pesos)**

**Claridge** Tucumán 535
**Plaza** Florida 1005
**Presidente** Avenida 9 de Julio
**Sheraton** San Martín 1225-1275

**Single from US$10 (98 pesos); double from US$15 (147 pesos)**

**Alvear Palace** Avenida Alvear 1891
**Crillón** Sante Fé 796
**Italia Romanelli** Reconquista 645/49
**Regidor** Tucumán 451
**Sussex** Tucumán

**Single from US$5 (49 pesos); double from US$9.50 (93 pesos)**

**Castelar** Avenida de Mayo 1152
**City** Bolívar 160
**Continental** Avenida R S Peña 725
**Argentino Grand** Carlos Pellegrini 37
**Gran Orly** Paraguay 474
**San Antonio** Paraguay 372
**Savoy** Callao 181

## USEFUL INFORMATION

**Banks:** Open Mon-Fri, noon to 4; closed weekends. Very few banks outside the big cities. Currency and travelers' checks can be changed only at banks and authorized agencies (travel agent or money exchange).

**Postage:** Mail can be posted at hotels or in street mailboxes.

**Telephone Tips:** Phones in booths and café bars. Useful numbers:

**Pam Am office,** 45-0111
**Airport Information,** 620-0156
**Tourist Information,** 32-2232
**Directories,** 110
**Time,** 113
**Weather,** 32-4480
**Police,** 101
**Fire,** 38-2222
**Urgent medical attention,** 34-4001

**Newspapers:** English-language newspapers and magazines are on sale in Buenos Aires. Local paper in English is the *Buenos Aires Herald.*

**Tipping:** Usual. A service charge of about 22% is usually included in the bill or check, but something extra is expected. About 15% of a bill up to 40 pesos, otherwise 10%. Tip taxi drivers 10% of fare; porters, 2 pesos per piece of baggage; hotel porter, 2 pesos; chambermaid, 5 pesos-10 pesos (only for stays of more than three days); restroom attendant, 2 pesos-5 pesos; hairdressers, 20% of bill. It is usual to tip movie and theater ushers. A tourist guide is tipped about 3 pesos per person.

**Electricity:** 220 volts, 50 cycles AC.

**Laundry:** Dry-cleaning and laundry services are good (dry-cleaning a suit, 8 pesos-12 pesos; laundering a shirt, 4 pesos).

**Hairdressing:** First-class hotels have salons (shampoo and set 25 pesos-30 pesos; man's haircut 15 pesos).

**Photography:** Color and black and white film available. Color costs 70 pesos, black and white 35 pesos. It takes 7-10 days to have color films developed.

**Clubs:** Rotary International; Lions; Kiwanis; Jaycees.

**Babysitting:** Hotels will usually oblige.

**Toilets:** No public toilets in streets but in bars, cafés, stores, restaurants and movie theaters. *Baño de Damas* for ladies; men's—*Baño de Caballeros.*

**Health:** Excellent British hospital in Buenos Aires (Pendriel 74). Some doctors and dentists speak English. Pharmaceuticals are expensive. Drinking water safe in large cities.

## TRANSPORTATION

Good, inexpensive but crowded buses in Buenos Aires; there are five subways and 50,000 taxis; flag one down or pick one up at any stand. Taxi fare is double the amount shown on the meter, but night fares are the same as day. A 20-block ride costs 30 pesos. Traffic is hectic. You can rent small European-type cars at an average daily rate (inclusive of 50 miles) of about 180 pesos-200 pesos. A chauffeur-driven car for eight hours costs about 200 pesos. An excellent railroad service links main cities and key resorts. There are four main line stations in Buenos Aires. The three domestic airline services are: **Aerolíneas Argentinas,** all major cities; **Austral Líneas Aéreas,** major cities in the south; and **LADE (Líneas Aéreas da Estado),** smaller cities of the south.

## FOOD AND RESTAURANTS

Argentina is a big beef country and you will find steak on every menu. For an Argentinian, the main meal would have six courses; hors d'oeuvres; soup; fish; meat; salad; dessert. For the visitor this is usually reduced to three. International cuisine is readily available in major cities but some of the local dishes are: as an appetizer, *parrillada,* mixed barbecued meats; *empanadas,* a sort of meat pie that you eat with your fingers, made of meat with raisins, hard-boiled egg and olives; *bife a caballo,* steak topped with fried eggs; *chorizo,* a spiced sausage—like a hot-dog; *churrasco,* a thick grilled beef steak; *asado,* barbecued ribs; *puchero,* a stew; *puchero de gallina,* chicken, sausages, chickpeas, potatoes, squash and bacon all cooked together. For a dessert try *dulce de leche,* like a sweet caramel custard, or *panqueques al rhum,* a crêpe suzette but very inexpensive.

Meal times are normal, though dinner is usually served later—at 9. Prices are average; dinner for one at an expensive restaurant costs 60 to 90 pesos; at a medium-priced restaurant, 40 to 50 pesos; at an inexpensive restaurant, 24 to 30 pesos. Hotel restaurants with good international cuisine are: **Claridge** (tel: 32-

4001); **Plaza Hotel** (tel: 31-0511). For a choice of both local and international cuisine: **El Aljibe,** in the Sheraton Hotel; **El Repecho de San Telmo** (Carlos Calvo 242—tel: 34-4473) in the old Spanish Colonial style—but not inexpensive; **Hostal del Lago** (Avenida Figueroa Alcorta 6400—tel: 76-8760), a 20-minute drive from town but worthwhile. For French cuisine—but still at the expensive end of the price scale—try **Au Bec Fin** (Arenales 1223—tel: 44-7201); **La Casserole** (Carlos Calvo 2000—tel: 23-3048); **Périgord** (Avenida del Libertado 15/350 San Isidro). You can eat economically at **El Palacio de la Papa Frita** (Lavalle 735) open 24 hours; **Los Immortales** chain restaurant with creole dishes, *empanadas* and *asado*; **El Ceibal,** chain restaurant with creole food; **El Colonial** (Marcelo T de Alvear 1206) for Argentinian food; **Munich Esmeralda** (Esmeralda 444—tel: 42-0644) for good Italian food. There are *bares lacteos,* the equivalent to a soda fountain and hundreds of *pizzerías* or pizza shops where pizza and *empanadas* cost about one-and-a-half pesos a serving. There are sidewalk cafés and tea rooms, called *confiterías.* Popular cafés are **El Molino,** (Rivadavia 1801), a tea room with a turn-of-the-century atmosphere, and **El Águila** (Callao 1120) with very good cakes.

## DRINKING TIPS

The national drink is wine. There is local beer, liqueurs and champagnes. Imported wine and Scotch are expensive. It is important to order exactly what you want, otherwise the barmen will serve you an undrinkable expensive 'cocktail.' A dry martini is called a *Clarito.* Women are welcome in all bars.

## ENTERTAINMENT

There are 250 movie houses in Buenos Aires. Foreign movies have Spanish sub-titles. Performance times are 4, 6, 8 and 10 pm. The **Teatro Colón** is the pride of Argentina and in the great tradition of La Scala and Covent Garden. On gala nights evening dress must be worn. The **Teatro Colón** houses the **National Symphony Orchestra** and its own opera and ballet companies. The season starts on 25 May with a gala performance attended by the President and his Cabinet. Internationally famous conductors, singers and dancers make guest appearances throughout the season.

There is an outdoor theater, **Anfiteatro Municipal,** in the Parque Centenario, which is open in the summer season from January to March. Serious music, often derived from early folk music, is played everywhere. And Argentina is the home of the tango. The legitimate theaters are open all year round but performances are in Spanish. There are also equvalents of off-Broadway experimental theaters.

Buenos Aires comes to life at night with discothèques, night clubs or folk entertainment. It all begins at 11 pm. Take off for the **Mau-Mau** (Arroya 866) the best discothèque in town, the **Afrika** for good beat bands. The **Michelangelo** has three different shows: tango, folk and beat, held in three caves. To see the top tango artists go to the **Tango Norte.** For folk try **Poncho Negro; El Rancho de Orchoa; El Mahgrullo; La Casa de Hernán; Figueros**

**Reyes; El Palo Borracho** or **Achalay Huasí,** all with typical Argentine music and dances. Nightclubs with stages shows are: **Karin; Karina;** and **King Club.** There are conducted night spot tours at 60 pesos to 80 pesos.

## SHOPPING

Shops open 9-7:30 (some close for lunch), Mon-Fri; 9-1, Sat; closed Sun. The shops nearly all specialize in one kind of merchandise each—or they are sophisticated boutiques. The exception is **Harrods** (Calle Florida). Best buys are leather goods and furs, alligator bags and handmade shoes to match. Nutria is a good fur buy and so is vicuña and guanaco fur made up as ponchos, and jackets of antelope suede. Souvenir treasures include a silver bowl, used for drinking yerba tea and the silver *Bombilla* or drinking tube that goes with it; rugs and carpets, guitars and, just for fun, a pair of *Bombanchas,* the baggy trousers worn by gauchos.

**Florida Street** is the main shopping area and is a pedestrian precinct. The fine shops are along **Avenida Santa Fé.** Furs are in **Suipacha Street;** rugs and carpets in **Viamonte Street.** There is no bargaining and no discount schemes. For small gifts (under 100 pesos) look for onyx carvings, alligator wallets, belts and gloves, ponchos and woollen goods. There is a flea market in Buenos Aires at the **Plaza Dorrego** in San Telmo, open Sundays only from 8am-1pm. Buenos Aires is also a center for the gems and silver of South America. **H. Stern & Ricciardi** in the Plaza have Brazilian precious stones and jewelry.

## SPORTS

National sports, apart from game hunting and trout and salmon fishing, are soccer, boxing, horse racing, polo and *pato*—a kind of basketball played on horseback. You can ride, play golf, tennis, swim or surf. Guest cards to the clubs can be arranged (contact the **Pan Am** office). Clubs include **San Isidro,** the **San Andrés,** the **Hurlingham,** the **Ituzaingo** and the **Don Torcuato.** Horseback riding is popular and horses can be hired from **Rustici's.** There is horse racing at **Palermo** and **San Isidoro** and polo matches at **Hurlingham, Palermo** and **Las Tortugas** Country Club. Horse shows are an important social event. Crowds of 100,000 go to the **River Plate Stadium** to watch soccer.

## WHAT TO SEE

In Buenos Aires the best way to sightsee is to take a conducted tour or rent a horse-drawn carriage for a ride round the beautiful **Palermo Park,** which has everything from a rose garden to a race course; from a fair ground to the beaches of Rio de la Plata. Take a ride down the **Avenida 9 de Julio,** said to be the widest avenue in the world. Or go out along the Avenida del Libertador to **Palermo Park,** visit the **Plaza de Mayo** and **Plaza del Congreso** and along the **Avenida General Paz,** or **La Costanera** along the waterfront. There are few old buildings in the capital; it is essentially a modern, rebuilt city. The waterfront district of **La Boca** is the Italian quarter, colorful, gay and noisy. It is full of Italian restaurants with writers and artists turning the street into a gallery. Take a look at **Casa Rosada,** the pink building in Plaza de Mayo, that houses the President's offices.

Among the old churches visit **Nuestra Señora de la Merced** (Our Lady of Mercy), the **Cathedral** on Plaza de Mayo, **Santo Domingo** and **Nuestra Señora de Pilar.** Take a launch trip to **El Tigre,** the delta of the Paraná River. It is a huge network of streams and canals, creating hundreds of small islands built up with luxury villas and strange buildings rising up from the water. It is only 17 miles from the city center, and there is a frequent and inexpensive riverboat service. Do not miss the chance to visit a cattle ranch or *estancia.* There is one within two hours of Buenos Aires.

The **National Museum of Fine Arts,** the country's largest and most important museum, is in Buenos Aires on the Avenida del Libertador. Along with the collection of paintings and sculptures by world masters you can see the major works of Argentinian artists (open daily 3-7 except Wednesday). Visit the **Museum of Decorative Arts,** a collection of paintings, antiques and tapestries (Avenida del Libertador). Do not miss the Museum of Spanish-American Art called **Isaac Fernández Blanco** (Suipacho 1422), a replica of an old colonial house and containing a collection of every kind of old silver, costumes and antiques (open daily except Wed). There is also the **Museum of Modern Art** (Corrientes 1530) and the **Museum of the Colón Theater** (Arturo Toscanini 1150). Museums of specialized interests are: the **National History Museum** (Defensa 1600), with historic military flags, uniforms and arms, with maps and documents covering the period of the Argentine struggle for Independence (open Sun, Wed, Thurs and Fri); and the **Argentine Museum of Natural Sciences** (Avenida Angel Gallardo 470), which is open on Sun, Tues and Thurs. For a really detailed list of all special interest museums, contact the **National Tourist Board** or the **Pan Am** office.

## NORTH ARGENTINA

These are the strongly traditional provinces of the country. In the west, in the provinces of Jujuy, Salta and Tucumán, is the beautiful, wild mountain country that was once the home of the early Inca civilization and, many years later, in the fight for independence, the place where a small group of gaucho soldiers held back the invading Spanish army. The mountains and ravines are fertile and rich in sugar cane and fruit. It is a place of music, laughter and endless festivals. Outside the capital city of **Salta,** the residents of the town pitch tents on the slopes of the hill and sing and dance all night. The flutes and *pincullos, charangos,* and guitars make a haunting music that follows the traveler wherever he goes. Argentina's National Independence was proclaimed in the province of Tucumán, from a house that has been preserved. In the province of **Jujuy** the mountains reach up to the blue sky. **Humahuca** is famous for its natural beauty and its historic Indian past. At **Pucara de Tilcara** there is an ancient Indian fortress with relics of the fighting days gone by; this is also the big-game hunting region. Salta has kept its colonial buildings and atmosphere. Hotels in Salta include the **Salta Hotel** (Calle Buenos Aires 1) single from US$10, and **Victoria Plaza Hotel** (16 Zuvina Street) from US$5 single.

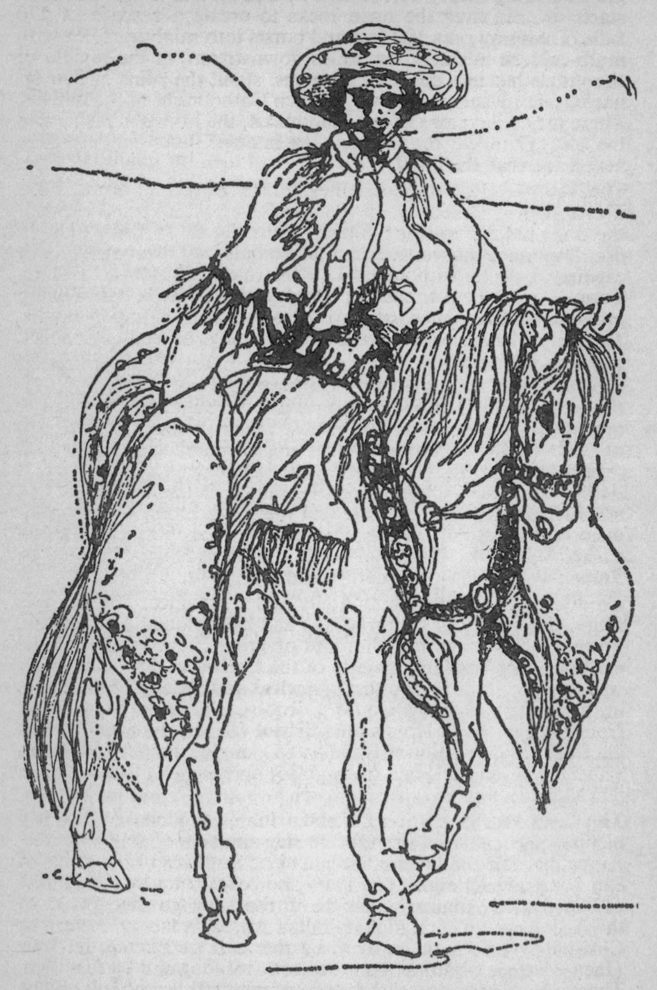

In the northeast, 1,300 miles from Buenos Aires, and deep into the jungle on the Brazilian border, is **Iguazú Falls.** The journey is 5½ hours by plane (or six days by boat). The falls are one of the most important sights in South America and are greater than either Niagara or Victoria. Twelve miles from the point where the Iguazú River joins the Paraná, is an amphitheater in the jungle measuring nearly 10,000 feet by 221 feet. It is here the river starts its race over the huge rocks to create a cascade of 270 falls. The spray rises 100 feet and bursts into rainbows filled with multi-colored birds. A few miles downstream, in the middle of the jungle but in a space of 25 acres, stand the ruins of **San Ignacio,** a Jesuit mission set up to teach Catholicism to the natives. There are the remains of the old church, the priests' college, and the homes built for the Indians. The **Iguazú Hotel** is an attractive new hotel near the falls.

**The Littoral Region** (Corrientes, Entre Ríos, and Santa Fé): This region is linked by the Paraná River, which runs between the three provinces. It is the land of the *dorado,* a fierce fighting fish. They usually weigh 25 to 35 pounds, but there have been catches of up to 55 pounds. The International Dorado Fishing Tournament is held annually in August at **Paso de la Patria** in the province of Corrientes, which is also the land of Indian myths. The people there speak the Guaraní language as well as Spanish.

**Entre Ríos:** This is a province of great beauty. The provincial capital Paraná is on the river, a city with a great cultural life. To the west of Entre Ríos is the province of **Santa Fé.** The large, modern and busy port of Rosario is on the right bank of the Paraná River and is the center of a thriving commercial and industrial region. The city has wide boulevards and magnificent theaters. It is also the place where General Manuel Belgrano hoisted the national flag for the first time and there is a monument to commemorate it. Hotels in the city of Corrientes are: **Gran Hotel Corrientes** (Junín 1549—tel: 4903) and the **Hotel Nacional de Turismo** (Avenida Costanera y Entre Ríos—tel: 3841).

**Córdoba:** The name of both a city and a province. The city was founded almost four centuries ago and has colonial architecture. Towers, bell-towers and churches of great beauty surround the extraordinary style and majesty of the **Cathedral.** The **University** was founded in 1613 and the **Historical and Colonial Museum** is in the former Viceroy's House. Córdoba City is one hour by air from Buenos Aires. Hotels are: **Bristol** (Rivera Inderta 72) single from US$5; **Crillón** (Rivadavía 85) single from US$10; **Plaza** (Buenos Aires 79) single from US$5; and **Sussex** (Buenos Aires 59) single from US$7.

**The Cuyo Provinces** (San Luís, San Juan, Mendoza): Cuyo is a picturesque region at the foot of the Andes mountains in west Argentina. It extends from the plains of San Luís to the peaks of San Juan and Mendoza. As the visitor climbs up to a height of 21,000 feet, the scenery changes to the snow-covered peaks of the **Aconcaqua.** There, high up in the Andes, is the monument to Christ the Redeemer, and nearby the famous **Puente del Inca** (Inca Bridge), a natural stone arc 150 feet long and 90 feet high. There are ski-runs and skating rinks making this a popular place for winter sports and there is an annual Snow Festival. In Mendoza a winter sports center is **Las Cuevas.**

The fertile lands below the Andes makes this the wine-growing region of Argentina. The world-famous Vintage Festival is held in **Mendoza** in March. Mendoza is a beautifully laid out modern city. Hotels are the **Plaza** (Chile 1132), single from US$7, and the **Sussex** (Avenida Sarmiento 250), single from US$6.

**Mar del Plata** (The Atlantic Beaches), is 250 miles south of Buenos Aires on the Atlantic coast. This is the leading beach resort and the Riviera of Argentina. It has the largest casino in the world, some 1,500 hotels, and apartments for rent. The visitor can rent a cabana at Bristol Beach, while St James and Playa Grande beaches are private. This is a great area for fishing and the seafood is excellent. You can ride or make the trip to the *Estancias,* the horse-breeding ranches at **Chapadmalal** and **Ojo de Agua.** Further south there is the beach resort of **Necochéa,** and inland is **Tandil,** in the cool of the hills.

**Mar del Plata** is known as "The Happy City." The season is late December through March. Among hotels are the **Benedetti** (Avenida Colón 2198), single from US$5; **Flamingo** (Moreno 2155), single from US$6; and **Gran Provincial** (Boulevard Maritimo 2300), single from US$12.50.

**The Southern Lakes** (Neuquén, Rio Negro, Chubut, Santa Cruz): Fly to **San Carlos de Bariloche,** the center for winter sports in this lake and mountain area. It looks like a Swiss village and, in fact, the Swiss were the original settlers. It is in the Nahuel Huapi National Park, an area that is divided into distinct regions. **Lake Nahuel Huapi** covers an area of 300 square miles and is at an altitude of 2,000 feet. It is surrounded by mountains rising to 12,000 feet. During the winter season (July to October) there is good skiing. The International competitions during the Ski Festival are followed by the Snow Festival. On Lake Nahuel Huapi there is densely forested **Victoria Island.** One popular place on the lake is the area of flowers and plants of every kind that fill the peninsula of **Llao-Llao,** where hotels include the **Llao-Llao,** single from US$22, and the **Tunquelén Hotel,** single from US$17.

**Bariloche:** Famous, as a region, for magnificent trout and salmon fishing. Best from mid-November to mid-April. There is a special fishing area at **Lake Traful,** four hours from Bariloche. Hotels in Bariloche include: **Bella Vista Hotel** (Sgto Rolando 351) single from US$21; **Cristal** (Avenida Bone Mitre 355) single from US$15; **Edelweiss** (Avenida San Martín 232) single from US$9 and **Pilmayquen** (Casilla Correo 191) single from US$10.

Take a boat trip to **Puerto Blest** at the end of a 10-mile fjord. You will pass **Casada Blanca,** a huge waterfall fed by the great glaciers. From Puerto Blest you can go to **Puerto Alegre** on the Chilean border and continue into Chile, or return to Bariloche and Buenos Aires.

Advance fishing and hunting arrangements can be made through either **Wenckheim Safaris Ltd** (PO Box 484, Bariloche) or **Lagos del Sur SA** (Santa Fé 861, Buenos Aires). The hunting season (for stag, Indian black buck, deer, boar, or geese, doves and ducks) is from March to July.

**Tierra del Fuego** (Antarctica): The capital of the territory of Tierra del Fuego is **Ushuaia,** the most southern city in the world. The scenery is made up of forests and lakes. Forests of *lenga,* a tree with deep red leaves, are a characteristic of this area. All roads lead to glaciers and snow-covered peaks. The rivers are filled with fish of every kind. The largest lake, the **Fagnano,** stretches across the island from east to west for 60 miles. It is a strange, wild country, still as mysterious today as it was to early explorers.

## SOURCES OF FURTHER INFORMATION

**Pan Am offices:** The Plaza Hotel, Florida 1001, Buenos Aires, and Avenida Roque Saenz Peña 832, Buenos Aires, and from any Pan Am office around the world; the **National Tourist Board,** Santa Fé 883, Buenos Aires; The **Argentinian Consulate,** 12 West 56th Street, New York, NY 10019; The **Argentinian-American Chamber of Commerce,** 11 Broadway, New York, NY 10004; The **Argentine Information Office,** 150 SE 2nd Avenue, Miami, Florida; The **Argentine Consulate,** 53 Hans Place, London SW1.

# Bolivia

**WHAT'S SPECIAL**

One thousand years ago, Bolivia was part of the fabled Inca Empire. Today you can see both the ruins of the great early civilization and many of the Incas' descendants. In the past, there was more of Bolivia to see. But by the beginning of this century, after internal troubles and numerous revolutions in the first 127 years of its independence, large chunks of the country had been parceled off to Argentina, Chile and Brazil, leaving Bolivia landlocked in the middle of the continent. In compensation it is called the "heart of South America."

Tourism is not Bolivia's prime concern at this stage of its history, and while there are perfectly acceptable places in the major cities (La Paz, for example) to cater to your need for "creature comfort," you might have to "rough it" elsewhere. Bolivia has the world's highest capital city, the highest golf course and ski run and the highest navigable lake.

**COUNTRY BRIEFING**

**Size:** 424,162 square miles
**Population:** 5,101,699
**Capital:** La Paz
**Capital Population:** 800,000

**Climate:** There is a great range of climate depending on the altitude. Winters are generally dry and sunny. It is dry and sunny in the Altiplano, sub-tropical in the Yungas, tropical around Oriente. Best time to travel is May through November.

**WEATHER IN LA PAZ**—Lat S16°30′—Alt 12,001 ft

| Temp | Jan | Feb | Mar | Apr | May | Jun | Jul | Aug | Sep | Oct | Nov | Dec |
|---|---|---|---|---|---|---|---|---|---|---|---|---|
| Ave Low | 43° | 43° | 42° | 40° | 37° | 34° | 33° | 35° | 38° | 40° | 42° | 42° |
| Ave High | 63° | 63° | 64° | 65° | 64° | 62° | 62° | 63° | 64° | 66° | 67° | 65° |
| Days of No Rain | 10 | 10 | 15 | 21 | 26 | 28 | 29 | 27 | 21 | 22 | 19 | 13 |

**Government:** A republic of nine departments.

**Language:** Spanish. Quechua and Aymara also spoken. English spoken in hotels.

**Religion:** 80% Catholic, 12% Protestant.

**Currency:** The Peso Boliviano; 100 centavos = 1 peso boliviano

| | 50c | PB 1 | PB 5 | PB 10 | PB 50 | PB 100 | PB 200 | PB 500 |
|---|---|---|---|---|---|---|---|---|
| US (Dollars.Cents) | .04 | .08 | .42 | .84 | 4.24 | 8.49 | 16.99 | 42.48 |
| UK (Pounds.Pence) | NOT AVAILABLE | | | | | | | |

**Public Holidays:**

New Year's Day, 1 Jan
Sea Day, 23 Mar
Holy Week, two days
Labor Day, 1 May
Corpus Christi, May
Independence Days, 5/6 Aug
Columbus Day, 12 Oct
All Souls' Day, 2 Nov
Immaculate Conception, 8 Dec
Christmas Day, 25 Dec

## HOW TO GET THERE

Fly Pan Am to Buenos Aires, Caracas or New York, then by connecting flight to La Paz, El Alto Airport. Flying time from Buenos Aires is 3 hours; Caracas 6¾ hours (via Bogotá and Lima); New York, 9¼ hours (via Lima).

## REQUIREMENTS FOR ENTRY AND CUSTOMS REGULATIONS

Valid passport, smallpox vaccination and 90-day 'tourist card' (renewable) are required for entry (tourist card can be obtained from Bolivian Consulates and air transport companies). There are no currency restrictions in operation; it is best to reconvert all money before leaving the country. When entering declare all personal items such as cameras or typewriters to avoid any difficulties when leaving the country. Otherwise one is permitted: one bottle spirits; 100 cigarettes or 200 grams of tobacco; one bottle wine; enough perfume for personal use. No restrictions on what you take out.

## AIRPORT INFORMATION

The airport is El Alto, 20 kilometers (12 miles) from La Paz. There is a free daily bus from the airport to the city center. Taxis are also available at all times and the fare to the city center is about PB20 per person. Taxis are used for journeys between airport. There is no arrival tax, but there is a departure tax, PB60. The only facilities are a hotel reservation counter. Airport porters are tipped PB6.

## ACCOMMODATIONS

For help in finding accommodations contact Dirección General de Turismo (tel: 27521/27522). Hotels in La Paz:

**Single from US$7.50 (PB88); double from US$10.50 (PB123.60)**

**Copacabana** Avenida 16 de Julio
**Crillon** Plaza Isabel la Católica
**La Paz** Avenida Camacho 1277
**Sucre Palace** Avenida 16 de Julio

**Single from US$1.50 (PB17.70); double from US$3 (PB35.30)**

**Avenida** Avenida Montés
**Grand** Evaristo Valle
**Tumusla** Calle Tumusla 580

## USEFUL INFORMATION

**Banks:** Open 9-12 and 2-4:30, Mon-Fri. Money can otherwise be changed at exchange offices.

**Postage:** Stamps available only at post offices.

**Telephone Tips:** Coin-operated telephone booths in restaurants and cafés. Useful numbers:

**Airport Information,** 59421/59320/59231
**Tourist Office,** 27521
**Tourist Information,** 27061/27521
**Directories,** 104
**Fire,** 119
**Police,** 110
**Ambulance,** 117
**Time,** 117

**Newspapers:** English-language newspapers can be bought. There is no local English-language publication.

**Tipping:** Customary; 10% in restaurants, 23% in hotels (included in bill). Otherwise: porter, PB1; cloakroom attendant PB5; hairdressers, PB2; hotel porter, PB2; chambermaid PB5; museum guides, PB12.

**Electricity:** 110-220 volts, 50 cycles AC in La Paz. In Potosí only it is 110 volts; 220 volts in the rest of the country.

**Laundry:** Dry-cleaning and laundry services readily available, fast and good. A 24-hour service in all major towns, and most hotels (dry-cleaning a suit cost PB14; laundering a shirt PB5.90).

**Hairdressing:** First-class hotels have salons (the Sucre Palace and Crillón) (shampoo and set PB30, tip PB2; man's haircut, PB5.90, tip PB1-PB2).

**Photography:** Reasonable selection of equipment; black and white and color film available in major cities, but expensive. Film can be processed in a couple of days, but some must be sent out of the country; it is advisable to take films with you.

**Clubs:** Rotary International and Junior Camara. Rotary meets at Club de la Paz; Automobile Club at Calacoto.

**Babysitting:** Services can be arranged through a few hotels.

**Toilets:** In hotels and restaurants. Ladies, *Damas*; men, *Caballeros*. Often advisable to use only hotel toilets.

**Health:** Doctors and dentists speak English. Imported pharmaceuticals are available but expensive.

## TRANSPORTATION

Good bus and taxi services available, but there are no other forms of public transport within cities. Payment for both is by cash. In a taxi you often rent only a seat—someone else who is going your way may join you. Taxis have fixed rates—PB1.50 per person for short trips. In La Paz there are *Trufis,* cabs with green flags, which follow fixed routes at fixed charges—a taxi-bus service. Extra charges: PB3 for luggage PB.50 per person and an extra PB2.50 at night. You can rent a car through Hertz, Benaro Trigo 429 (tel: 25591). Average rate for rent-a-car is around PB70.50. For chauffeur-driven car it is about PB50 per hour. Drive on the right. Outside cities roads can be very bad. The train service is quite comprehensive and has sleeping cars and food service, but trains are slow (e.g.—two days from Sucre to La Paz) and inefficient, but they do go through spectacular scenery. The new ferrobus is more efficient with reclining seats and meals served on board. The internal airlines are **Lloyd Aéreo Boliviaro** and **Transportes Aéreos Militares,** which link most principal cities. There are now hydrofoil cruises on Lake Titicaca.

## FOOD AND RESTAURANTS

Bolivia and more specifically La Paz, is not the place to go expecting the best in international cooking. The first-class hotels do have good food and sometimes international cooking, but you can probably eat as well, if not better and more interestingly, elsewhere. Meal times are normal American or European. Price range from about US$5 (PB59) for a meal in an expensive restaurant to US$1 (PB12) in an inexpensive one. It is not a good idea to try green salads or uncooked vegetables and bottled water is definitely preferable to tap water.

Some of the best national dishes can be bought cheaply from stalls on street corners. *Empanada salteña,* a combination of meat, chicken, olives, raisins, potatoes, pepper and hot sauce squeezed inside a cylinder of dough about the size of a hot dog is one of the most popular dishes and is available from most roadside stalls. Watch out for the word *picante* as a descriptive word (e.g. *picante de pollo*)—it means that the food is highly spiced with chili peppers. If you go for highly spiced foods however, try the *picante de pollo,* a chicken ('southern fried') with rice, fried potatoes, hot peppers and *chuno* or dried potato. Or have a mounted steak, *lomo montado,* which is a fried tenderloin with eggs, rice and banana; or again, the *parrillada,* a kind of Bolivian mixed grill. If you prefer a restaurant try the **Daiquiri** (16 de Agosto 1965) for *parilladas.* The **Cafetería Ely,** run by German immigrants (16 de Julio, esquina Bueno) serves good American-style food at low prices; the **China** (16 de Julio 1549) and **Mandarin** (6 de Agosto 2570) do a great business in Chinese specialties. Or try the restaurants in the larger hotels.

## DRINKING TIPS

Local whisky is good, as is wine and beer. Imported wines and spirits are available but there is now a law prohibiting the importation of whisky; it does get smuggled in and when available should cost about US$1 (PB12). A bottle of ordinary red wine is about US$1 (PB12) a bottle. Licensing hours are either all day or from 2pm to midnight and the sale of liquor is unrestricted. Ladies should be accompanied in bars. Hotels and coffee shops are good places for leisurely drinking, or look for places called *Confiterías* which are all over La Paz. Some of the more popular *confiterías* are the **Club de La Paz** (Avenida Camacho, Esquina Ayacucho); **Confitería Galey** (Avenida Camacho 1299); **Confitería Daiya** (Calle Mercado 801) and the **Confitería Toko** (Avenida 16 de Julio 1832).

## ENTERTAINMENT

There is a resident symphony orchestra and a resident ballet company. La Paz has a musical theater where these and local dramatic companies perform. La Paz also has many movie houses where foreign movies are shown, usually subtitled, but they are likely to be as much as four years old. Some of the clubs are **Club 21, Mau Mau Club, Don Pépe** and **Patachou.** There are also *peñas folklóricas* (native folk music shows) at the **Los Escudos** (Avenida Mariscal Santa Cruz) **Edificio Club de La Paz** (tel: 22028) or the **Kory-Thika** (Juan de la Riva 1435 —tel: 21363).

## SHOPPING

Shops open 9-12 and 2-6, Mon-Fri; 9-12 Sat. Best buys are vicuña ponchos, alpaca sweaters, gold and silver jewelry, wood carvings, hand-woven fabrics, pottery, native dolls and rugs. The main shopping street is **Calle Comercio. In Comacho, Lanza** and **Sopocachi** markets the leather-faced women vendors are noted for their bowler hats, intelligence and aggressiveness. They expect you to bargain. Some shops are: **Artesanias Bolivianas** (Avenida Sánchez Lima 2320) for jewelry and rugs; **Flora** (Avenida Sagárnaga) for sweaters; **Fotrama** (Avenida 16 de Julio 1764) for handicrafts and rugs; **Titikada Ltd** (Avenida Sánchez Lima), handicrafts; **Anticuario** (Calle Mercado) for antiques.

## SPORTS

Spectator sports are soccer, football, tennis and volleyball. The hunting in eastern Bolivia is probably about the best in the world today. To do it really properly you can go on a safari complete with bow and arrow and an Indian to play the drums. The trout fishing at **Lake Titicaca** is also gaining world renown. Skiing is tremendous at 17,000 feet, but make certain you are acclimatized first. Tennis clubs in La Paz and Sucre both welcome foreign visitors. Otherwise, horseback riding, yachting (Lake Titicaca, all year), mountaineering (**Club Andino** at Chacaltaya) and golf are all available. Try the **Mallasilla Golf Course** on the outskirts of La Paz—the highest golf course in the world, you should add 30 or 40 yards to your drive!

## WHAT TO SEE

The central road through La Paz is the **Prado** or 16th of July Street. Here, near the Plaza Murillo, are the presidential palace, legislative palace and cathedral. Further along, at **Plaza Venezuela,** is the 16th-century **San Francisco Church** and the monastery. See also the **National Museum of Art,** the open-air museum, and the collection of Tiahuanaco arts. In January each year there is the Indian fair, the *Alacitas.*

The ruins of **Tiahuanaco,** 42 miles from La Paz on the plain of Kalasasaya, are from one of the earliest civilizations of America. Their precise date is unknown, although estimates range from 10,000 BC to 1,000 BC. See the **Temple of Kalasasya** and the **Gates of the Sun and the Moon,** fantastic remnants of the sophisticated civilization that disappeared.

Not far from Tiahuanaco is **Lake Titicaca** (highest navigable lake in the world) half of which is in Peru. Here Indian reedboats share the waters with modern yachts and motor boats and two of the lake's 36 islands are called the Islands of the Sun and the Moon, paying obvious homage to the ruins of Tiahuanaco. The fishing and shooting here are good, the lake having more than four varieties of edible fish and the surrounding land is stocked with gulls, duck, geese, widgeon, woodcock, grebe, plover, ibis and gallinule.

On the shores of the lake is **Copacabana,** a city that existed at

the time of the Inca civilization and was used as a place of recreation by the royal family. The climate here is pleasant and temperate, the waters are warm enough for swimming, and the 17th-century city itself is one of the most pleasant old cities in Bolivia. See the **Statue of the Virgin** (which is said to possess miraculous powers), the Franciscan Fathers' **Monastery** and the 17th-century sanctuary with its numerous paintings and jewels. The celebration of the Festival of the Virgin of Copacabana is on 5 August.

Another city of interest is **Sucre,** called the 'white city' because of the white towers of its many churches and once the capital of Bolivia. It is still the legal capital of the nation. Pleasantly quiet and isolated, there are many gracious buildings here of both the Spanish colonial and republican periods, in addition to which Sucre has the second oldest 17th-century university in Latin America. Hotels are: **Hotel Municipal** (Avenida Venezuela) single from US$3; **Hotel Paris** (Calle Calvo 116) single from US$2 and **Hotel Londres** (Avenida Venezuela) single from US$1.50.

**Cochabamba,** an agricultural center, is a popular resort city as well as being Bolivia's second city. The market place and shopping centers here are comparable to those in La Paz. Hotels are: **Hotel Cochabamba** (Zona La Recoleta) single from US$5; **Hotel Ambassador** (Calle España 5006) single from US$4.76; **Hotel Capital** (Calle 25 de Mayo) single from US$5 and **Colón Hotel** (Plaza Colón 179) single from US$4.

**Potosí** is yet another of the old Spanish colonial towns, full of corkscrew streets and old mansions with colonial coats of arms. It was one of the first great cities of the Americas, early in the 17th century due in large part to the silver mines, which kept the Spanish treasury solvent. Stay at the **Central Hotel** (Calle Bustillo 1230) single from US$3.

## SOURCES OF FURTHER INFORMATION

From any **Pan Am** office around the world; **Dirección General de Turismo,** Avenida Camacho, La Paz; **Consulate General of Bolivia,** 10 Rockefeller Plaza, New York, NY 10020; **South American Travel Organization,** 100 Biscayne Boulevard, Miami, Florida 33132; **Embassy of Bolivia,** 106 Eaton Square, London SW1.

# Brazil

## WHAT'S SPECIAL

Occupying nearly half of South America, Brazil is the fifth largest country in the world and is bigger than the continental United States. Everything is on a scale to match . . . the sprawling Amazonian jungles with broad-leafed trees and enormous shrubs . . . great pine forests in the Rio Grande . . . parched deserts in the northeast . . . the Iguaçú Falls, higher and larger than Niagara . . . no fewer than 4,603 miles of Atlantic coastline . . . and the tall, white buildings of Rio de Janeiro reaching up between bare, purple mountains.

And then there are the people; as racially mixed as any in the world; friendly, hospitable and uninhibited. They work hard—and play hard as well on the beautiful beaches and their Carnival is the gayest in the world. Diamonds, sugar, coffee and rubber all come out of Brazil and there are still huge areas of the country that have scarcely been opened up. Some historians have suggested that Sir Thomas More was inspired by travelers' tales of Brazil when he dreamed up his Utopia. And the historians could be right because this land of the exhilarating samba and superb cuisine will probably inspire you too.

## COUNTRY BRIEFING

**Size:** 3,286,473 square miles
**Population** 94,500,000
**Capital:** Brasília
**Capital Population:** 500,000
**Rio de Janeiro:** 4,500,000
**São Paulo:** 6,200,000

**Climate:** Generally mild in Rio with plenty of sunshine; summer months December to February can be very warm. Best time to visit March-November.

**WEATHER IN RIO DE JANEIRO**—Lat S22°55′—Alt 201 ft

| Temp | Jan | Feb | Mar | Apr | May | Jun | Jul | Aug | Sep | Oct | Nov | Dec |
|---|---|---|---|---|---|---|---|---|---|---|---|---|
| Ave Low | 73° | 73° | 73° | 69° | 66° | 64° | 63° | 64° | 65° | 66° | 68° | 71° |
| Ave High | 84° | 85° | 83° | 80° | 77° | 76° | 75° | 76° | 75° | 77° | 79° | 82° |
| Days of No Rain | 18 | 17 | 19 | 20 | 21 | 23 | 24 | 24 | 19 | 18 | 17 | 17 |

**Government:** Federation of 22 States, a Federal district and four Territories. Since 1964 a military régime in power.

**Language:** Portuguese, but English and French understood, specially in Rio and São Paulo.

**Religion:** Roman Catholic, but many places of worship of all denominations in Rio and São Paulo.

**Currency:** The Cruzeiro; 100 centavos = 1 Cruzeiro

| | c50 | Cr1 | Cr5 | Cr10 | Cr50 | Cr100 | Cr200 | Cr300 |
|---|---|---|---|---|---|---|---|---|
| US(Dollars.Cents) | .09 | .17 | .85 | 1.70 | 8.48 | 16.95 | 33.90 | 50.85 |
| UK(Pounds.Pence) | .04 | .07 | .35 | .70 | 3.50 | 7.00 | 14.00 | 20.99 |

**Public Holidays:**

New Year's Day, 1 Jan
Carnival, 4 Days before Ash Wednesday
Good Friday
Tiradentes, 21 April
Labor Day, 1 May
Independence Day, 7 Sept
All Souls' Day, 2 Nov
Christmas Day, 25 Dec

## HOW TO GET THERE

Fly Pan Am direct to Rio de Janeiro, Galeão Airport, from New York; Miami via Caracas; San Francisco via Los Angeles, Guatemala City and Panamá City; and from Montevideo via Buenos Aires. Flying time from New York is 9¾ hours, Miami 8½ hours, Caracas 5½ hours, San Francisco 14½ hours, Los Angeles 13¼ hours, Guatemala City 8¾ hours, Panamá City 6¾ hours, Montevideo 3½ hours, and Buenos Aires 2¾ hours.

## REQUIREMENTS FOR ENTRY AND CUSTOMS REGULATIONS

A passport (visa not required); a round-trip ticket to the country of origin and a valid international smallpox certificate. Also advisable to have vaccination against typhoid and paratyphoid. You may take in as much currency as you wish, but cannot take out more money than you brought in. Banks permitted to sell foreign currency to departing visitors up to a maximum of 30% of amount changed through authorized dealers, for which receipts are held. Duty-free allowances are: 200 cigarettes, half-pound pipe tobacco, three quarts wine, two quarts champagne, two quarts liquor or gin; small amount of cosmetics and food for personal use; articles of personal use valued up to US$100; used portable radio, movie camera, typewriter, tape recorder and binoculars.

## AIRPORT INFORMATION

The two main international airports are Galeão (Rio de Janeiro) and Viracopos (São Paulo). Domestic flights in Rio land at Santos Dumont Airport and in São Paulo at Congonhas Airport. Pan Am provides free de luxe bus service to Congonhas in down town São Paulo. There is no bus service from Galeão Airport but taxis are plentiful. Fares are Cr 25.00 to the heart of Rio and Cr 30.00 to Copacabana, plus 10% tip. Porters are tipped Cr 2.00 per bag. Duty-free goods can be bought at the airport. No airport arrival tax, but on international flights there is a departure tax of Cr 19.00 and Cr 5.00 departure tax on domestic flights.

## ACCOMMODATIONS

Hotel rates are very flexible throughout the country. If you want a good view from your window you will have to pay more. Rio is extremely noisy. An inside room is less expensive and much quieter. Rates in Rio are higher during Carnival. Service charge of 10-15% (20% in Petrópolis) and a hotel tax of 10% will be added to the bill. The Federal University puts up men during vacations for about US$0.18. Hotels in Rio:

**Single from US$14 (Cr82.60); double from US$18 (Cr106.20)**

**Copacabana Palace** Avenida Atlântica 1702
**Excelsior Copacabana** Avenida Atlântica 1800 (MAP)
**Gloria** 632 Rua do Russel (CP)
**Leme Palace** Avenida Atlântica 656 (CP)
**Mirimar Palace** Avenida Atlântica 3668 (CP)
**Nacional Rio** Avenida Niemeyer 769 (MAP)
**Trocadero** Avenida Atlântica 2064 (CP)

**Single from US$10.75 (Cr63.40); double from US$14.50 (Cr85.50)**

**Ambassador** Rua Senador Dantas
**California** Avenida Atlântica 2616 (CP)
**Regente** Avenida Atlântica 3716 (CP)
**Savoy Othon** Avenida NS Copacabana 995 (CP)
**Toledo Copacabana** Rua Domingos Ferreira 71 (CP)

**Single from US$7 (Cr41.30); double from US$9.50 (Cr56.00)**

**Grande Sao Francisco** Rua Visconde de Initaúma 95
**Guanabara Palace** Avenue Pres. Vargas 392 (CP)
**Novo Mundo** Rua Richuelo 201

## USEFUL INFORMATION

**Banks:** Most are open 10-4 Mon-Fri, though some vary hours. You can also change currency or travelers' checks at shops marked *Câmbio.*

**Postage:** Buy stamps and mail letters only at post offices (look for the sign *Corrêio*); there are no mailboxes.

**Telephone Tips:** In many shops, restaurants, cafés and bars. Token operated and can be used only for local calls with a *Ficha* (token) costing Cr0.25. Useful numbers in Rio:

**Pan Am Offices,** 252,-8070
**Airport Information,** 230-9946
**Tourist Information,** 236-6609
**Emergencies,** 232-1234
**Fire Department,** 234-2020
**Police,** 222-2121
**Operator,** 100 or 101
**Directory Enquiries,** 102

For long distance telephone calls other than from your hotel, look for the sign *Cia Telefônica.*

**Newspapers:** You can get *Time* and *Newsweek* from almost any large newsstand in Rio and São Paulo, but newspapers are harder to come by. The local English-language newspaper is *The Brazil Herald.*

**Tipping:** Very much a Brazilian way of life, so you can be quite casual about it. Give your tip and no matter how generous it is, say *Para um Cafézinho* (for a little cup of coffee). A service charge of 10-15% is already included in restaurant checks but a tip of 5-10% is still expected. Porters Cr. 1.18 per piece of luggage; taxi drivers, at least 59 centavos or 10% of fare; hairdressers, Cr4.76; hotel porters, Cr1.18 per bag; chambermaids,

Cr2.45; cloakroom attendants, 90 centavos; museum guides, Cr1.48 or more.

**Electricity:** Rio and São Paulo—110 volts 60 cycles AC; Brasilia —220 volts, 60 cycles AC; Salvador, Manaus and Curitiba— 127 volts, 60 cycles AC. Check locally elsewhere. Some hotels have converters.

**Laundry:** Dry-cleaning and laundry services are of a very high standard in major cities; 24-hour dry-cleaning service available, mainly in hotels (dry-cleaning a suit Cr6.00; laundering a shirt 59 centavos).

**Hairdressing:** Most first-class hotels have good salons. (Shampoo and set about Cr18.00; man's haircut Cr9.00).

**Photography:** Good selection of equipment but usually expensive. Black and white film costs about Cr10.66 and a color film Cr20.65. Developing services quite reliable: black and white film takes two to three days; color, four to five days.

**Clubs:** Rotary and Lions.

**Babysitting:** Most hotels have a service.

**Toilets:** In hotels, restaurants, bus and ferry terminals. No charge and no tip expected; ladies, *Senhoras* or *Damas*; men, *Cavalheiros.*

**Health:** Many doctors have also trained in the US or Britain and speak good English. Pharmaceuticals available. Drink only bottled water. Outside main cities, mosquitoes can be a nuisance.

## TRANSPORTATION

Rio and São Paulo are extensively covered by bus services, but in town they can be crowded, uncomfortable and noisy. Rio also has a fleet of mini-buses (*Lotação*) but metered taxis are the quickest form of city transport. You can hail one in the street almost any time, day or night, but finding one in the rush hour is difficult. For longer journeys and excursions, agree on the price with the driver. Extra charge of 25% for night fares and on Sundays. Heavy trunks will cost you Cr1.48 each. You can rent a small car for about Cr59 a day or a larger car for Cr112 and a chauffeur-driven car for Cr148 a day (more with an English-speaking driver). An international driving license is required. Traffic lights are high over the middle of the roads and go from green to red surprisingly quick.

Train services connecting Rio, São Paulo and Belo Horizonte are quite reasonable, with sleepers and food available. Express bus services link most Brazilian cities. By bus from Rio to São Paulo and Belo Horizonte is 6½ hours (fares Cr15.25). A luxury bus service from Brasilia takes 20 hours.

Air travel is the most convenient form of transportation. Brazil has one of the largest domestic networks in the world. Main internal airlines are Cruzeiro do Sul, Varig, Vasp and Transbrasil. Air taxis are available between main centers. Advance reservations between Rio and São Paulo and Rio and Brasília (Ponte Aérea) are not required. Aircraft leave every 20 minutes to half an hour. Flying time to São Paulo, 45 minutes.

## FOOD AND RESTAURANTS

Brazilians are natural gourmets; the native food is very spicy and strongly influenced by their Portuguese and African origins. A good introduction to the local diet is the *feijoada*—rice, black beans cooked with jerked beef and a variety of other meats; manioc meal and slices of orange. It is not too rich. Then move on to *vatapá*—a porridge-like stew with fish and shrimps as the main ingredients; caruru—a traditional dish from Bahia; *cosido*—an enormous meat and vegetable stew. Simpler fish and shrimp dishes are numerous. Try *camarões a bahiana*—shrimps in a thick spiced tomato sauce, served with rice. The quality of meats is excellent and beef dishes are superb. Even a simple steak and french fries (*bife com batatas fritas*) tastes good. But *churrasco gaucho*—barbecued steak, pork and sausages, served with peppers, onions and manioc meal—is a must. Desserts are very sweet: try *goiabada*, a sweet made from guavas; delicious light coconut *quindins* and *dôce de leite*, which looks like fudge.

International cuisine is available in all good hotels. There are also numerous French, Italian, Hungarian and Chinese restaurants. In downtown Rio, try the **Mesbla** (Rua do Passeio 42, 11th floor) and **Museu de Arte Moderna** (Avenida Beira Mar) for international cuisine. The **Vendôme** (Avenida Franklin Roosevelt 194-A) is a first-class French restaurant, closed on Saturdays and Sundays. **Vergel** (Rua da Alfândega 176) for vegetarian meals and the **Leiteria Mineira** (Rua São José 82) for good business lunches and prompt service. In Copacabana **Flag** (Rua Xavier do Silveira 13) is outstanding for its international cuisine, **La Fiorentina** (Avenida Atlântica 290) for Italian Food—very popular with theater and movie stars; **Le Bec Fin** (Avenida Copacabana 178) and **Le Bistro** (R. Fernando Mendes 7) are good French restaurants and **A Poloneza** serves the best *boeuf Strogonoff* in town (Rua Helário de Gouvêia 116). In Botafogo you must go to **Chalé** (Rua da Matriz 54) for traditional Brazilian cooking and in Tijuca, just outside town, there is **Rincão Gaúcho,** an excellent *churrascaria.* If you like Japanese food, try **Akasaka** (Avenida Copacabana 1142) and **Le Chalet Suisse** (Rua Xavier da Silveira 112) is an expensive Swiss restaurant. Inexpensive counter restaurants and lunch bars can be found all over Rio. Recommended lunch bars are **Bob's** (scattered all over town); **Kid's** (Praça Mahatma Gandhi); **Pizzalândia** (Rua Senador Dantas); **Googies** (Avenida Copacabana) and **Zig-Zag** (Rua Santa Clara). Try *Kibon* ice-creams, sold in the streets. For a European tea try **Confeitaria Colombo** (Rua Gonçalves Dias 32).

Breakfast is usually served from 8-10; lunch from noon-2, dinner from 7 to the early hours of the morning, A dinner for one in an expensive restaurant will cost approximately US$8.00; in a medium priced restaurant, US$5.00 and in an inexpensive restaurant, about US$4.00.

## DRINKING TIPS

Beer, bottled or draft, is superb; favorite brands are *Pilsner, Brahma* and *Antarctica. Malzbier* is a good Brazilian stout.

*Cachaca*, the local sugar-cane brandy, is delicious and very potent. Mixed with lemon or coconut, sugar and ice it is called *Batida*. Local wines (*Precioso, Grandpierre, Château, Duvalier*), gin and whisky are very good. Imported spirits are expensive. Average price of a whisky and soda varies from US$0.60 (for local Scotch) to US$3.00 (for imported Scotch). A bottle of ordinary red wine will cost about US$1.50. There are no liquor restrictions but no alcoholic drinks for those under 21. Bars open from 7 am to the early hours of the next morning.

Local bottled soft drinks are worth a try and most bars and cafés serve ice-cold fresh fruit drinks. *Mate*, a strong Brazilian tea, is very refreshing and is served along the beaches in Rio by barefooted boys carrying large drums on their backs and shouting *mate gelado*' (iced mate). Coffee drinking is a national custom, and is served black in tiny cups.

## ENTERTAINMENT

Most large cities are very lively, but Rio and São Paulo most of all. There are always plenty of good theater shows to be seen, from lavish musicals to small experimental groups—all performed in Portuguese. Opera, concerts and ballet are performed at the **Teatro Municipal** and music recitals at the **Sala Cecilia Meireles.** Movies are very popular in Brazil, tickets are inexpensive (around US$1.00) and queues long, so get there early. International movies are shown with original sound track. Nightclubs are plentiful and many top performers appear regularly. In Rio try **Fred's** (Avenida Princesa Isabel), which has a first-class show; **Zum-Zum Club** (Rua Barata Ribeiro), a psychedelic disco; **Sacha's** (Avenida Atlântica 928), which shows silent movies, closed circuit TV and slides; **Canecao** (Rua Lauro Muller, Botafogo), a wild stadium-sized club very popular with the locals; **St Tropez** (Rua Almirante Gonçalves 5), a cozy "in" spot; **Crazy Rabbit** (Avenida Princesa Isabel 185), designed for the sophisticated and good for the single person; **Sucata** (Avenida Borges Medeiros 1426), which is very good for Brazilian music. For the single man **Big Al's** (Rua Fransisco Sa 35), is very free and easy and **Bolero** (Avenida Atlântica 1910), for very good looking dance hostesses. A trip to the suburbs to watch an *Escola de Samba* rehearse for the Carnival is unforgettable—information from the **Tourist Office.**

## SHOPPING

Shops and stores are open weekdays from 8-6 or 6:30—half day Saturdays. There are many large department stores, thousands of boutiques, shopping arcades, record stores, jewelry and gift shops. At **Importadoras** you can buy any assortment of imported goods, usually very expensive. It is not advisable to buy ready-made clothing, as the workmanship may be poor. Cottons are of excellent quality and fabrics are colorful. Best buys are leather goods (shoes are highly fashionable and well made), alligator bags, wallets, cigarette cases, antique silver (the delicate little coffee spoons with a semi-precious stone set in the handle make beautiful gifts), wood carvings, and above all, precious and semi-precious gems, pendants, necklaces and bracelets. Topaz, amethyst, aquamarine and tourmaline cut or uncut, are very popular and inexpensive. Brazilian handicraft shops are well stocked with unique native goods: rosewood bowls and trays, unusual beads, wooden dolls and latex figures from the Amazonian Indians, clay sculptures and miniature balsa rafts from the northeast; native musical instruments; framed butterflies and tarantula spiders, soapstone carvings and stuffed baby alligators. Children will love the Papagaio kites, which are lightweight and easy to pack. It is not customary to bargain in shops, but you will usually get a 10% discount if you ask for it. Main department stores are **Mesbla** (off Praça Mahatma Gandhi), **Sears** (Praia de Botafogo), **Sloper** (Rua do Ouvidor). For jewelry: **H. Stern** (Avenida Rio Branco) and **Maximino** (Rua Santa Clara); for handicraft and souvenirs: **Casa Hugo** (Rua Buenos Aires) and **Casa do Folclore** (Avenida Rio Branco). **Perfumarias Carneiro** (Rua do Ouvidor) and **Casa Hermanny** (Rua Gonçalves Bias). An open-air market known as the **Hippie Fair** is open every Sunday 9 am to sunset, at the Praça General Osório (Ipanema) —artists display paintings, woodcarvings and handicrafts, leather and metal work.

## SPORTS

Soccer is the Brazilian national sport. There are fierce league championships and the **Maracaña Stadium** is the world's largest, holding 200,000 people. The amateur soccer championships are held on the spotlit beaches of Copacabana, Ipanema and Flamengo. Watch them from the mosaic sidewalks, free of charge. Boxing, volleyball and basketball matches at the **Maracañazinho Stadium**; horse racing at the **Jockey Club** on Thursdays and Sundays (pari-mutuel betting), admission charges 40c (about Cr1). The biggest race is the Grande Premio Brasil, held on the first Sunday in August.

There are innumerable sports and social clubs in Rio, all with first-class facilities. Most offer temporary membership to visitors at reasonable rates but require introduction from current members. English-speaking residents in Rio belong to the **Payssandú Tenis Clube** (tennis, bowls, swimming), **Rio Country Club** (tennis, swimming); **Gávea Golf and Country Club** (golf and polo) or the **Yacht Clube do Rio de Janeiro** (sailing and water-skiing). Visiting cards can be obtained for the **Itanhangá Golf Course** from the Avenida Rio Branco 26, 16th floor (tel: 243-2175). Across the Guanabara Bay, in the city of Niterói, there is the **Rio Cricket Club** (swimming, soccer, cricket, rugby) and the **Rio Sailing Club** (swimming and yachting).

## WHAT TO SEE

**Rio de Janeiro:** Tourist agencies offer a wide range of well-organized tours of the city. If you would rather explore on your own, include in your itinerary a trip by cog-railroad to the **Corcovado Mountain**, which is crowned by the 1,200 ton, 130-foot-high statue of Christ the Redeemer. By cable car, you can go up the **Sugar Loaf**; there is a playground and a restaurant at the top. There are lines at the week-end, so go early or be prepared for long waits. A stroll you will not easily forget is along **Copacabana beach,** with its world famous mosaic walks, as the sun rises. Rio's gardens and parks are luxurious: the **Jardim Botanico** (Botanical Gardens) has over 7000 varieties

of exotic plants and 600 types of orchids—open every day from 8-5. The **Quinta da Bôa Vista** is the largest park in Rio and houses the **National Museum,** the **Zoo** and a tropical aquarium. Open from noon-4:30—closed on Mondays. Among the many churches, be sure to see the **Candelária,** on Praça Pio X, which has beautiful interior decorations and paintings; the **Convent of Santo Antonio** on the Largo da Carioca has a magnificent sacristy; the church of **Nossa Senhora de Glória do Outeiro** (on Glória Hill) has fine examples of Brazilian blue-faced tiling. The **Museum of Modern Art and War Memorial,** Avenida Beira Mar, is virtually all glass—open Mon. to Sat. noon to 7. Sundays and holidays from 2 to 7. The **Museum of Fine Art,** on the Avenida Rio Branco opposite the Teatro Municipal, has exhibitions by contemporary artists and many old masters, open daily noon to 9, closed on Sundays. The **National Historical Museum,** on Praça Marechal Ancora, has a collection of historical treasures, colonial sculptures, armor and silver—open noon to 5, closed Mondays. The **Museum of the Indian** illustrates the life of the Brazilian Indian, on Rua Mata Machado—open weekdays from 11-5.

Carnival in Rio is wild. For the four days preceding Ash Wednesday (late February, early March) the city goes mad. There are all night costume balls in hotels and clubs; processions by the *Escolas de Samba* in their traditional colors; *Mascarados* (hooded clowns); floats and communal dancing in the streets. Everybody joins in. On New Year's Eve, go down to the beaches to watch the *Macumbeiros* making offerings to Yemajá, the goddess of the sea (Macumba is a relatively mild form of Brazilian voodoo). But beware of pickpockets in the candlelit gloom. In September and October, Rio holds an **International Song Festival** that is very popular.

**Petrópolis, Teresópolis** and **Nova Friburgo** are mountain resorts not far from Rio. In Petrópolis, see the **Hotel Quintandinha,** which used to be a gambling casino and is now a private club, open to visitors: there are 20-foot bird cages, indoor Roman pools, a theater, a marble entrance hall and a restaurant. The **Imperial Museum** houses the old Empire's Crown Jewels—open Tuesday to Sunday, noon to 5. The **Cathedral** houses the tombs of the Emperor and Empress. Buses leave the Nova Rio bus station every 30 minutes and the journey takes 90 minutes. Hotels are: **Casablanca** (Avenida 7 de Setembro 286) and the **Quitandinha Hotel,** now a private club but with restaurant open to visitors.

Ferries leave from the Praça XV de Novembro every 20 minutes for **Niterói,** a quiet residential city across Guanabara Bay, much preferred by the British and American communities. Beyond Niterói you can reach the deserted beaches of **Saquarema, Marica** and **Cabo Frio.** Ferries also leave the Praça XV for the island of **Paquetá.** Cars are not allowed on the island, but you can rent horse-driven carriages and bicycles. It is a traditional meeting place for lovers. There are also full-day and half-day boat tours around **Guanabara Bay,** operated by Bateau Mouche, in the Botafogo section. Fares include lunch on board.

## SOUTH OF RIO

Traveling south of Rio, the weather gets cool: severe frosts in winter are not unknown and bother the large coffee plantations. This region has been very much in favor with settlers from Italy (São Paulo), Germany, Austria and Switzerland (Santa Catarina), Poland, Russia and the Ukraine (Paraná). São Paulo also has the largest Japanese colony outside Japan. In the deep south, bordering Argentina, Paraguay and Uruguay, you will find the romantic gauchos, handling one of the largest cattle herds in the world.

**São Paulo,** lying on the Tropic of Capricorn, is South America's leading industrial center, the fastest growing city in the world. *Paulistas,* as they are called, pride themselves on their cosmopolitan way of life, their splendid skyscrapers, highways, viaducts and modern shopping arcades. You get a superb view of the city from the 41-story **Edificio Italia,** the highest building in the city. You will not miss the Anhangabaú valley spanned by imposing *Viadutos.* Visit the new **Catholic Cathedral,** the **Municipal Stadium of Pacaembú,** the **Jockey Club** (races on Saturdays and Sundays), the **Teatro Municipal** and the **Museum Paulista,** in the suburb of Ipiranga (open Tuesdays, Thursdays, Sundays and holidays, noon to 4). The famous **Butantâ Snake Farm** and **Museum** is just outside the suburb of Pinheiros, open daily from 8 to 4. Take a bus or taxi to **Ibirapuera Park:** there is an up-to-date **Planetarium,** a velodrome for cycle and motorcycle racing, the new **Legislative Assembly** and the **Museum of Contemporary Art,** where the **São Paulo Biennial Exhibition** is held, the most important show of paintings and art in South America.

São Paulo is the gourmet's paradise. Restaurants of most nationalities can be found. For international cuisine try **Paddock** (Rua Sao Luiz 258); **A Baiuca** (Praça Roosevelt, 256); and **Terraço Italia** (Avenida Ipiranga 344), in town or the **Piccolomondo** (Rua Romilda Margarida Gabriel 142) in Jardim Europa. For first-class French cooking, go to **La Casserole** (Largo do Arouche 346); **Patachou** (Rua Augusta 926); **Chalé** (Rua Carlos Samaio 189) and **Maria Fulô** (Rua São José 563) for Brazilian dishes.

Entertainment in the city is thriving. For good shows (in Portuguese) there are many modern comfortable theaters, among them **Teatro Oficina; Teatro Cacilda Becker; Teatro Maria Della Costa** and **Teatro Brasileiro de Comedia.** Nightclubs are first-class. There is **Baiuca; Michel's** (very expensive); **Stardust;** and **Captain's Bar,** all highly recommended. And there are hundreds of movie houses all over town.

If you enjoy auto racing, the magnificent course at **Interlagos** is a must: the 500 kilometer race is held in September and the 1000 in November. Hotels in São Paulo:

**Single from US$18 (Cr106.20); double from US$20 (Cr118)**

**San Raphael** Avenida São Joao 1173
**Sao Paulo Hilton** Avenida Ipiranga and Epitácio Pessôa
**Vila Rica** Avenida Vieira de Carvalho 167 (CP)

**Single from US$13 (Cr76.70); double from US$18 (Cr106.20)**

**Alevear** Rua Gaspar Libero 65 (CP)
**Excelsior** Avenida Ipiranga 770 (CP)
**Grand Ca'd'Oro** Rua Avanhandava 308
**Danúbio** Avenida Brig Luiz Antônio 1099 (CP)
**Jaraguá** Rua Major Quedinho 44 (CP)
**Normandie** Avenida Ipiranga 1187 (CP)

**Othon Palace** Praça do Patriatca 65
**Samambia** Rua 7 de Abril 422 (CP)

**Single from US$8 (Cr 47.20); double from US$13 (Cr 76.70)**

**Comodora** Rua Duqne de Caxias 525 (CP)
**Marabá** Avenida lpiranga 757 (BB)
**Sao Paulo Hotel** Praça das Bandeiras 15 (CP)

**Santos** can be reached in leisurely way by ocean steamers from Rio in 12 to 15 hours or by car from São Paulo in less than two hours. This is one of Brazil's largest ports and has fine seaside resorts. The best is **Guarujá,** with luxurious apartment homes and good hotels and a magnificent beach. Try the fresh oysters, sprinkled with lemon juice, sold from little stalls along the beach. To stay in Santos there is the **Parque Balneario Hotel,** single from US$10.00.

**Iguaçú Falls,** one of the marvels of the world, can be heard from 25 kilometers away. (See also **Igazú Falls,** in the section on Argentina. They are two-and-a-half miles wide, larger and higher than Niagara, grander than Victoria Falls.) Fly by **Sadia** or **Varig** in two hours, or travel by train and river boat (about two days). Skilled guides can take you for a rather terrifying close-up view of the falls.

**Blumenau** (Santa Catarina) is a prosperous agricultural and manufacturing district settled mainly by Germans. **Florianópolis,** on the island of Santa Catarina, is joined to the mainland by Brazil's largest steel suspension bridge; **Campos de Jordão,** the leading resort for São Paulo is excellent for horseback riding and golf; **Porto Alegre** is a busy river port on the **Lagôa dos Patos,** the most important commercial center south of São Paulo; **Vila Velha** in the state of Paraná: see the 'old village built by nature'—an enormous extension of rocks carved by the wind and the rain.

## WEST OF RIO

To the west of Rio lies the state of **Miñas Gerais,** with its beautiful colonial towns and spa centers and the dense forests of the **Mato Grosso,** where hunting is superb. In the state of Goiás, in the Federal District, lies **Brasília,** the new capital of Brazil, lying about 4,000 feet above sea level and 580 miles from Rio. It was inaugurated on 24 April 1960. André Malraux once called it 'the capital of hope.' The buildings were designed by architect Oscar Niemeyer. They include the **Presidential Palace,** 100 yards from a huge artificial lake; the **Praça dos Tres Poderes** (housing the three powers of the government); the **Catholic Cathedral;** the **National Theater;** the **Acoustic Bowl** and the vast residential blocks. From the observation deck of the **Television Tower** you will see that the city is shaped like a large aircraft or cross. There is an international airport and domestic flights from Rio (fares US$38) take two-and-a-half hours. An inter-regional system of highways links Brasília to **Belém** and **Porto Alegre.** There are many first-class hotels serving international cuisine, but try the **TV Tower Restaurant.** Hotels in Brasília include the **Alvorada,** single from US$10; **Brasília Palace,** single from US$9; **Itamaratí Parque,** single from

US$9; **Nacional Brasília,** single from US$17 and the **Naçoes,** single from US$10.

**Belo Horizonte,** the capital of the state of Miñas Gerais, is in the heart of the mining and steel industries and has mysterious caves and grottoes: **Maquiné** cave near Cordisburgo was once occupied by prehistoric Indians. There are fine museums to be visited: **Museu da Cidade,** in town, and **Museu de Arte Moderna,** facing lake Pampulha, in a fashionable district. The **Igreja de São Francisco de Assis** was designed by Niemeyer and has blue-tile murals by Portinari, a leading Brazilian exponent of modern art. From Belo Horizonte you must take a day tour to **Ouro Preto,** a beautiful colonial town, 60 miles away. Its cobblestone streets, charming houses and 13 churches are preserved as a national monument. **Congonhas do Campo** is also a must. Here, Aleijadinho ('the little Cripple') a leprosy-stricken genius of the XVIII century, ringed the Church of Bom Jesus with incredible life-sized soapstone figures of the 12 apostles (you can get miniature replicas, also in soapstone, from good handicraft stores). South of the city lie the quiet spa towns of **São Lourenço, Poços de Caldas** and **Caxambú.** Hotels in Belo Horizonte: **Del Rey** (Praça Alfonso Arinos 60) single from US$12; **Excelsior** (Rua Cretes 753) single from US$70; **Normandy** (Rua Tamoios 212) single from US$12.

## NORTH AND NORTHEAST

Northwards towards the Equator lies the basin of the great São Francisco River; the **Sertão,** the dry region where the earth is burned dry by an implacable sun, and the Amazon jungle. **Salvador** is a dream city, famous for its 365 colonial churches, its rainbow-tinted houses and colorful markets. It is divided in two: **Cidade Baixa** (lower city) with the **Mercado Modelo** near the Praça Cairú and the old port, and **Cidade Alta** (higher city), 200 feet above, which can be reached by steep roads and by four public lifts. Here are the **Government Palace,** the **Custom House** and many other buildings. Scattered through the city are about 640 *Terreiros,* where rites of the Candomblé worship are conducted by Afro-Brazilian priests and priestesses. An important local festival is the **Festa do Bonfim,** in January. See the *Copoeira,* a dance developed by the blacks to practice fighting with their legs and look out for the *Berimbau,* a musical instrument resembling a bow with a coconut attached to it. Hotels in Salvador are: **Hotel da Bahia** (Praça 2 de Julho 1) single from US$16; **Plaza da Salvador** (Avenida Sete de Setembro 212) single from US$20.

**Recife,** 'the Venice of America', is laced with waterways crossed by numerous graceful bridges. The city is famous for its primitive balsawood fishing fleet (*Jangadas*—you can go out to sea with a fisherman for US$2.00), and for the *Frêvo,* an athletic native dance. At the **Museu do Açucar** (Sugar Museum) see models of colonial mills and devices for torturing slaves. Recife is three days from Rio by mail steamer and can be reached by main national airlines.

**Belém,** at the mouth of the Amazon, 90 miles from the open sea, just south of the Equator. It has an 18th-century **Cathedral,** a beautiful theater and one of the most moving and remarkable popular festivals: **Festival of the Candles** in October. Stay at the **Excelsior Grão Pará** (Praça da República 718) single from US$11.

**Manáus,** where the mean temperature is 80 degrees, is 1000 miles up the Amazon, in the heart of the jungle. From this river port, with its Opera House where Caruso and Bernhardt appeared (at the **Teatro Amazonas,** a relic of the rubber boom of 60 years ago), you can charter small river boats to take you into 'the last page of the Book of Genesis' as writer Euclides da Cunha described this mysterious region. Parrots, exotic birds and athletic monkeys chatter in the forest. You can hunt the fierce jungle cat, the onça: the giant relative of the pig, the tapir: or fish for a 500-pound piracuru, the largest fresh-water fish in the world. A place for the adventurous minded. A swim in the warm waters of the Amazon, however, it is not advisable: there are shoals of Piranha, a small, vicious fish with razor-sharp teeth. The **Hotel Amazonas** organizes inexpensive fishing and hunting expeditions. Air services from most Brazilian cities. Hotels in Manáus: **Manáus Amazonas** (Praça Adalberto Valle, S/N) single from US$14.50; **Lord** (Rua Quintino Bocaiuva/ Marcilio Dias) single from US$11.

## SOURCES OF FURTHER INFORMATION

**Pan Am Office,** Nacional Brasília Hotel, Loja 56, Brasília, Avenida Presidente Wilson 165-A, Rio de Janeiro, and from any Pan Am Office around the world; **Secretaria de Turismo,** Rua Real Grandeza 293, Rio de Janeiro; Avenida Paulista 326, São Paulo; **Departamento de Turismo,** Ed. Venancio IV, 4th floor, Brasília; **Brazilian Consulate General,** 630 Fifth Avenue, New York, NY 10020; 6 Deanery Street, London W1.

# British Honduras

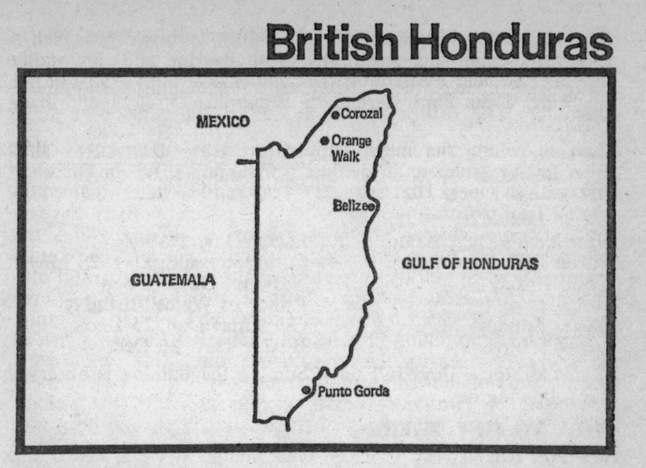


**WHAT'S SPECIAL**

Southern sub-tropics and a dry, dusty north give British Honduras a wide variety of scenery for a small country. From the beautiful coastal strip with its excellent beaches to the sharply rising Mountain Pine ridge and the Maya mountains in the west, the country is virtually new to tourism. The mosaic of islands off the barrier reef, one of the largest in the world, provides marvelous opportunities for scuba-diving and game fishing, while inland there is hunting and history. One of the oldest civilizations in the world, the Mayan, is only now being discovered with its sophisticated system of mathematics, astrology and religion.

British Honduras is famed for its orchids and wildlife. Some 150 varieties of bird make this an ornithologist's paradise. The limestone formations give rise to fascinating cave systems, often with evidence of primitive use. Hunting, mainly for jaguar, is a favorite sport. In all there is a lot to do and see.

**COUNTRY BRIEFING**

**Size:** 8,867 square miles
**Capital:** Belmopan
**Largest City:** Belize City
**Population:** 120,000
**Capital Population:** 38,000

**Climate:** The climate is sub-tropical but with a brisk wind prevailing from the Caribbean, which is especially invigorating from November to March.

**WEATHER IN BELIZE**—Lat N17°31′—Alt 17 ft

| Temp | Jan | Feb | Mar | Apr | May | Jun | Jul | Aug | Sep | Oct | Nov | Dec |
|---|---|---|---|---|---|---|---|---|---|---|---|---|
| Ave Low | 67° | 69° | 71° | 74° | 75° | 75° | 75° | 75° | 74° | 72° | 68° | 68° |
| Ave High | 81° | 82° | 84° | 86° | 87° | 87° | 87° | 88° | 87° | 86° | 83° | 81° |
| Days of No Rain | 18 | 22 | 27 | 25 | 24 | 17 | 16 | 17 | 15 | 15 | 18 | 18 |

**Government:** A self-governing colony. So long as the government receives budgetary aid from the British Government, an

English governor is responsible for defense and external affairs.

**Language:** English. Spanish also widely spoken.

**Religion:** Roman Catholic, Anglican and Methodist predominate.

**Currency:** The British Honduras dollar; 100 cents = 1 dollar

| | 10c | 50c | 1 BH$ | 5 BH$ | 10 BH$ | 20 BH$ | 40 BH$ | 80 BH$ |
|---|---|---|---|---|---|---|---|---|
| US (Dollars.Cents) | .05 | .25 | .50 | 2.50 | 5.00 | 10.00 | 20.00 | 40.00 |
| UK (Pounds.Pence) | .02 | .10 | .21 | 1.06 | 2.12 | 4.25 | 8.51 | 17.02 |

**Public Holidays:**

New Year's Day, 1 Jan
Baron Bliss Day, 9 Mar
Good Friday
Holy Saturday
Easter Sunday
Queen's Birthday
Labor Day, 1 May
Commonwealth Day, 24 May
National Day, 10 Sep
Prince of Wales' Birthday
Christmas Day, 25 Dec
Boxing Day, 26 Dec

If any of these days fall on a Sunday the holiday is observed the following day.

## HOW TO GET THERE

Fly Pan Am to New Orleans, Guatemala City, San Pedro Sula or San Salvador, then by connecting flight to Belize, Stanley International Airport. Flying time from New Orleans, 2 hours; Guatemala City, ¾ hour; San Pedro Sula, ½ hour; San Salvador ¾ hour.

## REQUIREMENTS FOR ENTRY AND CUSTOMS REGULATIONS

Passport; proof of citizenship only required from US citizens whose journey originated in the US or from British citizens whose journey originated in a British possession provided stay does not exceed six months. Visa required by nationals of some countries. Visitors' permits are obtainable at all points of entry to the country, without prior application. All tourists should have sufficient funds for their stay and a round-trip or onward ticket to another country. Smallpox vaccinations are compulsory and yellow fever and cholera injections if traveling from an infected area. Immunization requirements change from time to time and should be checked before departure. Typhoid, tetanus and polio vaccinations, though not necessary, are recommended. Visitors are not permitted to import more than £10 sterling but there is no limit to the amount of other currencies brought in. No fruit, firearms or ammunition may be taken in. Duty-free allowance: one bottle spirits; one bottle wine; 200 cigarettes or half a pound tobacco; a reasonable amount of perfume. There are restrictions on exporting Mayan antiques.

## AIRPORT INFORMATION

Stanley International Airport is about 10 miles northwest of Belize. No entry tax but departure tax of about US$2, Each airline has its own bus service to the center. Taxis are readily available at a cost of about US$1. There is a duty-free shop at the airport.

## ACCOMMODATIONS

The Belize Tourist Board (12 Regents Street—tel: 3013), provides assistance. Hotels in Belize:

**Bellevue Hotel** 5 Southern Foreshore (single from US$18.50 AP)
**Bliss Hotel** 1 Water Lane (single from US$12)
**Fort George Hotel** 2 Marine Parade (single from US$17 MAP)
**Golden Dragon** Queen Street (single from US$6.60)
**Palms Motel** Western Road (single from US$8 AP)

## USEFUL INFORMATION

**Banks:** Open 8-11 and 1-2, Mon, Tues, Thurs and Fri. 8:30-11:30 Wed and Sat. Money can also be changed in hotels. Branches of banks in all major towns.

**Postage:** Stamps from the post office or hotels; mail can be sent only from the post office.

**Telephone Tips:** Phones mainly in hotels and bars. Street booths are uncommon. Useful numbers:

**Tourist Office:** 3013
**Tourist Information:** 2999
**Operator:** 0
**Directories:** 0
**Police:** 2222
**Fire:** 0

**Newspapers:** English-language newspapers are the *Beacon* (weekly), the *Billboard* (irregular), the *Belize Times* (daily except for Tues and Sun) and the *Reporter* (weekly).

**Tipping:** Customary but optional; the usual 10% for hotels and restaurants (no service charge included). Porters, BH25—40c.

**Electricity:** 110-220 volts, 60 cycles AC.

**Laundry:** Hotels offer a good express service. There is a dry-cleaning service in Belize City (dry-cleaning a suit about BH $1.50; laundering a shirt, BH35c).

**Hairdressing:** Major hotels have salons and there are inexpensive ones in the towns (shampoo and set, BH$5; man's haircut, BH$1 to BH$1.50).

**Photography:** A good selection of equipment and black and white and color films in all major towns. For developing, color film has to be flown to Miami and back.

**Clubs:** Rotary.

**Babysitting:** Hotel staff will usually oblige.

**Toilets:** Always marked in English, found in restaurants, hotels and bars.

**Health:** Medical standards are high and specialists available. The main general hospital is in Belize City. Pharmaceuticals available but supplies can be erratic. Boil all drinking water.

## TRANSPORTATION

Only out-of-town bus services are available so, for Belize City itself, it is a matter of walking a short distance or taking a taxi, with a fixed rate of BH6 cents per person, from point to point. A small addition is made for night journeys. Car rental is available and details should be obtained from the **Belize Tourist Office.** There are no railroad services. A good long-distance bus service links most of the major towns, such as San Ignacio,

Orange Walk Town and Corozal Town. **Maya Airlines** operate internal flights linking Stann Creek, Orange Walk Town, Punta Gorda and Corozal Town.

## FOOD AND RESTAURANTS

Try the national dishes, composed of rice, beans and lobsters cooked in a variety of ways. Also *conch* and *tamales*—corn-flour with meat or fish wrapped in the *waha* leaf. These are all available in the main restaurants.

Similar to western traditions, an average meal consists of three courses; the hors d'oeuvres, the main course of meat or fish and the dessert and coffee. International cuisine is readily available in Belize and the first-class hotels. A service charge is not generally added to the bill and tipping is usually in the order of 10%. Breakfast in Belize hotels is usually quite early, between 7:30 and 8, lunch is from noon, and dinner from 7.

In Belize City both the **Bellevue** and **Fort George Hotel** have good restaurants. Other popular eating places are: **Talk of the Town** (Gabourel Lane); **Caribbean** (Regent Street); **China Inn** (Euphrate Avenue); **Raúls** (Bishop Street).

## DRINKING TIPS

The national drink, as everywhere in the Caribbean, is rum. Imported wines, spirits and beers are available. A bottle of Scotch costs in the region of BH$12.75 (US$6.37) and drinks can be sold in bars from 6am-9pm, and in clubs from 9am-midnight. Restaurant bars are open for 24 hours a day. Rum punch and Rum Popo are drunk as appetizers. The former is made with fruit juices and the latter with egg and nutmeg. It is not usual for women to be seen in the street bars though they are not unwelcome. For a leisurely thirst-quencher, try the numerous saloons and cafés. Visitors tend to congregate in the **Fort George Hotel.**

## ENTERTAINMENT

There are two movie houses, the **Majestic** and the **Palace,** showing English-language movies. Night life is definitely Caribbean style. Recommended spots are the **Palms Motel** on the Western Highway just outside Belize; the **Cross Roads Hotel,** the **New Town Club,** and the **Pickwick Club.** The **Continental Hotel** also offers evening entertainment.

## SHOPPING

Shops open from 7:30-11am, Mon-Tues; 7:30-noon, Wed; 1-4 Thurs; 8:30-1pm Fri and Sat. While you are in the British Honduras you must take back home some of their famed wood carvings, tortoiseshell items, straw hats and other handicrafts. Also a good buy are slippers made from Spanish towelling. For souvenirs the best place must be the **National Craft Center** (13 Vernon Street); also selling high-quality goods is the **Cottage Industries** shop (26 Albert Street, Belize). Well-stocked department stores are to be found along Albert Street and Queen Street. Also go to Belize's market in the center of town, by the sea, where prices are lower. It is not the custom to bargain.

**SPORTS**

Most sports are catered for; tennis at **Tropical Park** and at the **New Town Club** and the **Pickwick**—guests welcome. There is horseback riding out in the Mountain Pine Forest, fishing nearby and excellent swimming in the cold-water streams and pools. The hunting is very good—the place to go is the village of **Santeneja,** though most of the hotels will be able to arrange this for you. The island of **Turneffe** provides good facilities for its deepwater yachting and great fishing, while skin-diving and scuba diving is popular off **Ambergris Cay.**

**WHAT TO SEE**

Sightseeing musts are the Mayan ruins, of which more are being discovered year by year. The tremendous wealth of history within the country is only just showing itself. Major sites include those at **Altun Ha,** 30 miles northwest of Belize City where the world's largest jade head was discovered only two years ago, **Xunantunich,** 80 miles southwest of Belize and **St Herman's Cave** on Humming Bird Highway on the way to **Stann Creek Valley.** Tours of particular interest to the visitor include those of **Mountain Pine Ridge,** with its varied wildlife, beautiful scenery and greenery, and orchids, and the beaches of **Turneffe Island** and **Ambergris Cay.** The **Belize Museum** has a fine display of Mayan relics.

**SOURCES OF FURTHER INFORMATION**

From any **Pan Am** office round the world; **Tourist Board,** 12 Regent Street, Belize City; **West India Committee,** 18 Grosvenor Street, London W1.

# Chile

## WHAT'S SPECIAL

Because of its curiously attenuated shape (2625 miles long, 56 miles across at its narrowest point), Chile embraces an enormouse variety of scenery and climate. The Andes mountains run the entire length of the country and occupy more than half its width, rising to an average altitude of 10,000 feet. The Atacama desert in the north is one of the driest places on earth and in some parts no rain has ever been recorded. An interesting feature of rural life are the *huasos,* Chilean cowboys, who appear at rodeos (November-March) in flamboyant costume, playing guitars and singing traditional cowboy songs. Very few Indians survive among the population which is predominantly of Spanish descent with a generous sprinkling of German, Italian, English, Irish and Yugoslav.

## COUNTRY BRIEFING

**Size:** 741,767 square miles
**Capital:** Santiago
**Population:** 9,268,584
**Capital Population:** 3,000,000

**Climate:** North Chile is dry, central Chile temperate and South Chile wet all year. Summer is Oct-Mar.

**WEATHER IN SANTIAGO**—Lat S33°27′—Alt 1,706 ft

| Temp | Jan | Feb | Mar | Apr | May | Jun | Jul | Aug | Sep | Oct | Nov | Dec |
|---|---|---|---|---|---|---|---|---|---|---|---|---|
| Ave Low | 53° | 52° | 49° | 45° | 41° | 37° | 37° | 39° | 42° | 45° | 48° | 51° |
| Ave High | 85° | 84° | 80° | 74° | 65° | 58° | 59° | 62° | 66° | 72° | 78° | 83° |
| Days of No Rain | 31 | 28 | 30 | 29 | 26 | 24 | 25 | 26 | 27 | 28 | 29 | 31 |

**Government:** Constitutional Republic: present ruling party Marxist.

**Language:** Spanish. Some people speak English.

**Religion:** Roman Catholic.

**Currency:** The escudo; 100 centesimos = 1 Escudo

| | 1 | 5 | 10 | 50 | 100 | 200 | 500 | 600 |
|---|---|---|---|---|---|---|---|---|
| US (Dollars.Cents) | .03 | .17 | .35 | 1.78 | 3.57 | 7.14 | 17.85 | 21.42 |
| UK (Pounds.Pence) | NOT AVAILABLE | | | | | | | |

**Public Holidays:**
New Year's Day, 1 Jan
Good Friday and Easter Sunday
Labor Day, 1 May
May Day, 21 May
Assumption Day, 15 Aug
Independence Day, 18-19 Sept
Columbus Day, 12 Oct
All Saints' Day, 1 Nov
Immaculate Conception, 8 Dec
Christmas Day, 25 Dec

## HOW TO GET THERE

Fly Pan Am to Buenos Aires, Caracas and New York, then by connecting flight to Santiago, Pudahuel Airport. Flying time from Buenos Aires is 1¾ hours, Caracas 8¾ hours (via Bogotá, Lima and La Paz) and New York 11¾ hours (via Lima and La Paz).

## REQUIREMENTS FOR ENTRY AND CUSTOMS REGULATIONS

Passport, smallpox vaccination certificates and a round-trip ticket. Escudos best bought abroad; currency should be converted before leaving. Duty-free allowance: two bottles of spirits; two bottles of wine; 200 cigarettes; duty-free purchases limit US$100.

## AIRPORT INFORMATION

Pudahuel airport (13½ miles from Santiago) is connected to the capital by a half-hourly bus service (11 escudos) and by taxis, which charge 105 escudos (any number of passengers). Airport arrival tax is 196 escudos and departure tax varies between 50-67 escudos. No hotel reservation counter.

## ACCOMMODATIONS

Although there are few luxury hotels in Chile, even the cheaper ones are noted for cleanliness and hospitality. There are good hotels in all major cities, but they are in short supply throughout the country. Rates are higher in the extreme north and south. Furnished apartments can be rented. Hotels in Santiago:

**Single: US$17 (476 Escudos); double: US$20 (560 Escudos)**

**Carrera Sheraton** Teatinos 180—Casilla 2272
**Sheraton San Cristóbal** Avenida Santa Maria 1742

**Single: US$13.20 (369 Escudos); double: US$17.60 (493 Escudos)**

**Crillon** Agustinas 1025
**El Conquistador** Miguel Cruchaga 920

**Single: US$5.00 (140 Escudos); double: US$6.50 (182 Escudos)**

**Emperador** Avenida Bernardo O'Higgins 853
**Gran Palace** Huérfanos, esquina Marande 1175
**Kent** Huérfanos 878
**Lido** Huérfanos 682
**Panamericano** Teatinos/Huérfanos
**Posada del Salvador** Avenida Elidoro Yánez 893
**Ritz** PO Box 920
**Santa Lucia** Huérfanos 779, esquina San Antonio
**Victoria** Huérfanos 801

## USEFUL INFORMATION

**Helpful Hints:** Tea customary at 5 and dinner therefore a late meal. Women should wear shorts and slacks only on the beach.
**Banks:** Open 9-2, Mon-Fri in all major cities.

**Telephone Tips:** Phones are operated by tokens, which are sold at stores and hotels that have phones. A local call costs 3 centesimos.

**Newspapers:** The Hotel Carrera publishes a free daily English-language newspaper. Foreign newspapers are hard to find. English-language magazines and books available.

**Tipping:** Taxi drivers not usually tipped; porters 3 centesimos per bag, hotel porters 10%; chambermaids 5%; hairdressers 10%.

**Electricity:** 220 volts 50 cycles AC.

**Laundry:** Good dry-cleaners in main towns. Laundromats everywhere in Santiago.

**Hairdressing:** Good barbers and hairdressers in the larger cities.

**Photography:** Film is available but expensive.

**Clubs:** Several branches of Rotary and Lions Clubs.

**Toilets:** No charge, but a small tip is customary.

**Health:** Most doctors and dentists speak English. Day and night medical and dental service available through the Laboratorio Clinico, Alameda O'Higgins 1616 (tel: 81921). Imported pharmaceutical goods scarce and expensive. Stick to bottled water.

## TRANSPORTATION

Municipal and private companies operate public transport in the main cities and towns. The capital is served by trolley-buses and *liebres,* minibuses seating 17, all of which are inexpensive and operate all night. Taxis (black and yellow) in Santiago have meters and private automobiles (with and without meters) can be flagged or phoned. Taxis are at a premium in the rush hours 12:30-1:30 and 7:00-8:30; there is a 50% night surcharge. Average daily rate for a rented car is US$12. A regular inter-city express bus serves the north-south Pan Am Highway and a fast and efficient train service (sleeper and restaurant cars) reaches from Arica in the far north to Punta Arenas in the distant south. The Northern Railway System issues a 30-day excursion ticket valid for travel in one direction. Regular Linea Aerea Nacional (LAN) flights to all main cities and to Easter Island. All coastal towns can be reached by sea and there are occasional cruises to outlying Pacific Islands including Juan Fernández, where a famous castaway provided Daniel Defoe with the model for Robinson Crusoe.

## FOOD AND RESTAURANTS

Seafood is excellent, particularly lobsters and oysters (May-August). *Caldillo de Congrio* is a fish soup and *chupe de mariscos* is a shellfish dish. Meat and poultry are good quality although restaurants are not allowed to serve beef from 1-13 of each month. *Cazuela de ave* is a chicken and vegetable broth. Chilean bullfrog is a delicacy. *Empanadas* are pies filled with meat, onions, eggs, olives and whatever the cook fancies. *Pancho villa* is beans and smoked sausage (*chorizo*) and *pastel de choclo* is a summertime green corn stew with ground meat and vegetables. *Humitas* are Chilean hot tamales. Fruit and vegetables in season are abundant, inexpensive and delicious. The average cost of a meal is US$7.00 (expensive); US$3.00 (medium) and in an inexpensive restaurant about US$1.50. Good international cuisine can be sampled at the **Maistral** (Mosqueto 485); the **International** at the Hotel Carrera Sheraton (dancing); **Jacaranda** (Huérfanos 612), with delightful open-air dining in summer and **Nuria** (Agustinas 705-715) with a good orchestra downstairs. Steaks are a speciality at **El Parrón** (Providencia 1184) and the **Las Brasas,** Apuquindo. Flambé dishes light up the glass dining room at **La Piramide,** San Cristóbal Hill and there is an orchestra for dancing. Situated in a forest out of town is the **Lo Curro** (Lo Curro Road) with excellent food and soft music and open for tea, cocktails, dinner and dancing. For one-course meals and snacks try *tallarines con lomito,* steak and noodle casserole, *bife lomo,* steak with rice and *bien essas,* a type of hot dog with tomato and onion relish.

## DRINKING TIPS

Bars officially open at 10 am, but most prefer 6pm-12. Clubs keep later hours. Local wine, excellent and inexpensive (36 escudos). Try *Santa Carolina* and *Macul* (white) and *Tarapaca ex-Zavala* (burgundy-type). Imported liquor is expensive: whisky and soda costs about 84 escudos. The native drink is the potent *Pisco,* a grape distillation best drunk as a Pisco sour cocktail or as a *Pichuncho,* mixed with sweet vermouth. *Aguardiente* is the brandy equivalent and is also very alcoholic. The delicious Christmas-time punch, *cola de mona,* is sold in many downtown bars. **Escudo** is the most popular beer. Tea parlors are crowded for the five o'clock ritual and most popular are the **Astoria, Santos** and **Waldorf,** on Ahumada and the **Oriente** on Plaza Baquedano. Customers sit for hours at the **Jamaica Coffee House** on Estado and Huérfanos and the **Haiti** on Ahumada serves a refreshing fruit milkshake called *leche con fruta* and unusual varieties of coffee.

## ENTERTAINMENT

There are many lavish movie houses in the cities showing recent American and English movies with sub-titles. Matinees generally begin at 3:30 and the evening performance at 10. During the winter season there are weekly symphony concerts and occasional ballet and opera presentations. The two universities of Santiago maintain professional theater groups and the capital is a regular stopping point for European and American touring companies. Popular nightspots are: **La Châtelaine** (Piazza Pedro de Valvivia 1718) with Latin American music and **El Pollo Dorado** (Estado 215) where you can see Chile's national folk dance, the *cueca.* The **Portada Colonial** is considered the best discothèque in town. Strip-clubs are the **Night and Day** (Agustinas 1022) and the **Tap Room** (Avenida Bulnes 135). Women should be accompanied.

## SHOPPING

Shops open late (between 9-10:30) and sometimes close between 1:00-1:30 for lunch. They close at 7 during the week (a little later on Fridays) and at noon on Saturday. Best buys are copperware, Chilean wine, *trarihues* and *trariloncos* (fabrics), woollen rugs, wooden carvings from Easter Island and leather goods, including saddles made in Raneagua and Chillau. Chile is noted for its black pottery and the town of Pomaire near Melipilla (37 miles from Santiago) produces attractive handmade ceramics. When there are no price-tags feel free to bargain, but not in the main stores. The biggest department store in Santiago is **Los Gobelinos** (Ahumada). And try **Falabella, Rosenblith, Flano,** and **Almacenes Paris. Chilean Art** has a wide range of copperware, **Chile Lindo** handles black pottery and **Chile Típico** a variety of souvenir items including ponchos. All three are on Agustinas and in the same street is **José Sánchez** with fine quality Chilean woollens and worsteds. **H. Stern** in the Carrera Hotel specializes in jewelry made from locally-mined lapis lazuli. At **Estado 310** is the old established jewelry store **Casa Barros. Flano** (Unión Central 1088 and Huérfanos 1024) stocks international fashions and local creations and **Leo Schanz** (Merced 535) will custom-make pants for the whole family in eight hours. Pottery, baskets, dolls and other typical souvenirs can be found at Santiago's **Central Market.**

## SPORTS

The most popular spectator sport is football, closely followed by horseracing. There are race-tracks in Santiago with meetings every Saturday and Sunday and feast-days, and the annual social event, **The Derby,** is held at the Vinã del Mar Track. The most famous ski resorts in South America are only a few hours by train from the capital and from June-Sept there is ample scope for the novice as well as the experienced skier. At the nearer ski centers of **Farellones** and **Lagunillas,** accommodations are *refugios* or private lodges. **Portillo,** the largest of the resorts has top instructors, chairlifts, wonderful trails, ski runs up to six miles long and a luxury hotel. A day trip to the peace memorial, **Christ of the Andes** affords uninterrupted skiing all the way back. Portillo is two-and-a-half hours fron Santiago by car or four hours in a scenic train ride. The southern lake area, rich in river trout and salmon offers excellent opportunities for fly-fishing and there is good surf casting off the Pacific beaches. Game fishers can try for tuna and sword-fish in the waters of the north. Skin-diving, yachting and water-skiing can all be practised at **Algarrobo** and tennis, surfing and riding are to be found in most centers. The **Prince of Wales Country Club** and **Golf Club** have fine golf courses and other sporting facilities and the **Polo Club** includes tennis courts and a swimming pool.

## WHAT TO SEE

**Santiago:** Set on a high plateau (1706 feet) with the snow-clad Andes as a clearly visible backdrop, Santiago, the fourth largest city in South America has the added attraction of spacious streets, lovely gardens and a sunny Mediterranean climate. It is the focus of the commercial, industrial and cultural life of Chile and tall modern structures rise alongside more venerable monuments. The hub of the city is the **Plaza de Armas** with the Cathedral, the archbishop's palace and Government Palace. The **Cathedral** houses a fine painting of the Last Supper and a 17th-century silver lamp weighing 50 pounds. The guard at the elegant **Moneda Palace** (the Presidential Palace) changes ceremonially every 48 hours at 10 am. In **Quinta Normal** park are the **Modern Art Museum** and the **National History Museum** (closed Monday) with Arab mummies and a perfectly preserved body of a pre-Incan boy. The **Historical Museum,** next to the National Library on Miraflores contains Indian, colonial and folklore exhibits. The first Spanish fort in Chile is on the picturesque central **Santa Lucia Hill,** delightfully laid out with ornamental and pleasure gardens. A funicular climbs the 1000-foot **Cerro San Cristóbal** to the observatory and restaurant. The views from this hill are particularly impressive at night. Widest of all the streets is the **Avenida Bernardo O'Higgins,** named after the Irish-Peruvian founder of Chilean independence. A few miles south is **Maipu** with a monument to commemorate the battle here in 1818. The outstanding museum is open Saturday and Sunday. There is also the temple to the Virgin of Carmen.

**Valparaiso,** founded in 1536, is Chile's principal port and is 115 miles from the capital by rail and some 90 miles by road. The old town and business section is built on a low terrace on land reclaimed from the sea and the residential part of the city rises in tiers on hills surrounding the crescent-shaped **Bay of Valparaiso.** Winding roads and cliff railways (*ascensores*) lead to the upper town. The cathedral, parks, theaters and the few remaining colonial buildings, such as the church of **La Matriz** are in the lower town. **Plaza Sotomayor** is the shipping front, **Calle Esmeralda** the main shopping center and **Avenida Pedro Montt** with cafés and theaters is the social hub. Stay at the **Condell Hotel,** single from US$10 or the **Prat,** single from US$4.

**Viña del Mar:** Coastal resorts stretch all the way from La Serena to San Antonio, but the most fashionable is the elegant Viña del Mar. High season January-March. An attractive city of flowers and trees, with the president's **Summer Palace** on Castle Hill (Cerro Castillo), its parks include the central **Plaza Vergara, Plaza Mexico** with illuminated fountains and the **Quinta Vergara,** an estate (the palace is now a **Museum of Fine Arts**) with large gardens where concerts and other events are held in summer. Drama and ballet are performed in the **Municipal Theater.** The famous **Casino,** open 15 September-15 March offers roulette, baccarat, a nightclub with excellent cabaret and floorshows and a restaurant with orchestra. Good restaurants are: **Chez Gerald, Eden Roc, Armandito** and **Los Lilenes,** on the lovely road to the seaside resort of **Concón** (about 20 miles). Hotels in Viña del Mar: **Alcazar** (646 Alvarez Street) and **Chalet Suisse,** both single from US$7; **O'Higgins** (Plaza F. Vergara) and **San Martín** (Casilla 568), both single from US$9; **New Miramar** (Caleta Abarca), single from US$13.50.

**Chilean Lake Country:** A region of mountain and lake scenery and offering top-rate fishing (rainbow and brown trout) in little fished waters, the Chilean Lake Country extends from Los Angeles 320 miles south of Santiago, to Puerto Montt. (Hotels here normally open only December-April). See the 200-foot **Laja**

**Falls,** just north of Los Angeles. Fishing competitions are held in Laja Lake. Further south is **Lake Villarrica.** Hotels here are the **Vista Hermosa,** single from US$8 and the **Yachting Club,** single from US$10 (AP). The **Puyeué Lake** with many islands and waterfalls, has abundant birdlife. Nearby is the **Antillanca** volcano with good ski slopes. Try the **Gran Hotel Termas de Puyehue** with hot thermal baths, single from US$12 (AP). **Osorno** is near lakes **Puyehue** and **Rupanco** (hot springs). This old-fashioned city was colonized by Germans and their language is still as commonly used here as Spanish. Hotels here are **Granhotel,** single from US$7 and **Waeger,** single from US$8.25. Another German town is **Puerto Varas** on **Lake Llanquihue,** largest of the lakes (320 square miles) and ringed with snow-capped volcanoes. The **Gran Hotel** has single rooms from US$8.50. **Puerto Montt** is a seaport and excellent seafood plays a major role in its cuisine. Stay at the **Hotel Pérez Rosales,** single from US$7.45. Ten-day boat trips are organized from here through a region criss-crossed with canals and inhabited mainly by fishing folk.

**Punta Areñas** is the most southerly city in Chile, the last stop for Tierra del Fuego and Cape Horn. The center of an area rich both in oil and agricultural produce, the city is also a whaling town. There is racing, tennis and golf and, close by, some great ski runs. You can take a cruise to **Tierra del Fuego** or visit the local ranches. Contact **Blanco Travel.**

**Antofagasta:** In northern Chile, in a province of desert (the driest in the world) and mountain ranges, is the unique city of Antofagasta. Although earth for its main square had to be brought as ballast in sailing ships and water has to be piped from the Andes, a city of lovely parks and plazas has sprung from the barren soil. Stay at the **Antofagasta Hotel,** single from US$7. The province of Antofagasta is rich in archeological remains and there is a pre-Columbian museum at **San Pedro de Atacama.** Other tourist attractions are the **Tatio** geysers and **Chuquicamatá,** the world's largest open-pit copper mine, near Calama. You need authorization for this particular trip; enquire from your travel agent or airline.

## SOURCES FOR FURTHER INFORMATION

**Pan Am Office,** Huérfanos 1164, Santiago; and from any Pan Am office around the world; **Dirección de Turismo,** Catedral 1165, Santiago; **The Chilean Consulate General,** 809 United Nations Plaza, New York, NY 10017; 3 Hamilton Place, London W1.

# Colombia

## WHAT'S SPECIAL

Placed astride the land routes to the South American continent, Colombia, though proud of her independence from colonial Spain and enshrining the memory of Simon Bolívar, the Liberator, remains the most Spanish of South American countries. It has beaches, Andean ranges, green valleys and dense jungles. Every variety of tropical flower can be found, there are jaguars, pumas, armadillos and tapirs and no single country in the world has so many different kinds of birds.

## COUNTRY BRIEFING

**Size:** 440,000 square miles
**Population:** 22,914,950
**Capital:** Bogotá
**Capital Population:** 2,700,000

**Climate:** On the Caribbean coast, the average temperature is 83°. Cities in the temperate zone (3000 to 6500 ft) have an average temperature of 65-70°; in Bogotá (8669 ft above sea level) it is usually cool. Rainy season April-November. Best time to go: December-February.

**WEATHER IN BOGOTÁ**—Lat N5°36′—Alt 8678 ft

| Temp | Jan | Feb | Mar | Apr | May | Jun | Jul | Aug | Sep | Oct | Nov | Dec |
|---|---|---|---|---|---|---|---|---|---|---|---|---|
| Ave Low | 48° | 49° | 50° | 51° | 51° | 51° | 50° | 50° | 49° | 50° | 50° | 49° |
| Ave High | 67° | 68° | 67° | 67° | 66° | 65° | 64° | 65° | 66° | 66° | 66° | 66° |
| Days of No Rain | 25 | 21 | 18 | 10 | 14 | 14 | 13 | 15 | 17 | 11 | 14 | 16 |

**Government:** A republic.

**Language:** Spanish. English widely spoken.

**Religion:** Roman Catholic.

**Currency:** The peso; 100 centavos = 1 peso.

| | 1 peso | 5 pesos | 10 pesos | 20 pesos | 50 pesos | 100 pesos | 500 pesos | 1000 pesos |
|---|---|---|---|---|---|---|---|---|
| US (Dollars.Cents) | .04 | .22 | .45 | .91 | 2.29 | 4.58 | 22.93 | 45.87 |
| UK (Pounds.Pence) | .01 | .09 | .19 | .38 | .97 | 1.94 | 9.73 | 19.47 |

**Public Holidays:**

New Year's Day, 1 Jan
Epiphany, 6 Jan
St Joseph, 19 Mar
Holy Week
Labor Day, 1 May
Ascension Day, 31 May
Corpus Christi, 21 June
Peter and Paul, 29 June
Independence Day, 20 Jul
Battle of Boyaca, 7 Aug
Assumption, 15 Aug
Columbus Day, 12 Oct
All Saints' Day, 1 Nov
Independence Day—Cartagena, 11 Nov
Immaculate Conception, 8 Dec
Christmas Day, 25 Dec

## HOW TO GET THERE

Fly Pan Am direct to Barranquilla, Ernesto Cortissoz Airport, from Miami and from Caracas via Maracaibo. Flying time from Miami is 2½ hours, Caracas 1¾ hours and Maracaibo ¾ hour. Then by connecting flight to Bogotá.

## REQUIREMENTS FOR ENTRY AND CUSTOMS REGULATIONS

Passport, round-trip ticket and 90-day tourist card (obtainable from airlines or Colombian consulates on production of two passport-size photos). Visa required if you are staying for more than 90 days. You must have a smallpox vaccination certificate (and a yellow fever certificate if coming from an infected area). A maximum of 500 pesos only may be taken out of the country. Customs allowances: two bottles of wine or spirits; 200 cigarettes or 50 cigars or 250 grams of tobacco; perfume for personal use and gifts to the total value of US$10. A typewriter, radio, binoculars, movie camera and equipment, provided these are not new. Permit needed for guns and ammunition: apply in advance to the Ministry of Defense.

## AIRPORT INFORMATION

Ernesto Cortissoz airport is six miles from Barranquilla. The taxi fare is about 44 pesos. El Dorado airport is eight miles from Bogotá. From 6am-10pm, buses run every 30 minutes, fare, 5 pesos. Tip the porter about 2 pesos per bag. Taxis available at all times. Fare to the center of town about 44 pesos. Hotel reservation center and duty-free shop at the airport.

## ACCOMMODATIONS

Throughout Colombia, luxury hotels charge about US$11.50 (250 pesos) for a single room, US$14.50 (330 pesos) for a double; moderate hotels, US$9.00 (195 pesos) single; US$9.20 (200 pesos) double; budget hotels, US$6.90 (150 pesos) single; US$9.20 (200 pesos) double. All rates for rooms with private bath. There is a 5% hotel tax, but no service charge. There are also motels, *hosterías* and bungalows. It costs 800 pesos a month, with breakfast, to stay in student accommodations. For assistance in finding accommodations in Bogotá go to the Corporación Nacional de Turismo de Colombia, Calle 19, 6-68 (tel: 810510). Hotels in Bogotá:

**Single from US$15 (327 Pesos); double from US$20 (436 Pesos)**

**Bogotá Hilton** Carrera 7, 32-16
**TEQUENDAMA INTER•CONTINENTAL** Calle 26, 10-42

**Single from US$10 (218 Pesos); double from US$13 (283 Pesos)**

**Bacata** Calle 19, 5-32
**Comendador** Carrera 18, 38-41
**Continental** Avenida Jiménez, 4-16
**Cordillera** Carrera 8a, 16-89
**Dann** Avenida 19, 5-72

**Single from US$3 (66 Pesos); double from US$5 (109 Pesos)**

**El Presidente** Calle 23, 9-45
**Steves** Carrera 10, 16-67

## USEFUL INFORMATION

**Banks:** Open Mon-Fri 9 to 3, some close between noon and 2:30 and close at 4.

**Postage:** Most good stores sell stamps. Internal surface mail unreliable; send all letters air mail. The main post office is on Carrera 7, near Calle 17.

**Telephone Tips:** Booths on main streets in hotels, restaurants and cafés. Useful numbers:

**Pan Am Offices:** Bogotá (Tequendama Hotel), 420-720
Barranquilla, 11-610
Cali, 821-154
**Airport Information,** 669-200
**Tourist Offices,** 810-510
**Accommodations Offices,** 669-200
**Directory Inquiries,** 13 and 14
**Time,** 17
**Fire,** 19
**Police,** 12
**Red Cross,** 453-333

**Newspapers:** Foreign magazines and newspapers available. Local English-language newspaper is the *Andean Times.*

**Tipping:** Customary in Colombia, but some exceptions—neither taxi drivers nor museum guides are tipped. In restaurants, 10% —if a service charge of 10% has been included in the check, a tip of 5% is still expected. Airport porter, 3 pesos per bag; porters and hotel porters, 2 pesos per bag; rest room attendants, 2 pesos.

**Electricity:** Bogotá—150 volts 60 cycles AC, but in most first-class hotels 110 volts 60 cycles AC; same in rest of country.

**Laundry:** Dry-cleaning and laundry services quick, efficient and inexpensive. First-class hotels have a 24-hour service (dry-cleaning a suit 15-20 pesos; laundering a shirt 6-10 pesos).

**Hairdressing:** First-class hotels have good salons (shampoo and set, 12-15 pesos; man's haircut, 10-15 pesos).

**Photography:** Equipment and films easily found in major cities, but expensive. Developing times; two to three days for black and white; from four to five days for color.

**Clubs:** Rotary and Lions.

**Babysitting:** Most hotels have services—ask the hotel clerk. Services include: **Guardería Infantil La Porciuncula** (tel: 497484); **Babylandia** (tel: 497310); **Centro Social Sta Magdalene Sofia** (tel: 583366) and **Gardería Infantil Pinocho** (tel: 692805).

**Health:** Many doctors are US-trained and speak good English. Except for large hotels, drink only boiled water. Eat only fruit and vegetables which have been peeled. Most pharmaceuticals and toiletries avaliable but expensive.

## TRANSPORTATION

Bogotá has a bus service with reasonable fares, but taxis are the most convenient form of city transport and a must after nightfall (Colombia has quite a crime problem). Taxis are metered with a minimum charge of 2 pesos; extra charges after 9 pm, on Sundays and holidays. You can flag one down in the street or phone **Taxi Real** (tel: 430580). You can rent a car from **Hertz**—who have branches at the airport and at the Tequendama Hotel arcade (tel: 347961). Hourly rates vary from US$1.70 to US $2.35 (with an additional US10-14c per kilometer). Traffic in cities is disorganized and difficult and cross-country roads poorly marked. Best bet is to rent a chauffeur-driven car. Rates are US$1.84 an hour within city limits.

Railroad services are interesting but rustic and not recommended. Long-distance bus services also connect main cities, but they too, are not very comfortable. Airways are the best way to travel. Avinanca, SAM, Aerocondor, TAO, TAC are the domestic airlines. Helicopter services are also available through **Helicol** (Helicópteros Nacionales de Colombia, an Avianca affiliate). **Avianca** has a "See Colombia" ticket for US$65.00, valid for 30 days' unlimited travel within the country, except to San Andrés, in the Caribbean, and Leticia, on the Amazon (you have to pay US$25.00 more to go there). Flying times from Bogotá are: Barranquilla—1 hour 10 minutes; Cartagena—1 hour 5 minutes; Santa Marta—1 hour 10 minutes; Cali—40 minutes and Medellín —35 minutes.

## FOOD AND RESTAURANTS

Colombians are specialists in soups and stews. Native dishes well worth trying, are *ajiaco,* a delicious chicken and potato soup, served with avocado pear or corn on the cob; *puchero Santa Fereno*: boiled chicken, brisket of beef and port with pumpkin and vegetables; *lechona*: stuffed pork; *arroz con pollo*: traditional chicken with rice; *viudo de pescado*: a fish stew, and *sacocho*: which could be compared with bouillabaisse. *Tamales*: spicy meat pies steamed in banana leaves, are extremely tasty and nutritious. But if you prefer international cuisine, good restaurants are plentiful. Top of the list in Bogotá are the **Monserrate Dining Room,** on the 17th floor of the Tequendama (tel: 812080); **La Hacienda** and **Le Toit** Supper Club (tel: 326020) at the Bogotá Hilton. **La Reserve** (Carrera 15, 13-15—tel: 459659); **Eduardo** (Carrera 11, 89-22—tel: 364387) and the **Unicorn Club** (Calle 94, 7-75—tel: 362641) are also first-class international restaurants. Go to **Koster** (Calle 35, 74-32) for French food or try the *boeuf strogonoff* or the *chicken kiev* at the **Balalaika** (Carrera 15, 32-83—tel: 320796); the *paella* at **La Zambra** (Carrera 3, 74-32) and other Spanish dishes are delicious; **El Emir** (Carrera 13, 67-00—tel: 496980) specializes in Arabian food. For native Colombian meals go to the **Casa Vieja** (3-73, Avenida Jiménez—tel: 346171) one of the oldest houses in town and **Los Arrayanes** (tel: 348908) in the same building; **La Pola** (Calle 19, 1-85—tel: 411343); **Mesón de Indias** (Calle 13, 3-53—tel: 438651) and **Zaguan de Las Aguas** (Carrera 3, 74-32). In Cali, the **Hotel Inter•Continental** has two restaurants, excellent both for international and local dishes; **Cali Viejo** has splendid atmosphere. In Medellín the **Hotel Bolívar** (Carrera 53, 45-99); **Hotel Veracruz** (Carrera 50, 54-22) and the **Inter•Continental Medellín,** five miles out of town, also have international cuisine. **Fondas Antioquenas** specializes in excellent Colombian food. In Cartagena, go to **Capilla Del Mar** (Carrera 3) for splendid lobster and fish. The **Club de Pesca,** at the Fuerte del Pastelillo, has superb sea food.

Breakfast is taken from 8 to 10, lunch from noon to 2:30 and dinner from 8 to 10. A meal in an expensive restaurant will cost about US$10 for one; in a medium-priced restaurant about US$8 and in an inexpensive one about US$5. For low-priced meals and snacks **Le Chalet Suizo** (Carrera 7, 21-51—tel: 341721); **Monte Blanco** (throughout the city); **Club Sandwich** (between Carrera 9 and 7); **Crem Helado** (Carrera 14, 31-49) are recommended: you can get hamburgers, sandwiches, *empanadas* (two layers of corn dough with filling) and hot *chile con carne,* etc. For late afternoon tea and pastries go to **La Suiza** (Calle 25, 9-41) or **Belalcázar** (Carrera 7). Most restaurants close on Sunday. Some can be fussy about dress: men may need a jacket and tie. Eating from street stalls is not recommended.

## DRINKING TIPS

The best beer is **Club Colombia,** which is now exported to the US. Local rums are good too, and inexpensive. **Ron Caldas** is similar to Jamaican rum, **Ron Medellín** is lighter. But try **guarapo** and the potent **aguardiente** ("firewater") both made from the sugar cane. There are some local wines but most are imported. The average price of a whisky and soda, or of a bottle of wine, is about 20 pesos. There are no liquor restrictions but ladies are not welcome in bars and cafés, except in top hotels. Visitors find alcohol has a much more immediate effect than at lower altitudes. Colombian coffee is perhaps the best in the world. At the **El Dorado Airport** there is a free coffee bar on the second floor.

## ENTERTAINMENT

Evening entertainment in Bogotá, specially in winter, is centered around the **Teatro Colón,** a Spanish colonial theater, where you can go for opera, concerts and ballet. There are usually two performances every evening, at 6:30 and 9:30. There are also several Spanish-speaking theater groups and an English-speaking group who perform in town. There are band concerts at the **Parque Independencia** on Sunday mornings; concerts (and art exhibitions) at the **Luís Angel Arango** library; and musicals, plays and native dances at **La Media Torta,** an open-air theater near Quinta de Bolívar. Movie-going is very popular. The best movie houses are on **Carrera 7.**

The most sophisticated night spots in Bogotá are the **Monserrate Room** in the Tequendama Hotel and **Le Toit,** on the 41st floor of the Bogotá Hilton. The **As de Copas** (Carrera 13, 59-24) features flamenco dancing; the **Unicorn** (Calle 119, 7-75) is a private club where tourists are welcome and the single person will not feel out of place; the popular **El Circo Eléctrico** (Carrera 10, 26-

77) has the best drinks in Bogotá; **Bar Santa Fé,** at the Tequendama Hotel has a "Western" atmosphere and **Candilejas** (off Carrera 13) is a Spanish nightclub. Discothèques are **Las Vagones,** across from the Tequendama Hotel, **Le Drugstore,** in the El Lago Shopping Center and **Discothèque Dumbo** (Carrera 13, 44-21). Others are **Tizca** on Calle 28, which has a strip show or the **Café Europa Billares** (Calle 22 near Carrera 8A). Women should not walk alone in the streets at night.

## SHOPPING

The main shopping area of Bogotá is on **Carrera 7:** shops and stores are open from 8.30 or 9-6.30, including Saturdays. Colombian clothing and shoes are inexpensive—linen shirts at less than US$8. Very fashionable and warm are the native *Ruanas,* woollen ponchos in brilliant colors worn by both men and women over their street clothes. Best buys are emeralds, of which Colombia is the world's greatest source. Good jewelers are in the Tequendama and Hilton Hotels and on Carreras 6, 12 and 13, where you'll find the **Jewelry Center.** A delightful gift is an 18-carat gold charm—a little basket enclosing an uncut emerald, which you can get for about US$7.50. For silver and leather goods or handicraft antiques the best store is the government-controlled **Artesanias de Colombia** (Calle 19, 5-59) where you can get leather duffle-bags, calfskin rugs, woven mats, heavy copper paella pans and many delightful pieces. For pre-Colombian artifacts go to **Jaime Errazuriz** in the Tequendama Hotel or **Galería Bogotá** (Carrera 13, 44-54). For antiques, brass and copper-ware **La Toma de Agua** (Calle 10, 2-7) or a delightful three-story shop called simply **Antiques,** on Plaza Bolívar. Try bargaining, except in the large department stores.

## SPORT

*Tejo,* played by throwing a metal disc at a "cap" which explodes (similar to pitching horseshoes), is the only native Colombian sport. You can watch this game at the **Campo Colombia** (Calle 32, 6-23). Football (soccer), cockfighting, tennis and basketball are popular. There is horse racing on Sundays at the **Hippódromo Techo,** in Bogotá; dog racing at **Autopista del Norte 20,** Puente. During the winter the best Spanish bullfighters are in South America: you can see them at **Plaza de Toros de Santamaría.** Among the many golf courses, **Bogotá Country Club** (two 18-hole courses), **Los Lagartos** and **San Andrés.** Baseball is played in Barranquilla and Cartagena, polo in **Medellín.** There is marlin fishing off **Barranquilla** and trout fishing in the lakes near Bogotá. Water skiing in **Santa Marta,** skin-diving in **San Andrés.** There are bears, jaguar, panther, tapir for the hunter: you need a license. Partridge, duck and geese are plentiful.

## WHAT TO SEE

**Bogotá:** Among the new skyscrapers of modern Bogotá are treasures of Colombia's colonial past: the **Palace of San Carlos,** where Simon Bolívar once lived, now the Presidential Palace (go at 5 pm and you will see the changing of the guard); the **Cathedral** in Plaza Bolívar, originally built in 1573, which holds a very fine collection of paintings from the colonial period; the churches of **San Francisco, San Diego** and **Veracruz** (which contains the remains of the heroes of the War of Independence with Spain); **La Toma de Agua,** in the district of La Candelaria,

is one of the finest old buildings in the city; also the **Teatro Colón** and the **Mint** (Calle 11, 4-93). An absolute must is the **Museo del Oro** (Gold Museum) on Carrera 6, Calle 16, where a collection of 15,000 pre-Colombian gold pieces is displayed. Museums are open from 10-6 from Tuesday to Saturday and on Sundays and vacations from 10-2. Worth a visit are the **Colonial Museum** (Carrera 6, 9-77), in the cloisters next to the Church of San Ignacio and the **National Museum** (Carrera 7, 28-66). Bogotá also has a modern **Planetarium** and **Museum of Natural History.**

Outside town you can go by cable car (*Teleférico*) to the top of Monserrate, for a spectacular view of Bogotá. Only 35 miles from the heart of town is one of the wonders of South America, the **Salt Cathedral of Zipaquira,** carved by the Chibcha Indians and half-a-mile below ground. It can hold 10,000 people and you can drive three miles into the mine, almost to the altar. But don't forget your coat—it's chilly.

## THE CARIBBEAN COAST

**Barranquilla:** On the mouth of the Magdalena River, this modern industrial city of 800,000 is the main port of the country. The **Country Club** has golf, tennis and swimming facilities and you can rent a boat from the Yacht Club for a day's deep sea fishing. The "South American Wimbledon" tennis championships are held in Barranquilla in March. For German cooking try **Brandes** and the **Fogón Gaucho** for meats Argentine style. Hotels are the **Caribana** (Carrera 41, 40-42) single from US$8; **Central** (Calle 38, 41-22) single from US$8; **EL PRADO INTER•CONTINENTAL** (Carrera 54, 70-10) single from US$11.50; **Genova** (Calle 44, 44-46) single from US$6.50; **Riviera** (Calle 34, 44-81) single from US$4.50.

**Cartagena:** The "golden gate to South America" is the most perfectly preserved example of a walled city in the New World. See the historic Castles of **San Felipe** and **San Fernando** and the imposing fortress of **San Sebastian** and **Bocachica.** Visit the **Vaults,** the **Clock Tower,** the **Inquisition Palace.** Hotels are the **Americano** (Boco Grande, Avenida San Martín) single from US$8; **Del Caribe** (Boco Grande, Carrera 1) single from US$9; **Bahía** (Boco Grande, Avenida San Martín) single from US$7.50; **Quinta Avenida,** single from US$8; **Flamingo** (Boco Grande, Avenida San Martín) single from US$6.

**Santa Marta** is a delightful year-round seaside resort, ideal for fishing, water-skiing, sunbathing and skin-diving and dune sliding on the **Rodadero Beach.** Just out of town is the **Hacienda de San Pedro Alejandrino,** a national shrine and museum with the room where Simon Bolívar died in 1830.

**San Andrés:** A lazy tropical island off the coast of Nicaragua. It is said that the pirate Morgan buried his treasure on the island and according to legend it is still there. You can see **Morgan's Cave,** in the southern part of the island.

## THE WESTERN (PACIFIC) COAST

**Medellín** is the second city of Colombia. Its **Cathedral** is said to be the largest brick building in the world. Do visit the orchid plantation at **La Finca El Ranchito,** just outside the city and the estate owned by Señor Ospina Pérez, which has 70,000 orchid plants of more than 300 varieties. Hotels are: **Europa-**

**Normandie** (Calle 53, 49-100) single from US$9; **MEDELLIN-INTER•CONTINENTAL** (Variante a las Palmas) single from US$13.05; **Nutibara,** single from US$10; **Vera Cruz,** (Carrera 50, 54-18) single from US$7.

**Cali:** It is said that the most beautiful women in Colombia come from Cali, which has an ideal climate. It has fine universities, good sports facilities and many social clubs. Among hotels are the **CALI-INTER•CONTINENTAL** (Avenida Colombia 2-72) single from US$13.05.

**Manizales:** Here on the peaks of El Nevado del Ruiz you can go skiing and tobogganing the year round.

**San Agustín:** The most important archeological zone in Colombia, with gigantic stone statues, pre-Colombian tombs and burial mounds.

## NORTH AND EAST OF BOGOTÁ

**Tunja:** In the Departamento of Boyaca, "the birthplace of Colombia," on the site of the citadel of the ancient Unza Indians, Tunja is another colonial city. Many of the Spanish Conquistadores settled here and their coats-of-arms, carved in stone, still adorn the façades of ancient mansions.

**Llanos Orientales:** A plain of 110,000 square miles, where with a Jeep and a tent you can enjoy a really inexpensive and adventurous holiday fishing, and hunting with a rifle, cougar, deer, alligator and crocodile.

## SOURCES OF FURTHER INFORMATION

**Pan Am** offices in Bogotá in the Tequendama Hotel (tel: 420720); in Cali at Calle 12, 5-30; in Barranquilla in the Colseguros and from any Pan Am office around the world; **Corporación Nacional de Turismo,** Calle 19, 6-68, Bogotá and in main cities; **Colombia Government Tourist Board,** 140 East 57th Street, New York, NY 10022; the **Colombian Consulate General,** 3 Hans Crescent, London SW1.

# Costa Rica

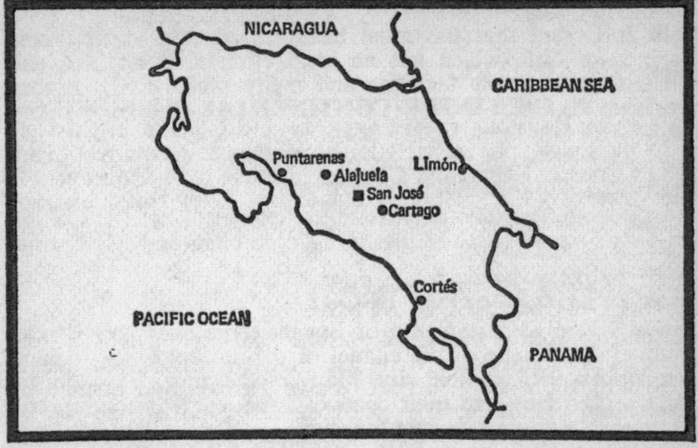


## WHAT'S SPECIAL

Bananas, coffee, cocoa, tobacco and honey all come out of Costa Rica, a country with no army and compulsory education. Here orchids bloom all year round and there are forests of rosewood, cedar and mahogany. Visitors can climb volcanoes and view two oceans, hunt jaguar, tapirs, ocelot and deer, go mining for gold, or fish for black marlin, tarpan, sawfish and lobster.

## COUNTRY BRIEFING

**Size:** 19,883 square miles
**Capital:** San José
**Population:** 1,811,290
**Capital Population:** 414,624

**Climate:** The dry season, December-May, is the best time to visit, but the climate is agreeable all year round.

**WEATHER IN SAN JOSE**—Lat N9°56′—Alt 3,760 ft

| Temp | Jan | Feb | Mar | Apr | May | Jun | Jul | Aug | Sep | Oct | Nov | Dec |
|---|---|---|---|---|---|---|---|---|---|---|---|---|
| Ave Low | 58° | 58° | 59° | 62° | 62° | 62° | 62° | 61° | 61° | 60° | 60° | 58° |
| Ave High | 75° | 76° | 79° | 79° | 80° | 79° | 77° | 78° | 79° | 77° | 77° | 75° |
| Days of No Rain | 28 | 27 | 29 | 23 | 12 | 8 | 8 | 7 | 6 | 6 | 16 | 15 |

**Government:** A republic.

**Language:** Spanish. English, German, French, Dutch and Italian frequently heard.

**Religion:** Roman Catholic, but other denominations represented.

**Currency:** The Colon: 100 céntimos = 1 Colón

| | 50 cént. | 1 Col. | 5 Col. | 10 Col. | 20 Col. | 50 Col. | 100 Col. | 400 Col. |
|---|---|---|---|---|---|---|---|---|
| US (Dollars.Cents) | .07 | .15 | .76 | 1.52 | 3.05 | 7.63 | 15.26 | 61.06 |
| UK (Pounds.Pence) | .02 | .04 | .24 | .49 | .99 | 2.47 | 4.95 | 19.80 |

**Public Holidays:**
New Year's Day, 1 Jan
Feast of St Joseph, 19 Mar
Anniversary of the Battle of of Rivas, 11 Apr
Easter
Labor Day, 1 May
Corpus Christi, June
St Peter and St Paul, 29 Jun

Anniversary of the Annexation of Guanacaste Province, 5 Jul
Our Lady of the Angels, 2 Aug
Assumption and Mother's Day, 15 Aug
Independence Day, 15 Sep
Columbus Day, 12 Oct
Immaculate Conception, 8 Dec
Christmas Day, 25 Dec

## HOW TO GET THERE

Fly Pan Am direct to San José, Santa Maria International Airport, from Houston via Mexico City and Guatemala City and some days also via San Salvador or Managua. Also direct flights from Caracas via Panamá City. Flying time from Houston, 4¾ hours; Mexico City, 3 hours; Guatemala City, 1¼ hours; San Salvador, 1¼ hours; Managua, ¾ hours; Caracas, 3 hours and Panamá City, 1 hour.

## REQUIREMENTS FOR ENTRY AND CUSTOMS REGULATIONS

Passport or Tourist Visa Card (valid for 30 days) available from Costa Rican Consulates, or at US Pan Am offices; plus means of identification and tickets for onward travel and a smallpox vaccination certificate. The visa costs US$2 but is free for US and UK citizens. No currency restrictions and no customs declaration necessary for passengers carrying only personal effects. Duty-free allowance: up to three liters of wine or spirits; half kilogram tobacco in any form, and other items not exceeding US$100 as a taxable amount.

## AIRPORT INFORMATION

Santa Maria International Airport is 11 miles from San José. Buses are frequent and cost 1.50Cs. Taxis plentiful and cost about 2Cs. Airport departure tax, 20Cs. Duty-free shop and hotel reservation counter.

## ACCOMMODATIONS

For help in finding accommodations there is the **Instituto Costarricense de Turismo,** Calle Alfredo Volio, Avenidas 4/6, Apartado 777, San José (tel: 23-2733). Inexpensive *pensiones* available from about 10Cs (US$1.50). Hotels in San José:

**Single from US$10 (65.50 Cs); double from US$14 (92 Cs)**

**Balmoral** Avenida Central, Calles 7/9
**Europa** Calle Central, 5a Avenida
**Irazú** PO Box 962
**President** Avenida Central, Calles 7/9
**Royal Dutch** PO Box 4258
**Crystal** PO Box 5570, Autopista Wilson

**Single from US$8 (52.40 Cs); double from US$11 (72.05 Cs)**

**Amstel** Calle 7, Avenidas 10/12
**Gran Costa Rica** 3a Calle, Avenidas Central/2

**Single from US$4 (26.20 Cs); double from US$6 (39.30 Cs)**

**Diplomat** Calle 6, Avenidas Oriente/2
**Pensión Canada** Calle 9, Avenida 9, Casa No 779
**Plaza** Avenida Central, Calles 2/4

## USEFUL INFORMATION

When giving directions the Costa Rican will give distances not in blocks, or yards, but in *varas*—a *vara* is some 33 inches.

**Banks:** Open 8-11 and 1:30-3, Mon-Fri; 8-11am Sat. Change currency and travelers' checks at hotels and stores.

**Postage:** Stamps at post offices, newsstands, bookshops.

**Telephone Tips:** Phones in streets, cafés and restaurants. Useful numbers:

**Pan Am office,** 23-2088
**Airport Information,** 41-0744
**Operator,** 113
**Time,** 112
**Weather,** 22-5616
**Police,** 118
**Fire,** 118
**Ambulance,** 21-5888

**Newspapers:** English-language newspapers available. Local English-language publications are the *Tico Times* and *The Grapevine.*

**Tipping:** A 10% charge is either included in the check or expected in restaurants. Porters, 50 céntimos per piece of luggage (minimum 1C); hotel porters, and chambermaids, 50 céntimos; taxi drivers do not expect tips.

**Electricity:** 110 volts, 60 cycles AC throughout the country.

**Laundry:** Good laundry and dry-cleaning services (dry-cleaning a suit, 6Cs; laundering a shirt, 1.25Cs).

**Hairdressing**: First-class hotels have salons (shampoo and set, 12Cs-15Cs; man's haircut, 2.50Cs).

**Photography:** Good suppliers in main cities. Black and white film costs about 4.50Cs and color 19.50Cs. Developing, 2-3 days for black and white, 4-8 for color.

**Clubs:** Rotary, Lions, Kiwanis, Jaycees.

**Babysitting:** None.

**Toilets:** No public toilets, but free in restaurants, bars, hotels, and gas stations. Ladies, *Damas* or *Señoras*; men, *Caballeros* or *Hombres.*

**Health:** Many English-speaking doctors and dentists. Imported pharmaceuticals are expensive. Tap water is drinkable in San José; fruit should be washed. Anti-malarial drugs should be taken when visiting some coastal regions.

## TRANSPORTATION

Good highway and bus services between San José and most places of interest. Slow but inexpensive railroad service. There are 232 local and private airports, the main ones served by **LACSA, APSA, AVE, ALPA** among internal airlines. Virtually all places are within 45 minutes flight of San José. Flights tend to leave in the morning only. Taxis in San José abundant and can be flagged in the street; cost, a fixed 3C within the metropolitan area. U-drive cars cost US$10 a day plus 10 cents per kilometer and US$2 insurance; another US$10 a day if you want a chauffeur. A few good highways, but elsewhere surfaces are fair. The ferry across the Nicoya Gulf from Puntarenas to Nicoya, cuts the three-hour road time in half.

## FOOD AND RESTAURANTS

Local dishes are tasty. Try *tamales*—made from meat, rice and corn with chili on top, wrapped in a banana leaf; *ceviche,* raw fish marinated in spices and lemon juice; *mondongo,* tripe in different sauces, and soups—*olla de carne* and *pozol*. Breakfast is from 6-9; lunch 12-2; dinner 6-8. You can get continental food at the **Royal Dutch Hotel,** The **Gran Hotel Costa Rica** (Calle 3, Avenida Central 2—tel: 21-4000); French food at **La Bastille** (Plaza Colón, Calle 22—tel: 22-4950). For national dishes try **Balcón de Europa** (Avenida Central, Calle 7/9—tel: 21-4841), and **Chavelona** (Avenida 10, Calle 10/12—tel: 21-6094), and if you like seafood, **Casino Español** (Calle 3, Avenida Central 2—tel: 21-4241).

## DRINKING TIPS

Rum is the national drink. Beer is popular and good. Whisky and soda costs between 2.50Cs and 5Cs. It is inadvisable for women to go into bars unaccompanied.

## ENTERTAINMENT

At the **National Theater** in San José there is drama, opera, ballet and concerts, often by international companies. Movie houses show English and American movies with original soundtracks. San José has several nightclubs including **Los Naranjos, Boîte Europa** and the **Dolphin Club** at the President Hotel.

## SHOPPING

Shops open 8-12 and 2-6, Mon-Sat. The best shops: **La Gloria, La Galería** and **Mil Colores** on Avenida Central, and others around the Central Market. The best souvenirs to buy are articles made from wood. Bargain in stores and markets.

## SPORTS

Soccer is the national sport, but there is also basketball, boxing, baseball and bullfights in the last week of every year. You can play tennis or golf, go horseback riding, yachting or fishing. The annual Holy Week tarpon tournament attracts many North American sportsmen who come for the marlin, sharks, sawfish, snook and tarpon. Guided safaris are arranged for big game hunting in the Sarapiqui region for jaguar, tapir, deer and alligator.

## WHAT TO SEE

In San José the 19th-century **National Theater** has a lavish interior with murals, gold decorations and fine marble staircases. Other interesting buildings are the **Metropolitan Museum** and the **National University** in the remarkable University City. The **Museo Nacional** (Calle 15/17, Avenida 2) has collections of pre-Columbian antiquities and the **Banco Central's Gold Museum** houses ancient gold ornaments.

Sugar mills, cocoa plantations, coffee and banana processing plants are all interesting and at **Sorche's** ox-cart factory wagons are still painted by hand. Not very far from San José is the oldest church in Costa Rica, the **Otosi Mission** built by the Spanish in 1743. On the Pacific coast are the white sand beaches of **Playas del Coco** and **Bahía de Culebra** (Coconut Beach and Snake Bay). The resort of **Ojo de Agua** is famous for its pure mountain spring.

Two-and-a-half hours' drive from the capital is the 11,000-foot-high **Irazú volcano,** still active. From the top on a clear day, both the Atlantic and Pacific oceans can be seen. **Poas Volcano** is also active and also in this direction is **Alajuela,** a good summer resort. Further west—15 minutes by air or four hours by train from the capital—is **Puntarenas,** a resort and center for great fishing. There are some good hotels here, including the **Tioga,** from US$4 single.

Two-hundred miles offshore is **Cocos Island,** whose legendary buried treasure has drawn hundreds of expeditions. Eastward from San José, a short trip by air, or a scenically exciting six-hour train ride, is the port of **Limón** where Columbus landed on his fourth voyage. From here, bananas, coffee, honey and other goods are shipped. Hotels are the **Park,** single from US$4, and the **Caribe,** single from US$5.

## SOURCES OF FURTHER INFORMATION

**Pan Am office,** Solera Building, Avenida 3, Calle 5, San José, and from any Pan Am office around the world; **Instituto Costarricense de Turismo,** Calle Alfredo Volio, Avenida 4/6, Apartado 777, San José; **Costa Rica Consulate General,** 211 East 43rd Street, New York, 10017; **Costa Rican Embassy,** 8 Braemar Mansions, Cornwall Gardens, London SW7.

# Ecuador

**WHAT'S SPECIAL**

Tiny Ecuador is full of natural beauty. From the north to the south run two imposing Andean Cordilleras—the backbone of the country, with magnificent volcanoes, some extinct but some only dormant, inhabited by the llamas, the giant condor and the handsome, large-beaked *huacamayos*. Between these two mountain ranges, at an altitude of 7,000 to 9,000 feet, lies the Central Valley, where over half of Ecuadorians live. Nearly 40% of all Ecuadorians are Indians and their life has changed little since their land was invaded by the Spanish Conquistadors. Between the Andes and the Pacific Ocean lie the sprawling plantations and the coastal plains of the Guayas River. Guayaquil largest city in Ecuador, is the commercial capital of the region. To the east of the Cordilleras lies the sparsely inhabited Oriente—the Amazonian jungles, where the recently discovered oil deposits are said to be larger than those in Venezuela.

**COUNTRY BRIEFING**

**Size:** 105,648 square miles **Population:** 6,973,100
**Capital:** Quito **Capital Population:** 600,000

**Climate:** Sharp contrasts according to altitude. On the coastal lowlands, equatorial, with average temperature 83°, a hot rainy season from November-May and a dry season for rest of year. Quito, in Central Valley (altitude 9,350 ft), has cool spring climate throughout year with average temperature 55°.

**WEATHER IN QUITO**—Lat SO°13′—Alt 9,446 ft

| Temp | Jan | Feb | Mar | Apr | May | Jun | Jul | Aug | Sep | Oct | Nov | Dec |
|---|---|---|---|---|---|---|---|---|---|---|---|---|
| Ave Low | 46° | 47° | 47° | 47° | 47° | 45° | 44° | 45° | 45° | 46° | 45° | 46° |
| Ave High | 72° | 71° | 71° | 70° | 70° | 71° | 72° | 73° | 73° | 72° | 72° | 72° |
| Days of No Rain | 15 | 11 | 11 | 8 | 10 | 18 | 24 | 22 | 16 | 13 | 16 | 15 |

**Government:** A republic.

**Language:** Spanish. English only in hotels, tourist centers and major shops.

**Religion:** Predominantly Roman Catholic.

**Currency:** The Sucre: 100 centavos = 1 sucre

| | 1 | 5 | 10 | 20 | 50 | 100 | 500 | 1,000 |
|---|---|---|---|---|---|---|---|---|
| US (Dollars.Cents) | .038 | .192 | .384 | .769 | $1.923 | $3.846 | $19.23 | $38.461 |
| UK (Pounds.Pence) | .016 | .082 | .165 | .330 | .827 | £1.65 | £8.27 | £16.522 |

**Public Holidays:**

New Year's Day, 1 Jan
2-day carnival on Monday and Tuesday preceding Lent
Maundy Thursday and Good Friday
Labor Day, 1 May
Battle of Pichincha, 24 May
Bolívar's Anniversary, 24 July
Independence Day, 10 Aug
Anniversary of Guayaquil, 9 Oct
Columbus' Day, 12 Oct
All Saints' Day, 1 Nov
All Souls' Day, 2 Nov
Independence of Cuenca, 3 Nov
Foundation of Quito, 6 Dec
Christmas Day, 25 Dec

## HOW TO GET THERE

Fly Pan Am to Panamá City or Caracas, then by connecting flight to Guayaquil, Simon Bolívar Airport or to Quito, Mariscal Sucre Airport. Flying time from Panamá City is 1¾ hours to Guayaquil and 1½ hours to Quito. Flying time from Caracas is 3¼ hours to Guayaquil (via Bogotá) and 3 hours to Quito (via Bogotá).

## REQUIREMENTS FOR ENTRY AND CUSTOMS REGULATIONS

Passport, smallpox vaccination certificate, ticket and tourist card valid for 90 days obtainable from Pan Am, Ecuadorian Consulates or on arrival, on production of three photos. Visitors are allowed to bring in duty-free: one liter spirits, seven ounces tobacco or 50 cigars or 300 cigarettes and personal effects. No restriction on amount of foreign currency brought in, but only same amount may be taken out.

## AIRPORT INFORMATION

The International Airport for Quito is Mariscal Sucre, five miles from the city center. Buses run infrequently but taxis available during day (no night flights into Quito). The fare to the city is 30 sucre. No arrival tax, but 62.50 sucre on departure. At airport duty-free shop, exchange office and a tourist information desk. Tip airport porter 2 to 5 sucre. Simon Bolívar Airport is three miles from Guayaquil. A taxi to the center costs 20-25 sucre.

## ACCOMMODATIONS

Quito has luxurious first-class hotels; the **HOTEL INTER•CONTINENTAL QUITO** is perhaps the most famous. But you will not have any difficulty in finding accommodations at very reasonable prices. Pensions and *residencias* are comfortable and clean; most offer full pension as an option. If there is no central heating make sure you have enough blankets as nights are quite chilly. The hotel reservation counter at the Airport is open daily from 7am-6. For help in finding accommodations go to the **Tourist Commission** on 1315 Av Manuel Larrea (in Guayaquil, at the Fiori Building, Av 9 de Octubre). All hotel bills are subject to 10% service charge and 10% tax. Hotels in Quito:

**Single from US$11 (286 sucre); double from US$15 (390 sucre)**

**Colón International** Avenue Amazonas/Patri 3103
**INTER•CONTINENTAL** 12 de Octubre Street, 2500

**Single from US$4 (104 sucre); double from US$8 (208 sucre)**

**Colonial** Maldonado 3035
**Embajador** Avenida Colón 1565
**Humboldt Capitol** Espejo Street 931
**Inca Imperial** 219 Bogotá Street
**Majestic** Independence Square

**Single from US$2.25 (58 sucre); double from US$4.50 (117 sucre)**

**Columbus** Avenida Colón 1664

## USEFUL INFORMATION

**Banks:** Open Mon-Fri from 9.00-noon; 2.30-4.00. Take travelers' checks in dollars, you can cash them in good hotels and major stores.

**Postage:** Stamps are available from post offices.

**Telephone Tips:** Phones in restaurants, hotels, shops.

**Useful Numbers: Tourist Information:** 570 040; **Ecuadorian Tours** (agency of the American Express): 219 000.

**Newspapers:** English-language magazines in Quito and Guyaquil.

**Tipping:** Restaurants generally include a 10% service charge in checks, but a 5% to 10% tip is still expected. If service charge not included, leave a tip of 15%. Porters, 2 to 5 sucre per bag; hairdressers, 20% of the bill; cloakroom attendants, 1 sucre. Taxi drivers not tipped.

**Electricity:** 110 volts, 60 cycles AC.

**Laundry:** Dry-cleaning and laundry service excellent and speedy in luxury hotels (dry-cleaning a suit, 45 sucre; laundering a shirt, 13 sucre).

**Hairdressing:** First-class hotels have good salons (shampoo and set 28 sucre plus 20% tip).

**Photography:** Equipment and film available in Quito and Guayaquil, but prices high. Developing not very reliable.

**Clubs:** Lions, Rotary and Jaycees.

**Babysitting:** Services can be arranged in good hotels.

**Toilets:** Rely on hotels and good restaurants. Ladies, *Damas*; Men, *Caballeros*.

**Health:** Good hospitals in Quito and Guayaquil, where some doctors speak English. Pharmaceutical and toiletries available in major cities, but expensive. Boil water before drinking. Avoid fresh fruit and vegetables, except in good hotels and first-class restaurants. Inoculation against typhoid and hepatitis advisable. Remember the high altitude and take it easy.

## TRANSPORTATION

Buses and *colectivos* (smaller buses seating up to 20) available but taxis are more convenient; you will find them at stands in the main plazas, or you can flag one down in the street. Average fare in the city is 10-15 sucres, but up to double at night. You can also rent a taxi by the hour for 50 sucre per hour. For a self-drive car the daily rate is US$12 (a deposit of US$25 is also usually required); chauffeur-driven US$2.50 an hour. Roads on the whole are good. If you have time to spare, the rail journey from Guayaquil to Quito is exciting but takes a long time—12 to 18 hours to cover the 288 miles, so do not forget to take sandwiches. Perhaps the most exciting part of the journey is the climb up the **Nariz del Diablo** (Devil's Nose) via a series of switchbacks, to a perpendicular ridge 1,000 ft above the river's gorge.

You can also travel from Quito to Guayaquil in comfortable air-conditioned buses via Transandina. The journey takes eight hours (reserve in advance). **CEA** (Companía Ecuadoriana de Aviación) and **Tame** (Ecuadorian Military Air Transports) have flights to Guayaquil and other cities and to the Galápagos Islands. Flying time from Quito to Guayaquil, 45 mins.

## FOOD AND RESTAURANTS

There are some native specialties that you ought to try. Favorites are *locro,* a stew made with potatoes, beef broth and a squash-like vegetable called *yuca,* served topped with an avocado pear; *llapingachos,* fried mashed potatoes with cheese and an egg; *humitas,* sweet corn tamales and *choclo,* corn on the cob. If you fancy something really typical, try *cuy,* which is baked guinea pig and, if you like fish, *ceviche de corvina,* white fish in lemon sauce. **La Choza** (Avenida 12 de Octubre) is perhaps the best restaurant in Quito, serving excellent native food as well as an international menu. **Epicur** (10 de Agosto) does not look very inviting, but the food is superb and the prices low. On the seventh floor of the **Quito Inter•Continental Hotel** you will find **El Techo del Mundo,** with first-class international cuisine, organ music, strolling guitarists and singers. It is expensive and sophisticated. For French cooking, go to **Le Bistro,** across from the Quito Hotel, or **Normandie; Rincón de Sicilia** (Avenida 10 de Agosto 971) is excellent for Italian food and you can have a delicious pizza at the friendly **La Vieja Europa** (Amazonas y Calama 458). **La Cueva de Luiz Candelas** (Benalcázar 709) is a Spanish-style restaurant with excellent food. **Pío Pío** (Avenida Colón) is a drive-in where you can get barbecued chicken, as well as hamburgers and tortillas. **Chiper** (Diego de Almagro 1170) serves a first-class steak and lobster. For Chinese food, go to **Chifa Chang** (Avenida 1110) or **Chanchang** (Chile 1050).

Four courses usually make up an average meal: soup, entrée, salad and dessert. Breakfast is usually from 7-9, lunch from 12:30-2:30 and dinner from 7:30-9:30. A meal in an expensive restaurant costs about US$1. Very popular for light meals and snacks are **Café Austria** (Avenida Chile), **Salón Vienes** (Venezuela 1045) and **Tía's** (on Guayaquil).

## DRINKING TIPS

Best beers in Ecuador are Pilsner, Club or the stronger Victoria Sport. A whisky and soda (or a bottle of red wine) will cost 25 sucres. Popular drinking spots are the **Techo del Mundo** (at the Hotel Quito), **El Conquistador Bar** (at the Hotel Colón),

**Quick Pick** (Amazonas y Veintimilla) and **La Fuente** (Av Orellana).

## ENTERTAINMENT

Visiting opera, ballet or theater companies or concert recitalists will perform at the **Teatro Colón,** where tickets range from 130 to 312 sucres. Movies are inexpensive and more popular. The most lively nightclubs in Quito are the **Tally-ho** (Calle Santa Prisca 120), **La Llama** in the Hotel Quito, **Le Toucan** (Camino al Inca), and the **Unicorn** discothèque at the Colón Hotel. For young people, the dimly-lit **Candil** (Cordero and Amazonas) is the place to go. The Quito and the Colón Hotels have small and sophisticated casinos. In Guayaquil there are nightclubs and restaurants at the **Atahualpa** and **Humboldt** hotels and **El Terminal,** at the airport, has a casino, dancing and floorshows.

## SHOPPING

The best shopping in Quito is to be found in the **Avenida Colón** and in the arcades under the Government Palace on **Avenida Guayaquil,** around the Plaza de Independencia. Shops are open on weekdays from 8:30 to noon and from 2:00 to 6:00 and on Saturdays from 8:30 to noon. For the best Panama hats (which are really made from Toquilla straw in Ecuador) go to **Donat's** (Calle Chile 1060) where you can pick one up for US$10—there are some very pretty ones for the ladies, too, for US$3. For thick handwoven woollen ponchos and rugs in brilliant colors and stripes go to **Folklore** (Av Colón 260—there is also a branch at the Hotel Quito), where you will also find embroidered blouses, silver work, balsa wood items, straw baskets and pottery. Handicraft store with a wide range of goods is the government-run **Ocepa—Artesanías del Ecuador** (Calle Carrion 1336), where prices are reasonable. For pre-Colombian and colonial antiques, go to the better shops like **Antiquedades** (Chile 1035) or **Artes,** 6 de Diciembre 1138)—there is a thriving trade in fake antiques and fake *Tsantas* (shrunken heads which are the trophies of the Jivaro head hunters) made out of goat skin. For silver and gold, go to **Hamilton** (Calle Chile 1067) and **H. Stern** (in the Hotel Quito): you can get rings made by the Octavalo Indians, gold brooches based on Inca designs and charms for bracelets. In the old section of town **La Ronda Street** has some nice tourist shops. At No 954 you can buy woven rugs. Except in the larger stores, bargaining is customary and haggling over prices is a must at the Indian markets. In Quito there is an **Indian market** on Calle 24 de Mayo, every Tuesday.

## SPORT

Soccer is very popular with Ecudorians and there are matches throughout the year. The main season is from June to November and the best places to go are the **Estadio Olímpico Municipal,** the **Estadio de la Concentración Deportiva** and the **Estadio Atahualpa.** Basketball and indoor sports at the **Coliseo,** local sport called *Pelota de Guante* (glove ball); watch it at the **Estadio Mejía,** in Mejía College, on Saturdays and Sundays—no admission charge. The bullfighting season is from February to March.

Cockfighting is also very popular. Horse racing on Sundays at **La Carolina** race track in Quito and at the **Hipódromo Santa Cecilia** in Guayaquil. Guayaquil and Quito have golf and tennis clubs and horseback riding: Ask at the local **Pan Am** office or at your hotel desk for guest cards. **Hotel Inter•Continental Quito** has a heated outdoor swimming pool. There is good pigeon shooting near Quito; partridges and deer are found in the *páramos* (highlands); jaguars, tapirs and alligators roam the Oriente. Excellent trout fishing in the rivers and brooks of Mount **Cotopaxi** and **Chimborazo**—but you will need a license—apply to the Ministry of Industry. If you like mountaineering, this is the place to be. The **YMCA** (Amazonas 113, phone 238 220) organizes climbing expeditions into the snow-covered Cordilleras. There is year-round swimming, yachting and other sea sports along the Pacific coast and deep-sea fishing off Playas, Salinas and Manta. Best time to go is January-May: boats can be chartered for US$80 to US$90.

## WHAT TO SEE

**Quito** is a city of white houses with balconies and woodwork painted blue (the colors of the Virgin—on 6 December, the festival of San Francisco de Quito, owners of houses in the old section of Quito must have their woodwork painted blue), Indians gather in front of buildings and the Calle La Ronda, but are averse to having their photos taken; do it casually and preferably from a distance. The Plaza de Independencia, lies in the shadow of the **Cathedral**, where the national hero Sucre is buried. Here is the *Descent from the Cross,* the famous painting by the Indian artist Caspicara. Nearby are the **Municipal Palace** and the **Government Palace.** Do not miss **La Compañía,** the Jesuit church, whose façade is so delicately carved it resembles lacework and whose high altar is made of solid gold. The **Church of San Francisco** has magnificent art treasures and cloisters and the **Church of Santo Domingo** has rich woodcarvings and a remarkable Chapel of the Rosary. The **Museum of the Monastery of Santo Domingo** and the **Franciscan Museum** next to the Church of San Francisco have splendid collections of colonial religious art; the **Museum of Archeology,** in the Banco Comercial (Avenida 10 de Agosto) has exhibits of Indian and colonial art as well as a fine gold museum, while the **Casa de la Cultura Ecuadoriana** has a unique collection of musical instruments. The **Municipal Museum of Art** (Calle Espejo) and **Casa Benalcázar** have fine collections of Ecuadorian paintings from the last four centuries, while the studio of Oswaldo Guayasamín, a highly appreciated Indian painter and designer, is like an art gallery and many items are for sale.

Take a picnic to the top of **El Cerro Panecillo,** the Little Breadloaf Hill, 600 feet above the city. If you like a swim, there are thermal pools at **Alaugasí** and **Tingo María** in the Valley of Chillos, half-an-hour out of Quito. Very popular is a trip to the Equator, 15 miles north of Quito. You can have your photograph taken with one foot in each hemisphere.

A must for the visitor to Ecuador is a trip to one of the Indian markets, in the neighboring townships: **Saquisilí** (Thursday is market day) is the nearest one to Quito, about 35 miles south of the city, where you can buy decorative fabrics with birds, cats and war gods woven into the design. On the way you will pass by the **Cotopaxi**, the largest active volcano in the world, and **Otavalo**, where the colorful market is very early on Saturday mornings. At **Santo Domingo** (market day on Sundays), three hours from Quito, the native Colorado Indians comb their hair into a helmet shape and paint their bodies red to ward off evil spirits. **Riobamba** has its market on Saturdays. **Ambato**, known as the "Garden City of Ecuador," holds a Festival of Flowers and Fruits from 6-10 February. The Indian Market, held on Mondays, is the largest in Ecuador. The **Villa Hilda Hotel** has single rooms from US$2.25. There is a farm on the road from Quito where you can

rent an arena, if you would like to try your luck with a baby bull. A short drive to the east of Ambato lies **Baños**, a summer resort and a natural health spa. **Guayaquil**, the largest city in Ecuador, is its most important seaport. Well worth seeing are the **Cathedral of San Francisco**, the **Church of Santo Domingo** (built in 1548) and the **Palacio Municipal**. There are tennis, golf and yachting clubs, many first-class movie houses, and the **Bogotá Theater**, with open-air performances and excellent restaurants. Recommended are those at the **Hotel Atahualpa**, which also has a casino and a nightclub and at the **Hotel Continental**; the **Trocadero Restaurant**, on Calle P Ycaza is good. Best time to go to Guayaquil is during the dry season from May to November. Hotels here are: single from US$8.50, **Cima's**, Avenida C. J. Arosemana; **Humboldt**, Malecón 2309; single from US$4.40; **Continental**, Ballen 319; **Palace**, Calle Chile 216.

From Guayaquil you can go on an excursion up the Guayas river into tropical jungle, with its exotic birds and large plantations; or to the popular seaside resorts of **Playas.** Stay at the hotel **Humboldt,** Balneario Victoria, single from US$7. At **Salinas** the deep-sea fishing in the Humboldt current is superb. The hotel **Miramar** has singles from US$7. **Punta Carnero,** the newest of coastal resorts, has a luxurious hotel, the **Punta Carnero Inn,** single rooms from US$15. There is a fleet of cruisers for deep-sea fishing.

**Cuenca** is the third largest city in Ecuador and is famous for its Panama hat industry (also known as Montecristi hats). There is a nightclub at the new **El Dorado Hotel,** single from US$6; or stay at the **Cuenca Hotel,** single from US$3.50. The Indian market is on Thursday.

**Galápagos Islands,** 650 miles off the coast of Ecuador, are one of the most extraordinary regions in the world. The 300 islands, only six of which are inhabited, are peaks of gigantic underwater volcanoes, rising 7,000 to 10,000 feet above the sea bed. The flora and fauna of this wildlife sanctuary inspired Charles Darwin to formulate his theory of evolution. You can fly from Quito to **Baltra Island** (**TAME** has flights every Friday and Tuesday) and then go on an excursion of the islands. Alternatively you can sail from Guayaquil to the **Island of Santa Cruz** and then rent a boat with guide for US$25 a day. The **Charles Darwin Research Centre** at Academy Bay on Santa Cruz can be visited from 9 to 4 from Mondays to Fridays. Tours of the islands are organized by **Lindbad Travel,** of New York, and **Metropolitan Touring,** of Quito.

## SOURCES OF FURTHER INFORMATION

From any **Pan Am office** around the world; **Ecuadorian Tourist Commission:** PO Box 2454, Quito, Ecuador; The **Ecuadorian Consulate General,** 1270 Avenue of the Americas, New York, NY 10020; The **Ecuadorian Embassy and Consulate,** 3 Hans Crescent, London SW1.

# El Salvador

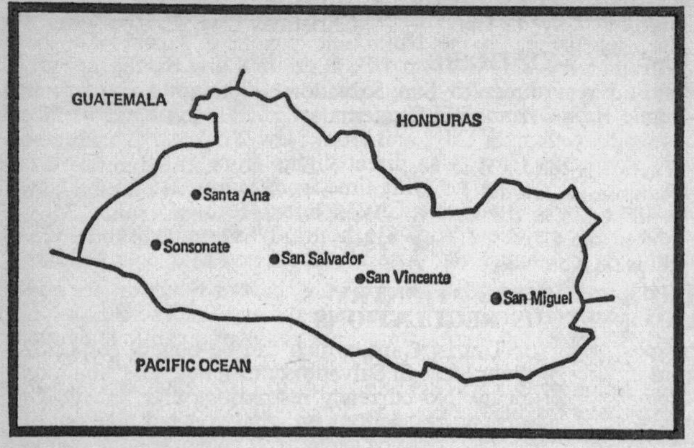


**WHAT'S SPECIAL**

El Salvador is the third most densely populated country in the world and the most industrialized country in Central America. There are six fine lakes, acres of coffee plantations, miles of beach along the Pacific coast and 22 volcanoes—some still active.

Originally El Salvador was populated by an Indian Nahoa race called the Pipils. In 1523, the Spanish invaded and the country remained under Spanish rule until the beginning of the 19th century.

**COUNTRY BRIEFING**

**Size:** 8,260 square miles
**Population:** 3,541,010
**Capital:** San Salvador
**Capital Population:** 340,500

**Climate:** Temperature varies according to altitude, but generally warm all year round. There is a warm, rainy season ('summer') May-November and a dry season November-May. Evenings cool.

**WEATHER IN SAN SALVADOR**—Lat N13°42′—Alt 2,238 ft

| Temp | Jan | Feb | Mar | Apr | May | Jun | Jul | Aug | Sep | Oct | Nov | Dec |
|---|---|---|---|---|---|---|---|---|---|---|---|---|
| Ave Low | 60° | 60° | 62° | 65° | 67° | 66° | 65° | 66° | 66° | 65° | 63° | 61° |
| Ave High | 90° | 92° | 94° | 93° | 91° | 87° | 89° | 89° | 87° | 87° | 87° | 89° |
| Days of No Rain | 30 | 27 | 30 | 27 | 18 | 11 | 12 | 12 | 10 | 15 | 26 | 29 |

**Government:** A Republic.

**Language:** Spanish.

**Religion:** Roman Catholic.

**Currency:** The Colón; 100 centavos = 1 Colón.

| | 10 | 50 | C1 | C5 | C10 | C50 | C100 | C125 |
|---|---|---|---|---|---|---|---|---|
| US (Dollars.Cents) | .04 | .20 | .40 | 2.00 | 4.00 | 20.00 | 40.00 | 50.00 |
| UK (Pounds.Pence) | .01 | .08 | .16 | .84 | 1.69 | 8.47 | 16.94 | 21.18 |

**Public Holidays:**

New Year's Day, 1 Jan
Labor Day, 1 May
Holy Week (Thurs, Fri, Sat)

Fiesta of the Patron of San Salvador, 4, 5 and 6 Aug
Independence Day, 15 Sept
Columbus Day, 12 Oct
Memorial Day, 2 Nov
First Cry of Independence, 5 Nov
Christmas Day, 25 Dec

## HOW TO GET THERE

Fly Pan Am direct to San Salvador, Ilopango Airport from Miami; New Orleans via Guatemala City; Houston via Mexico City and Guatemala City, and from New York via Washington and Guatemala City. Also direct flights from Panamá City via San José and Managua. Flying time from Miami 2½ hours, New Orleans 3 hours, Guatemala City ½ hour, Houston 4 hours, Mexico City 2 hours, New York 6½ hours, Washington 5 hours, Panamá City 2¼ hours, San José 1¼ hours and Managua ¾ hour.

## REQUIREMENTS FOR ENTRY AND CUSTOMS REGULATIONS

Passport, visa (or Tourist Card, which can be bought for US$2 from airlines, or your local El Salvador consulate), and smallpox vaccination certificate. No currency restrictions and, except for archeological pieces, no restrictions on what you can take out of the country. Currency should be exchanged before leaving. Duty-free allowances are: two bottles of spirits; 2.2 pounds of tobacco or 600 cigarettes; enough perfume for personal use.

## AIRPORT INFORMATION

Ilopango International Airport is eight miles from San Salvador. The link-up from airport to city is by bus or taxi. Buses run every 10 minutes from 5.00 am-11 pm. The fare is 50 centavos. Taxis available at all times; the fare to town 6-7.50¢. No arrival tax, but departure tax of 10% of air fare (if round trip ticket bought in San Salvador). Duty-free shop and hotel reservation counter.

## ACCOMMODATIONS

For help in finding accommodations go to the Instituto Salvadoreño de Turismo, Calle Rubén Darío, 619 San Salvador, or Tío, Ilopango Airport (tel: 27-0888). Hotels in San Salvador are:

**Single from US$15.00 (37.50C); double from US$20.00 (50C)**

**Camino Real** Boulevard de los Héroes
**EL SALVADOR INTER•CONTINENTAL** PO Box 1067-68, Colonía Escalón

**Single from US$8.00 (20C); double from US$14.00 (35C)**

**Gran Hotel San Salvador** Avenida España/1a Calle Oriente
**Parker House** 17 Calle Oriente 217

**Single from US$6.00 (15C); double from US$10.00 (25C)**

**Morazán** 1a Calle Oriente 17
**Nuevo Mundo** 1a Calle Oriente 217

## USEFUL INFORMATION

**Banks:** Open 8.00-4.00 Monday-Friday, 8.00-noon Saturday (always open at the airport). Change travelers' checks and currency in hotels, restaurants.

**Postage:** Stamps only at post offices.

**Telephone Tips:** Phones in restaurants, hotels, cafés etc. Also booths. Useful numbers:

**Pan Am Office,** 23-0188/23-5055
**Tourist Information and Accommodations,** 23-2077
**Airport Information,** 27-0135; 25-7039 and 27-0888
**Operator Service** and **Directory Inquiries,** 14
**Time,** 17
**Police,** 23-5011
**Fire,** 21-8661
**Red Cross,** 21-9406
**Emergency Clinic Center,** 25-1871

**Newspapers:** English-language newspapers are obtainable.

**Tipping:** Customary; no service charge on bills. In restaurants 10-15%; porter, per piece of luggage, 25 centavos in airport, 20 centavos in other places; taxi drivers, 25 centavos; hairdressers, 10-15%; chambermaids, optional; cloakroom attendants, 25 centavos and museum guides, optional.

**Electricity:** 110 volts, 60 cycles AC.

**Laundry:** Good dry-cleaning and laundry services available, 24-hour in most shops, express in major hotels (dry-cleaning a suit, C3.00; laundering a shirt 75 centavos).

**Hairdressing:** First-class hotels have salons (shampoo and set C5.00-C7.50; man's haircut about C2.50).

**Photography:** Good selection of equipment, black and white and color film, available in major cities. Black and white costs C1.25, color C2.55. Black and white processing takes about 24 hours, color three days.

**Clubs:** Lions and Rotary.

**Babysitting:** Services possible but difficult.

**Toilets:** In bars, restaurants, hotels, movie houses, gasoline stations, etc. Ladies, *Damas*; men, *Caballeros.*

**Health:** Some doctors and dentists speak English. Imported pharmaceuticals available but expensive. Boil drinking water. Fruit and vegetables should be washed. Take precautions againt malaria in a few areas.

## TRANSPORTATION

Buses and taxis are the only transportation. Taxis are easily flagged down in the street or can be ordered by 'phone. They have fixed rates, and night fares are higher. It is possible to rent a car for US$10-16 per day, plus US$0.10 per mile, extra charge for an English-speaking driver. The Pan American Highway, which connects San Salvador with La Libertad and Acajutla is paved; many other roads can be used only in the dry season. Railroads used primarily for freight. No internal airline.

## FOOD AND RESTAURANTS

Breakfast is from 6-9; lunch from 12-3 and supper from 6-midnight. You can eat either international cuisine or Salvadorean specialties. Try the *gallo en chicha,* a rooster cooked in hard cider, or *pupusas,* little corn cakes filled with cream cheese or ground pork. Among fresh fish sole is particularly good and you can often get small fresh oysters and lobsters in season at the port of **La Libertad.** For a real taste of Central America have a hot *tamale* from a street stall.

A first-class meal is available at the **Rendezvous Room** in the INTER•CONTINENTAL HOTEL (tel: 23-62-77), where there is dancing and a floor show as well as good food. Or try something with its roots in San Salvador itself—**Migueleño** (Calle Gerardo Barrios 708—tel: 21-5429) or **La Curbina** (33 Calle Oriente Bis 424—tel: 25-6650). Other restaurants include: **La Fonda,** Paseo General Escalón (Avenida Norte 85—tel: 23-1861); **Rosticería Americana** (2a Avenida Norte/9a Calle Oriente—tel: 21-8635); **Le Mar** (Paseo General Escalón 4357—tel: 23-2990) or **La Diligencia** (Paseo General Escalón/83a Avenida sur,—tel: 23-4765). Prices range from US$12 for an expensive meal to around US$4 for an inexpensive one.

## DRINKING TIPS

The local drinks are Tick-Tack, Espiritu de Caña, Ron Atlacatl. Imported wines, spirits and beers are available—C22.50 per bottle whisky, C12.50 per bottle of red wine. A whisky and soda costs about C1.50. The local beer is good.

## ENTERTAINMENT

October and November are good months for music, as the **International Music Festival** is held in November. There is a **National Symphony Orchestra** and two theater groups, one organized by the University and the other by the English-speaking community. Several movie houses. Performances generally begin at 1, 3, 6:15 and 8:45. Nightclubs are few, but the **Rendezvous Room** at the EL SALVADOR INTER•CONTINENTAL is good. Some interesting discothèques are: **Discothèque Hilltop Inn,** Colonía La Providencia; **Discothèque El Coche Rojo** on the road to Sta Tecla; **Discothèque Orni,** Boulevard Hipódromo, Colonía San Benito; **La Roca,** Paseo General Escalón and **El Cisne,** 24 Avenida Norte 21 Calle Poniente.

## SHOPPING

Shops open 8:00-noon and 2:00-6:00 Monday-Friday, and 8:00-noon Saturday. Best buys are ceramic work, wooden ornaments, pottery, native dolls, leather goods and cotton clothing. Ceramics and textiles good regional buys. Bargain in markets, but not shops. Places to buy are **Insafi,** Calle Rubén Darío, **Almacen Europa,** Calle Arce; **Almacenes Simán,** Calle Rubén Darío; **Almacen Europa,** Calle Arce; souvenir shop at the INTER•CONTINENTAL HOTEL; **Souvenir Las Gardenias,** Avenida Cuzcatlán, souvenir shop at **Ilogano Airport.**

## SPORTS

Baseball and basketball, soccer and football are all spectator sports. For swimming there are many public and private pools, several lakes and the ocean. The best pools are in **Los Chorros,** 'Garden of the Poets.' There is a riding club on the road to Santa Ana and polo is played during the dry season. Golf and tennis are popular—available at the **Club Campestre** all the year round to visitors with cards. Try volcano climbing at San Salvador, Izalco, Santa Ana, San Miguel and San Vincente.

## WHAT TO SEE

Much of San Salvador is new; only the center has a jumble of buildings and people. You can get an overall view of the city from the surrounding hills which are called **Los Planes de Renderos.** Here, in **Balboa Park,** climb to the highest peak. 'The Devil's Door,' and see San Salvador spread out. The **National Museum** (David J. Guzman), the **National Palace** and the **Monument of Our Savior** are worth seeing and the Children's Park, Zoo Park, Cuzcatlán Park and Liberty Park.

Not far from San Salvador is **Izalco,** an Indian town whose inhabitants still live a traditional life in native costumes. Nearby is a 7,000 foot, still-active volcano of the same name. One mile to the east, at the same height, is **Cerro Verde** or Green Mountain. From the top of Cerro Verde you can watch the volcano in action, belching out fire and rocks.

The crater lake of **Coatepeque** forms a background to the volcano at Izalco, and here you can swim, fish or go boating.

There are a number of pre-Columbian ruins in El Salvador; most of the excavated ones are centered around **Tazumal** and **San Andréas.** There is also a small museum. Among old towns there is **Nahuizalco,** populated by Indians. Another old town, **Panchimalco,** still bears traces of its colonial settlers, although the people living there are Indians.

**Los Chorros,** near San Salvador, is a park with waterfalls, pools and reservoirs surrounded by bright flowers and exotic plants.

On the Pacific Coast, beaches and coves include those in Acajutla, Las Flores, Los Cóbanos, Amatecampo, El Pimental, Los Blancos, El Cuco, Estero de Jaltepeque, El Tamarindo, and Barra de Santiago.

**Santa Ana,** second city of El Salvador, is in the heart of the coffee-growing country and has a famous cathedral. The **Roosevelt Hotel** has single rooms from US$4.

## SOURCES OF FURTHER INFORMATION

**Pan Am** Office, Edificio La Centro-Americana, Alameda Roosevelt 3107, San Salvador, and from any Pan Am office around the world. **Instituto Salvadoreño de Turismo,** Calle Rubén Darío 16, San Salvador; **El Salvador Tourist Information Office,** 708 Market Street, San Francisco, California 94103; **Consulate General,** 211 East 43rd Street 1205, New York, NY 10017; **Embassy of El Salvador,** Edinburgh House, 9b Portland Place, London W1.

# French Guiana

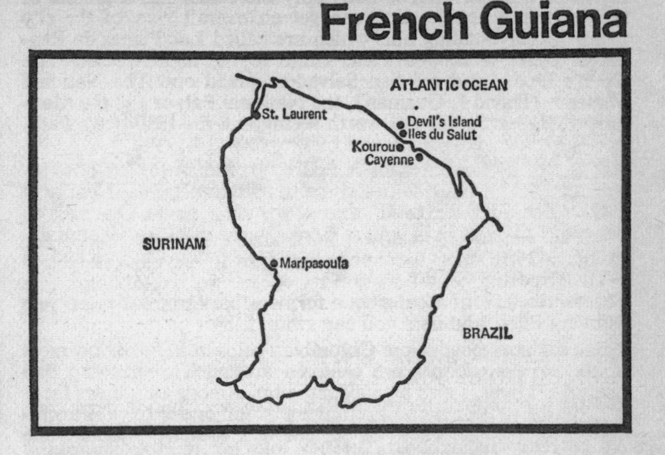


**WHAT'S SPECIAL**

This wild, primitive land has twice been chosen to play a distinctive part in the affairs of France. In the 19th-century Devil's Island, six miles off shore, became the site of the notorious former French penal colony. In 1968 France moved her space research center from Algeria to the sandy coast of Kourou, 26 miles from French Guiana's capital, Cayenne. An instant town with ultra-modern facilities, including several hotels, was built there and has given a big boost to the country's tourist trade. Other parts of the country are still undeveloped. Tropical jungle covers most of the interior and the forests are dissected by a great spread of rivers. Haka tigers, ocelots, jaguars and tapirs roam the hills and more than 1,000 Indians of six different tribes, including the famous Arawaks, live in picturesque settlements. Gold was discovered in 1855 and is still one of the biggest exports.

**COUNTRY BRIEFING**

**Size:** 35,135 square miles
**Population:** 48,000
**Capital:** Cayenne
**Capital Population:** 19,668

**Climate:** Hot and humid with temperatures averaging 80°. Heavy rainfall from April to July. Best to visit August to December.

**WEATHER IN CAYENNE**—Lat N4°56′—Alt 20 ft

| Temp | Jan | Feb | Mar | Apr | May | Jun | Jul | Aug | Sep | Oct | Nov | Dec |
|---|---|---|---|---|---|---|---|---|---|---|---|---|
| Ave Low | 74° | 74° | 74° | 75° | 74° | 73° | 73° | 73° | 74° | 74° | 74° | 74° |
| Ave High | 84° | 85° | 85° | 86° | 85° | 87° | 88° | 90° | 91° | 91° | 89° | 86° |
| Days of No Rain | 11 | 22 | 9 | 9 | 5 | 7 | 13 | 22 | 26 | 27 | 19 | 13 |

**Government:** French Overseas Department.

**Language:** French. Very little English spoken.

**Religion:** Roman Catholic.

**Currency:** French Franc; 100 centimes = 1 Franc.

| | 5c | 10c | 50c | 1F | 10F | 50F | 100F | 250F |
|---|---|---|---|---|---|---|---|---|
| US (Dollars.Cents) | .01 | .02 | .10 | .20 | 2.00 | 10.00 | 20.00 | 50.00 |
| UK (Pounds.Pence) | — | — | .04 | .08 | .84 | 4.23 | 8.46 | 21.15 |

**Public Holidays:**

New Year's Day, 1 Jan
Mardi Gras
Mi-Carême
Good Friday
Easter Monday
Labor Day, 1 May
Whitsun
National Day, 14 Jul
Assumption 15 Aug
All Saints' Day, 1 Nov
Christmas Day

## HOW TO GET THERE

Fly Pan Am to Georgetown, Paramaribo, Fort de France and Pointe à Pitre, then by connecting flight to Cayenne, Rochambeau Airport. Flying time from Georgetown is 1½ hours (via Paramaribo), Paramaribo ¾ hour, Fort de France 2 hours and Pointe à Pitre 2 hours.

## REQUIREMENTS FOR ENTRY AND CUSTOMS REGULATIONS

Passport, round-trip ticket and smallpox vaccination certificate. Yellow fever inoculation. No visa for stay up to three months. No currency regulations; currency may be freely exchanged at local banks. Duty-free: 200 cigarettes, or half-pound tobacco, perfume for personal use.

## AIRPORT INFORMATION

Rochambeau Airport is 15 kilometers from Cayenne. Airport buses meet planes; free except for excessive luggage. Taxi fare to Cayenne, 35 francs. Arrival and departure taxes of 5 francs. No duty-free shop, no nursery, no hotel reservation counter.

## ACCOMMODATIONS

Two miles outside Cayenne is the excellent hotel **Du Montabo** on Montabo Hill and there are several recently-built hotels near the space center at Kourou. Outside the main towns, hotels are generally less expensive. The **Syndicat d'Initiative** (tel: 919) will help with finding accommodations. Hotels in Cayenne: **Hotel du Montabo** (Route de Montabo) single from US$20.00 MAP; **Neptima** (Rue Félix Eboué) single from US$10.00 and **Ket-Taï** (Boulevard Jubelin 1120) single from US$10.00.

## USEFUL INFORMATION

**Banks:** Open 7:30-1 Mon-Fri. Closed Sat and Sun. You can change currency and travelers' checks at hotels.

**Postage:** Stamps at post offices and in hotels.

**Telephone Tips:** Phones in post office, street booths, hotels and restaurants.

Useful Numbers:

**Tourist Information,** 919
**Operator,** 453
**Directory Inquiries,** 477
**Airport Information,** 20
**Police,** 18

**Newspapers:** English-language publications available.

**Tipping:** Service charge not usually included in restaurant checks; tip 10%; porters, 1 franc per piece of luggage; taxi drivers, hotel staff, museum guides do not expect tips.

**Electricity:** 220 and 127 volts, 50 cycles AC.

**Laundry:** Major hotels have good services (dry-cleaning a suit, 10F; laundering a shirt, 1F).

**Hairdressing:** No facilities in hotels (shampoo and set, about 5F; man's haircut, about 3F).

**Photography:** Good selection of black and white and color films in main cities. Developing: one week for black and white, two months for color.

**Clubs:** Rotary and Lions.

**Babysitting:** None.

**Toilets:** In hotels, restaurants, cafés. Ladies, *Dames*; men, *Hommes.*

**Health:** Many doctors and dentists speak English. Imported pharmaceuticals available, reasonable prices. Drink bottled water.

## TRANSPORTATION

There is a bus service between Cayenne and Kourou but otherwise one cannot rely on public transport. Taxis are readily available by phone (tel: 307/357 or 770), but are expensive. Complete taxi tour of the city and island of Cayenne costs about 55F. Rented cars are available from Hertz. Roads not good outside Cayenne. Internal airlines serve Cayenne, Saint Laurent and Maripasoula.

## FOOD AND RESTAURANTS

Much of the food is imported from France, so in general meals are expensive. Breakfast is from 7:30-8:30, lunch from 12-2 and dinner from 7:30-9. Best international food is at the **Hotel Montabo** and at **Guilbaud's and Montjoly** bar-restaurants in Cayenne. Creole specialties include *Bouillon d'Awaras,* Colombo curry and several dishes with red kidney beans. These can be tried in Cayenne at **Le Tatou** (Rue Chaussée Sartines); **Le Snack Créole** (Rue Félix-Eboué); and **La Bonne Cervoise** (Route de Gallion). Chinese restaurants in Cayenne include **Chen Teng You** (Cité Mirza—tel: 292); **Le Dragon d'Or** and **Coq d'Or** (Avenue Général de Gaulle—tel: 183); **Ket-Taï** (Boulevard Jubelin—tel: 1080); **Kimelone** (Rue Lallouette—tel: 90); **La Baie d'Along** (Route de Mont Joly); has Vietnamese specialties.

## DRINKING TIPS

Rum is the national drink. Bars open all day, ladies welcome. No licensing restrictions for those over 21. Rum and Scotch cheaper than in the States.

## ENTERTAINMENT

Cayenne has four movie houses. There is dancing at most hotels in the evenings. The **Hotel Montabo** has a discothèque and nightclub and there is a nightclub at **Hotel Ket-Taï.** Other night spots in the Cayenne area are **Le 106** and **Le Cric Crac.** In Kourou there is a jazz club at the **Hotel des Roches** and **Le Cachin** has a creole band.

## SHOPPING

Best buys are jewelry, ceramics and Indian arts and crafts such as woodcarvings and dolls. Good stores in Cayenne are mostly around the **Avenue Général de Gaulle.**

## SPORTS

Most popular spectator sports are basketball, football, tennis and cockfighting. For visitors there is swimming, river fishing, yachting, golf (at Cayenne) tennis (clubs at Cayenne and Kourou) riding and hunting. Canoes can be rented for hunting waterfowl. Guns must be declared and need a permit.

## WHAT TO SEE

Cayenne has a Museum and Botanical Gardens. To the north is the official residence of the Prefect, the hospital and government offices. Nearby is the sports stadium. From **Fort Ceperou** there is a good view of the city, countryside and sea. Excursions to the space center can be organized from **Kourou,** which lies less than 5° north of the Equator and is thus an ideal place for rocket launching. The **Hotel des Roches,** at Kourou (single room from US$11), also organizes trips to the **Iles du Salut** including **Devil's Island.**

Further east the little town of **St Laurent** on the Maroni River bordering Surinam also has an infamous old prison. Jungle tours are available from Cayenne—ask at Hotel Montabo. On these you can visit remote Indian villages, bivouac in the forest or fish in the lakes and rivers and walk over the orchid-studded mountains. On river trips you rough it overnight in primitive jungle shelters It is also interesting to fly right across country for a week-end in **Maripasoula,** a remote town amid the waterfalls and lakes of true Indian country.

## SOURCES OF FURTHER INFORMATION

From any **Pan Am** office around the world; inquire at **Hotel Montabo Cayenne** or **Hotel des Roches,** Kourou for trips and excursions; **Air France,** 5 Place de Grenoble, Cayenne; **Cie. Le Transatlantique,** 80 Place de Grenoble, Cayenne; **French Government Tourist Office,** 610 Fifth Avenue, New York, NY 10020, and 178, Picadilly, London W1.

# Guatemala

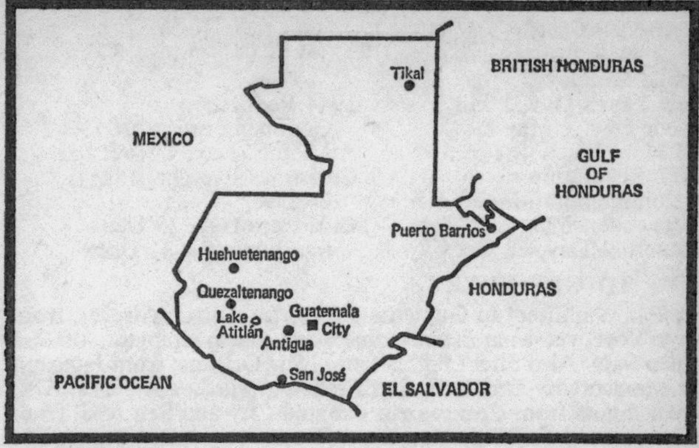


## WHAT'S SPECIAL

For archeologists or anyone with a sense of history, Guatemala has unique attractions. The northern part of the country was the home of the Mayan civilization, one of the most sophisticated in the ancient world. Some idea of their staggering art and architecture can be had at Tikal. Here is one of the world's greatest archeological sites—miles of great pyramids, temples, palaces—and still only a fraction of it unearthed. The Maya-Quiché Indians, descendants of those great temple-builders, are a friendly, dignified people whose way of life has changed little in centuries.

The climate is another attraction: the country is called "the land of the eternal spring." While the weather is sub-tropical, it is never oppressively humid or hot. There is wild life in plenty—ocelot, puma, wild boar and alligator—and rare birds, one of which, the quetzal, is the national bird and gives the currency its name.

## COUNTRY BRIEFING

**Size:** 42,042 square miles
**Population:** 5,000,000
**Capital:** Guatemala City
**Capital Population:** 800,000

**Climate:** Good all year. Not much rain or humidity.

**WEATHER IN GUATEMALA CITY**—Lat N14°37′—Alt 4,855 ft

| Temp | Jan | Feb | Mar | Apr | May | Jun | Jul | Aug | Sep | Oct | Nov | Dec |
|---|---|---|---|---|---|---|---|---|---|---|---|---|
| Ave Low | 53° | 54° | 57° | 58° | 60° | 61° | 60° | 60° | 60° | 60° | 57° | 55° |
| Ave High | 73° | 77° | 81° | 82° | 84° | 81° | 78° | 79° | 79° | 76° | 74° | 72° |
| Days of No Rain | 26 | 26 | 28 | 25 | 16 | 17 | 10 | 10 | 8 | 13 | 23 | 27 |

**Government:** An independent republic.

**Language:** Spanish. The Indians speak over 20 dialects. English understood in hotels and shops in larger centers.

**Religion:** Roman Catholicism predominates.

**Currency:** The Quetzal, which is at par with the US Dollar; 100 centavos = 1 quetzal

| | 5c | 10c | 25c | 1Q | 5Q | 10Q | 20Q | 50Q |
|---|---|---|---|---|---|---|---|---|
| US (Dollars.Cents) | .05 | .10 | .25 | 1.00 | 5.00 | 10.00 | 20.00 | 50.00 |
| UK (Pounds.Pence) | .02 | .04 | .10 | .41 | 2.08 | 4.16 | 8.33 | 20.83 |

**Public Holidays:**

New Year's Day, 1 Jan
Labor Day, 1 May
All Holy Week
1871 Revolution Commemoration, 30 Jun
Independence Day, 15 Sept
Columbus Day, 12 Oct
1944 Revolution Commemoration, 20 Oct
All Saints' Day, 1 Nov
Christmas Eve (half day), 24 Dec
Christmas Day, 25 Dec
Fiesta Bancaria, 31 Dec

## HOW TO GET THERE

Fly Pan Am direct to Guatemala City, La Aurora Airport, from New York via Miami and some days via Washington or San Pedro Sula. Also direct flights from New Orleans; from Houston via Mexico City and from San Francisco via Los Angeles. Also direct flights from Caracas via Panamá City and San José, from Managua and San Salvador; from Buenos Aires, São Paulo, Rio de Janeiro and Brasília (all routing via Panamá City). Flying time from New York is 5 hours, Miami 2½ hours, New Orleans, 2½ hours, Houston 3½ hours, San Francisco 5¾ hours. Flying time from Caracas is 4¼ hours, Panamá City 2¼, San José 1¼ hours, Managua 1 hour, San Salvador ½ hour, Buenos Aires 8½ hours, São Paulo 9¼ hours, Rio de Janeiro 8¾ hours and Brasília 7¼ hours.

## REQUIREMENTS FOR ENTRY AND CUSTOMS REGULATIONS

Passport and a tourist card or visa obtainable from Guatemala Consulates or your Pan Am Office. It costs US$3. An international smallpox vaccination certificate is required. US dollars readily accepted, so no need to convert into local currency. Currency controls allow you to change only Q20 back to dollars on departure. A permit is needed for firearms and ammunition: inquire at a Consulate. Duty-free allowance: two bottles spirits; 200 cigarettes. Archeological relics and jade are restricted exports.

## AIRPORT INFORMATION

La Aurora international airport is about five miles south of Guatemala City center. You can take a local bus—uncomfortable but adequate—into town for 10 centavos or, easier, a taxi, available at all times. There is an official fixed fare of Q2.50 to the center of town or Q1.50 to the Camino Real Hotel, nearer to the airport. No airport taxes. Duty-free shop and hotel reservations desk. Tip porters 25 centavos per bag; 50 centavos for a large piece.

## ACCOMMODATIONS

The range is from luxury hotels to inexpensive, but clean and comfortable, pensions. For advice ask at the Tourist Information Bureau at the airport. Pensions cost about Q3 a day each for a room, but mostly operate on the American plan of room and all meals. Hotels are crowded at the peak of the two tourist seasons (June-August and January-March) so it's best to reserve ahead. Hotels in Guatemala City:

**Single from US$13.00; double from US$20.00**

**Camino Real** Avenida La Reforma, 14a Calle, Zona 10
**Guatemala Biltmore** Avenida La Reforma, 15a Calle, Zona 10
**Ritz Continental** 6a Avenida 'A' 10-13, Zona 1

**Single from US$6.00; double from US$8.80**

**Maya Excelsior** 7a Avenida 12-46, Zona 1
**Pan American** 9a Calle 5-63, Zona 1
**Motel Plaza** Vía 7, 6-16, Zona 4

**Single from US$3.30; double from US$6.00**

**Centenario** 6a Calle 5-33, Zona 1
**Colonial** 7a Avenida 14-19, Zona 1
**Palace** 12a Calle, 4a Avenida, Zone 1

## USEFUL INFORMATION

**Banks:** Open 8:30-12:30 and 2-4, Mon-Fri. First-class hotels will change travelers' checks.

**Postage:** Stamps at post offices and hotels.

**Telephone Tips:** Phones in public booths, hotels and cafés. Useful Numbers:

**Pan Am Office,** (reservations 82181 & 22144), (airport 61481)
**Airport Information,** 62083/7 and 64281/5
**Tourist Information,** 81250/81156
**Operator,** 00
**Directory Inquiries,** 14
**Time,** 16
**Fire,** 12 & 13
**Red Cross,** 15

**Newspapers:** English-language papers available. Local English-language news bulletin, *Headlines,* is published six days a week.

**Tipping:** Luggage porters, 25 centavos per bag, or more for a large item; taxi drivers, no tip except for extra service; hotel porters, cloakroom attendants, hairdressers and museum guides, 25 centavos; hotel chambermaids, 5% of the bill. In restaurants service charges are not generally included, so leave about 10 centavos.

**Electricity:** 110/120 volts, 60 cycles AC.

**Laundry:** Guatemala City has reliable and prompt laundry and dry-cleaning services and luxury hotels can provide express service (dry-cleaning a suit, Q2; laundering a shirt, 30 centavos).

**Hairdressing:** Facilities in major hotels and outside salons (shampoo and set, Q3; man's haircut, Q1).

**Photography:** Black and white film available in most places, but color film hard to find outside the capital. Processing of color can be slow and expensive.

**Clubs:** Rotary, Lions and Jaycees.

**Babysitting:** Larger hotels can arrange.

**Toilets:** Only in good hotels, cafés and restaurants. Ladies, *Damas* or *Señoras*; Men, *Caballeros, Hombres* or *Señores.*

**Health:** Good doctors and dentists and many speak English.

**The Medical Center** (tel: 65061/2) and the **Herrera Llerandi Hospital** (tel: 66771/5) give emergency treatment—both are private. Medical charges can be quite high so it is wise to be insured. Imported medicines and toiletries expensive. Immunization against typhoid and tetanus is recommended. Precautions should be taken against diarrhea and dysentery. If going to the interior take Chloroquine tablets for malaria prevention. Wash all fruit and vegetables bought in markets. Tap water chlorinated and considered safe in Guatemala City, but elsewhere bottled water is best.

## TRANSPORTATION

There is a comprehensive bus network in Guatemala City, crowded but inexpensive. Unmetered taxis numerous and relatively expensive. It is easy to rent a car. For a Hertz Volkswagen the cost would be Q10 per day plus 8 centavos per Km. Addresses: Hertz, 19a Calle 7-07, Zona 1 (tel: 80202/85460) at the Ritz Continental Hotel and at the airport; Avis's main office is at 12a Calle 2-73, Zona 9 (tel: 67469). There are no traffic lights so traffic on the avenues (north to south) has priority over that on the streets (*calles*). On mountain roads use the horn. There is a good long-distance bus service linking Guatemala City with major towns; fares are very reasonable. Trains are inadequate and not recommended. The best way to visit Tikal is by air: Aviateca, the internal airline, will fly you there in 45 minutes.

## FOOD AND RESTAURANTS

There is no national cuisine; most local dishes are Mexican-style, but bananas in various guises are a specialty. Try *tamales* (banana leaves stuffed with meat and corn), *rellenitos de platano* (fried bananas stuffed with black beans), *chiles rellenos* (stuffed peppers) and *gallo en chicha* (chicken cooked in cider). Guatemalan coffee is among the best in the world. International cuisine is available in all the tourist centers. In the capital try **Vittorio** (7a Avenida 14-68, Zone 9—tel: 62440) and the **Petit Suisse** (7a Avenida 3-04, Zona 9—tel:65659)—both relatively expensive, around Q10. **La Ronda** (tel: 681271) in the Camino Real Hotel is fun for an evening's entertainment; music, dancing and floorshow. The **Ritz Continental Hotel** also has a good, medium-priced restaurant, **La Taberna de Don Pedro** (tel: 81671). Try **La Parrillita** (Plazuela España, Zona 9—tel: 61485) and **El Fogón** (Calle Montúfar 4-23, Zona 9—tel: 61485) for steaks. If you like seafood go to **La Quebrada** (6a Avenida 4-60, Zona 4—tel: 66754) or **Auto Mariscos** (via 9, 5-04, Zona 4—tel: 63018) for charcoal-grilled lobster and shrimps. **El Tamal** (20a Calle 1—50, Zona 10—tel: 680535) offers typical Guatemalan food, and so does **El Ranchón Antiqueño** (13a Calle 3—50, Zona 1). There are several places for quick, inexpensive meals and snacks in the main shopping district (around 6th Avenida).

## DRINKING TIPS

Bars are open from noon till late—some to 5am. Ladies should be accompanied. Imported spirits and especially wines are expensive, so try the local product. Best local beer is Monte Carlo. Guatemalan rum has a high reputation and the adventurous can sample *aguardiente* (sugar cane liquor). It is one of the ingredients, with grenadine and kümmel liqueurs, of an El Jaguar cocktail (fiery red and garnished with lime) at the **El Jaguar** bar in the Hotel Camino Real. The Biltmore, Ritz Continental and Pan American Hotels also have popular bars.

## ENTERTAINMENT

The **National Symphony Orchestra** gives concerts from May to October and the ballet season starts in August. There are theater performances all year round, in Spanish and English and several movie houses. The Ritz Hotel has a nightclub, **The Brasília** and **Bodegón** and **Pigalle,** both on the Plazuela España, are also recommended. For dancing there are a few discothèques: **La Manzana** (Edificio Maya, Zona 4), **Tijuana** (Avenida Las Américas, Zona 13) and **El Gato Pardo** (20 Calle 0-76, Zona 10).

## SHOPPING

Shops generally open from 8:30-12:30 and 3-7, Monday to Saturday. Best buys are handwoven Indian textiles, (both sold by the meter and made up into dresses, jackets, ponchos, purses, etc), wood carvings, silver jewelry, leather goods and ceramics. You'll find a wide choice of attractive handicrafts for presents under US$10; look in the market (on 12th Street from 4th to 6th Avenidas). Other good places for native crafts are: **Sombol** (Avenida La Reforma 14-14, Zona 9) textiles, dresses, furniture; **Mayatex** (12a Calle 4—56, Zona 1) textiles and silver jewelry; **San Antonio** (6a Avenida 11—58, Zona 1) silver jewelry; **La Regional** (8a Avenida 6—75, Zona 1) textiles, leather goods; **La Dama** (12a Calle, 4—44, Zona 1) specializes in handmade wooden furniture. For general shopping, the two main department stores are **Almacenes Paiz** (Centro Comercial, Zona 4) and **Almacén Mi Amigo** (Centro Comercial, Zona 9). Bargaining is customary in markets, but not in stores.

## SPORTS

**Golf** is popular and you can play at the Country Club or the Mayan Golf Club. Both also offer **tennis** and **swimming** facilities. Hotels can arrange temporary membership for their guests. Several other clubs have tennis and swimming all the year round. There is also swimming on the coasts, and you can try **water skiing** and **skin-diving** on Lakes Atitlán and Amatitlán. There is some fresh-water fishing on the lakes and rivers but deep-sea fishing is better. Mountaineers can try the many volcanoes: Agua, Fuego and Pacaya are the most popular. The many beautiful trails on the outskirts of the capital make **horseback riding** a rewarding way to explore the countryside and you can hire horses from the stables of the Association Hípica de Guatemala. **Wild game** is abundant in the forests and hunting is excellent; travel agents in the capital can arrange expeditions or ask the *Caza, Tiro y Pesca* (hunting, shooting and fishing club) 3a Avenida 8—35, Zona 2, for advice.

## WHAT TO SEE

In Guatemala City, do not miss the **Museum of Archeology and Ethnology** (Building 5, La Aurora, Zona 13) a magnificent collection of Mayan art; the **Museum of History and Fine Arts** (same area) and the **Museum of Popular Arts and Crafts** (10a Avenida 10—72, Zona 1) have interesting exhibits of Indian handicrafts. The country's colonial past has left a heritage of fine churches: see the **Cathedral** and **La Merced church. The National Palace,** in pale green stone, and the **Torre del Reformador** (like an illuminated Eiffel Tower at night) are prominent landmarks. In the **Hipódromo del Norte** a relief map displays the contours of the country. Children will enjoy the zoo.

**Antigua** is the former capital. Severely damaged by an earthquake in 1773, it still preserves something of its colonial grandeur, with ornate ruined churches and other fine 16th-century buildings. The **Colonial Museum** is housed in the former University, one of the first to be founded in the Americas. Try to go on a Saturday, Monday or Thursday—market days—when you can bargain for hand-wrought silver, pottery and Indian textiles. Antigua is about half-an-hour by car from the capital, or you can go by bus, or take one of the tours organized by local travel agents. The high point of the year is Holy Week when processions take place in the main streets over intricate carpets made all of colored sawdust. Stay at the **Hotel Antigua,** single from US$11.00.

**Chichicastenango,** the central market town for the Indians in the surrounding highland villages, is also famous for its markets held on Thursdays and Sundays. The **Mayan Inn** (tel: 86661) is a pleasant place to stay—and a good base for trips by car or on horseback into the surrounding hills, single from US$16.50 (AP).

**Lake Atitlán** must not be missed: one mile high, deep turquoise water ringed by high green hills and volcanoes with cascading waterfalls, it must be one of the most spectacularly beautiful lakes in the world. Around it are 12 Indian villages named after the 12 apostles. The new **Hotel Atitlán** (single from US$10) is recommended for its fine position on the lake. The **Tzanjuyu,** single from US$12 (AP) and Regis, single from US$6 can also be recommended.

The second city of Guatemala is **Quetzaltenango,** meaning "place of the quetzal"; a cool, highland town with springwaters said to be medicinal. Another center for visiting Indian villages, its market is held every day and the week of 15 September is fiesta time. You can stay at the **Hotel Bonifaz** (4 Calle 10—50, Zona 1) single from US$7. Undoubtedly, Guatemala's greatest treasure is the ruined Mayan city of **Tikal,** one of the world's most fascinating archeological sites. The Mayan people, whose ancestors are thought to have come from Asia some 10,000 years ago, developed an astonishingly advanced civilization and independently invented sciences of astronomy and mathematics. Tikal has only recently begun to be excavated and only a fraction of its huge extent has been uncovered from the jungle growth of centuries. But you will see miles of massive pyramids and temples, plazas and intricately carved pillars. Its treasures—carvings, painted vases, jade ornaments—are on show at the archeological museum. You can go to Tikal and return in one day by air, but to make the most of your visit it is worth staying a day or so. **The Jungle Lodge,** single from US$16 (AP), is fairly primitive or try the new **Mayan International** near Flores.

In the northeast, towards the Mexican border, is **Huehuetenango,** another rewarding place for ruin hunters, with the temples,

forts and ball courts of **Zaculeu** ("white land") just outside the city. Stay at the **Hotel Zaculeu,** 5a Avenida 1—14, Zona 1, single from US$3.50. On the Atlantic coast **Puerto Barrios** is the major port, about five hours by road through the jungle on the new Atlantic Highway, or 30 minutes by air. The **Hotel del Norte,** single from US$7 (AP) is recommended. From here you can take a pleasant trip by launch on the Rio Dulce to **Lake Izabal,** famous for its flora and fauna, and the castle of San Felipe de Lara, built as a defense against English pirates.

The Pacific coast at San José, two hours by car from the capital on the first-class highway, is popular for deep-sea fishing. The new luxury hotel club **Chulamar,** single from US$15, also on the Pacific, offers golf, fishing and swimming in pools on the private beach; you can get there in 90 minutes by special bus from the capital (Q5 each way) or take a day tour arranged by one of the travel agencies.

## SOURCES OF FURTHER INFORMATION

**Pan Am Office,** 6a Avenida 11-41, Zona 1; Guatemala City, or from any Pan Am Office around the world; **National Tourist Bureau,** 6a Avenida 5—34, Zona 1, Guatemala City; **Guatemala Tourist Commission,** 9393 Wilshire Boulevard, Beverly Hills, California 90212.

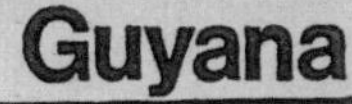

## WHAT'S SPECIAL

Guyana is a "land of waters"—of rivers and creeks, where the fishing is superb; of canals, dikes and waterfalls. The spectacular Kaieteur Falls, five times higher than Niagara, are one of the natural wonders of the world. There are tropical forests, cattle-ranching savannahs and vast sugar plantations; bauxite mines and many picturesque towns inhabited by people of Amerindian, African, East Indian, Chinese and European origins.

## COUNTRY BRIEFING

**Size:** 83,000 square miles
**Capital:** Georgetown
**Population:** 763,000
**Capital Population:** 190,000

**Climate:** Fairly equable, mild tropical. Best time to visit is from July to September.

**WEATHER IN GEORGETOWN**—Lat N6°50′—Alt 6 ft

| Temp | Jan | Feb | Mar | Apr | May | Jun | Jul | Aug | Sep | Oct | Nov | Dec |
|---|---|---|---|---|---|---|---|---|---|---|---|---|
| Ave Low | 74° | 74° | 75° | 76° | 75° | 75° | 75° | 75° | 76° | 76° | 76° | 75° |
| Ave High | 84° | 84° | 84° | 85° | 85° | 85° | 85° | 86° | 87° | 87° | 86° | 84° |
| Days of No Rain | 14 | 15 | 19 | 19 | 11 | 6 | 10 | 15 | 23 | 22 | 20 | 11 |

**Government:** A co-operative Republic.

**Language:** Only English-speaking country in South America.

**Religion:** Christian (57%); Muslim (8.8%) and Hindu (33.5%).

**Currency:** The Guyanese dollar; 100 cents = 1 Guyanese dollar

| | G25¢ | G50¢ | G$1 | G$5 | G$10 | G$20 | G$50 | G$100 |
|---|---|---|---|---|---|---|---|---|
| US (Dollars.Cents) | .10 | .20 | .40 | 2.00 | 4.00 | 8.00 | 20.00 | 40.00 |
| UK (Pounds.Pence) | .04 | .09 | .19 | .95 | 1.91 | 3.83 | 9.59 | 19.19 |

**Public Holidays:**
New Year's Day, 1 Jan
Republic Day, 23 Feb
Eid-ul-Ah'sa, Feb
Phagwah, Mar
Good Friday
Easter Monday
Labor Day, 1 May
Youman Nabi, 18 May
Independence Day, 26 May

Commonwealth Day, 3 Aug
Deepavali, 29 Oct
Christmas Day, 25 Dec
Boxing Day, 26 Dec

## HOW TO GET THERE

Fly Pan Am direct to Georgetown, Timehri Airport, from New York, via Barbados and Port of Spain. Flying time from New York, 6¼ hours; Barbados, 1¾ hours; Port of Spain, 1 hour.

## REQUIREMENTS FOR ENTRY AND CUSTOMS REGULATIONS

Passport, ticket to leave the country and a smallpox vaccination certificate. Visas not required for US and Commonwealth visitors. Cholera and yellow fever immunization if coming from an infected area. Duty-free allowance: one-sixth of a gallon of spirits (except gin and vodka); one-sixth gallon of wine; one-half pound of tobacco. Firearms need a license from the Ministry of Home Affairs, Georgetown. Information on exchange control regulations available from the Bank of Guyana in Georgetown.

## AIRPORT INFORMATION

The International Airport for Georgetown is Timehri, 25 miles from the city center. There are buses into town and the taxi fare is G$3.50. Departure tax: G$3. Timehri Airport has a duty-free shop and a hotel reservation counter. Tip the porter about G$1 per suitcase.

## ACCOMMODATIONS

If you need help in finding accommodations, call the **Guyana Development Corporation** (tel: 3096 and 3099). There are several boarding houses, but make sure you get an air-conditioned room. Hotels in Georgetown:

**Pegasus** Sea Wall Road, Kingston (single from US$17.50)
**Woodbine** New Market Street (single from US$11 CP)
**Tower** 74/75 Main Street (single from US$7.50)
**Park** 38 Main Street (single from US$7 CP)

## USEFUL INFORMATION

**Banks:** Open 8-noon, Mon-Fri; 8-11, Sat.

**Postage:** Stamps must be obtained from post offices. For overseas telegrams and radio telephone services go to Cable & Wireless Ltd at the Bank of Guyana Building.

**Telephone Tips:** Booths available, and in restaurants and cafés.
Useful Numbers:
**Pan Am agents,** 6-2067
**Tourist Office, Information, and Accommodations Offices,** 3096 and 3099
**Operator,** 0
**Directories,** 91
**International Operator,** 94
**Time,** 97
**Emergencies,** 999

**Newspapers:** *The Daily Chronicle*, *Evening Post*, and *The Sunday Chronicle* and *Mirror* on Sundays.

**Tipping:** In restaurants 10%; porters G50¢ per piece of luggage; hotel porters and chambermaids G$1. Unnecessary to tip taxi drivers.

**Electricity:** 110-220 volts, 50 cycles AC, in Georgetown. Elsewhere 110-220 volts, 50 or 60 cycles AC.

**Laundry:** Dry-cleaning and laundry services available and inexpensive.

**Hairdressing:** Good salon in Pegasus Hotel (shampoo and set about G$3-G$4; no tip).

**Photography:** Equipment and films imported and expensive. Black and white film developed in three to four days; take color film to a larger capital or back home.

**Babysitting:** Services arranged through your hotel.

**Toilets:** Available but best to use your hotel.

**Health:** Good general practitioners and some specialists in Guyana and good dentists. Imported pharmaceuticals available and not necessarily expensive. Water in Georgetown is safe to drink, but elsewhere water and milk should be boiled. Malaria has been eliminated, but mosquitoes can be a nuisance. Cooked food from street vendors not recommended.

## TRANSPORTATION

Bus services in the city are fairly good; taxis scarce in rush hours and at night. Taxi stands in the main centers. Fares in Georgetown generally about G$1, but check with driver before setting off. Taxis can also be hired by the hour for G$3. The average daily rate for a rented car is G$8: go to Ramahan's Esso Station opposite Stabroek Market. Traffic drives on the left and watch out for bicycles, donkey-carts and animals.

Railroad services have been suspended, but long-distance bus services are good, especially along the coast. **Guyana Airways Corporation** operates scheduled services within the country, including to Kaieteur Falls. There are ferries across the Demerara, Berbice and Essequibo Rivers and steamer services from Georgetown to towns on the coastal strip.

## FOOD AND RESTAURANTS

International cuisine is available in hotel restaurants—**El Dorado** in the Pegasus Hotel, the **Cactus Club** in the Tower Hotel, the **Moonglow** at the Woodbine Hotel. **Palm Court** and **Belvedere** hotels also have fine restaurants. The **Club Diabolique,** in Church Street, provides French food and wines and the **Rendezvous** has excellent steaks and chicken. Try the **Chinese Dragon** and **Bamboo Gardens** for Chinese meals. If you wish to sample local dishes you must try *metamgee,* a concoction of yams, plantains and cassava cooked in coconut milk; or *pepperpot,* a sort of perpetual stew. Garlic pork is a tasty Portuguese dish. Food is generally inexpensive and even in an expensive restaurant, dinner for one will not cost more than US$2. Breakfast is from 6:30-7:30; lunch 11:30-12:30; and dinner after 6.

## DRINKING TIPS

Local beers and rums are very good: **Russian Bear** rum and **King of Diamonds** are excellent. Gin and vodka are produced locally. **Diamond Club** is a Guyanese whisky. Imported wines, spirits and beers, when available, are expensive. Ladies are welcome in bars but should have an escort. Best places to go for a drink are the hotel bars.

## ENTERTAINMENT

For evening entertainment there are occasional concerts and theater performances: the **Theater Guild,** which has a high reputation, stages about eight plays a year. There are several movie houses in Georgetown and one drive-in movie six miles east of the city. There is dancing at weekends in most restaurants. The Government is being reasonably successful in keeping "choke and rob" gangs off the streets, but it is still inadvisable to wander off the main streets at night.

## SHOPPING

Shops are open 8-11:30 and 1-4, Mon-Sat. Best buys are Amerindian wares and curios, bead aprons, blow pipes, basketwork and pottery. Recommended are **Margarita Gift Shop,** (92 Middle Street); **Scandinavian Shop, Oleander Boutique** and the **Minor Industries Center** in High Street. **Correia's** jewelry establishment (159 Charlotte Street) specialists in Guyanese diamonds and other jewelry. The best place in Georgetown to haggle over local arts and crafts is the **Stabroek Market,** where you should bargain.

## SPORTS

There are dozens of cricket grounds in and around the city, but the **Georgetown Cricket Club** is one of the finest in the tropics. Soccer, tennis, hockey, boxing and horse racing are also very popular. Motor racing at the **South Dakota** circuit in Atkinson Fields attracts big crowds. There is swimming at the municipal pools at **Fort Groyne** and **Luckhoo Park.** Water skiing, yachting, motor and sailboat racing can be arranged at the **Demerara Rowing Club.** The annual rodeo, held on **Rupununi** cattle ranches on Easter weekends, is a big tourist attraction. Freshwater fishing is marvelous and you can go night hunting from boats on the coastal regions.

## WHAT TO SEE

**Georgetown** is a pleasant and attractive city. Of its many beautiful Georgian-style wooden buildings, the Anglican **St George's Cathedral** is said to be the highest wooden building in the world. The **City Hall,** painted bright blue, is a Gothic extravaganza and you must also see the **Law Courts** and the Gothic tower over the colorful and lively **Stabroek Market.** Miniature diamond and gold mines are displayed at the **Guyana Museum** and there is an important collection relating to the history of the Amerindians at the **Carnegie Free Library.** The **National History Museum** has now reopened. A must is a visit to the 180-acre **Botanical Gardens,** which has one of the best collections of palms in the world. Here, too, you can see the giant Victoria Regia and lotus lillies, experimental rice fields, tropical flowers, like the cannonball flower—and in the garden's **Zoo,** there are manatees, Guyanese sea cows, ugly-looking tapirs and many other animals.

Outside the capital, the country's main attractions are the huge cane plantations and sugar factories; the bauxite mines of **Mackenzie;** the ruins of a 300-year old Dutch fort at **Kyk-over-al,** near Bartica. Hotels in Bartica are the **Berner's Croft** and the **Moderne,** both from about US$5 for a single. See the **Timehri** rock paintings in the River Mazaruni area; the **Rupununi Savannahs,** where you can go fishing for the arapaima, the largest freshwater fish in the world; and the almost incredible 741-foot high, 300-foot wide **Kaieteur Falls,** on the Potaro River, Guyana's main tourist attraction. There are daytrips from Georgetown by **Guyana Airways Corporation,** which include a picnic by the magnificent falls, one of the highest in the world—G$35 for everything. The seaplane leaves at 9:30am and you are back in town by 5. You can also stay the night and in the morning visit the Guyana Consolidated Goldfields at **Mahdia.** Reserve tours and excursions well in advance from **Guyana Travel Tours** (A 102 Issano Place East, Bel Air Park) or from **Guyana Overland Tours** (38 Main Street, Georgetown).

## SOURCES OF FURTHER INFORMATION

**Pan Am** agents: **Bookers Shipping** (Demerara) Ltd, Bank of Guyana Building, Georgetown, and from any **Pan Am** office around the world; **Tourist Development Officer,** Guyana Development Corporation, 4th Floor, Bank of Guyana Building, Georgetown; the **Guyana Consulate General,** 355 Lexington Avenue, New York, NY 10017; **Guyana High Commission,** 28 Cockspur Street, London SW1.

# Honduras

**WHAT'S SPECIAL**

Christopher Columbus reached Honduras in 1502 and gave the country its name, a Spanish word for 'depths,' after the deep waters off its Caribbean coast. It is one of the more mountainous, beautiful and fascinating countries in Central America, with forests, volcanic peaks, fine beaches, coffee plantations, cotton, tobacco, and of course bananas. The remains of the Mayan civilization at Copán show that Honduras was highly developed about the time the Vikings were tentatively beginning to sail out of sight of land.

**COUNTRY BRIEFING**

**Size:** 43,227 square miles
**Population:** 2,582,000
**Capital:** Tegucigalpa
**Capital Population:** 267,470

**Climate:** Hot and humid in coastal regions. More moderate inland. Tegucigalpa is rather hot in March and April. Rainy season May-Nov.

**WEATHER IN TEGUCIGALPA**—Lat N14°03′—Alt 3,294 ft

| Temp | Jan | Feb | Mar | Apr | May | Jun | Jul | Aug | Sep | Oct | Nov | Dec |
|---|---|---|---|---|---|---|---|---|---|---|---|---|
| Ave Low | 43° | 40° | 41° | 50° | 54° | 58° | 52° | 51° | 53° | 53° | 66° | 48° |
| Ave High | 78° | 81° | 82° | 88° | 91° | 85° | 85° | 87° | 87° | 86° | 84° | 84° |
| Days of No Rain | 30 | 26 | 30 | 27 | 21 | 18 | 23 | 22 | 19 | 23 | 27 | 30 |

**Government:** Independent republic.

**Language:** Spanish. Many speak English.

**Religion:** Predominantly Roman Catholic.

**Currency:** The Lempira; 100 centavos = 1 lempira.

| | 10c | 50c | 1 lemp. | 5 lemp. | 10 lemp. | 20 lemp. | 50 lemp. | 100 lemp. |
|---|---|---|---|---|---|---|---|---|
| US (Dollars.Cents) | .05 | .25 | .50 | 2.50 | 5.00 | 10.00 | 25.00 | 50.00 |
| UK (Pounds.Pence) | .02 | .10 | .21 | 1.06 | 2.12 | 4.25 | 10.63 | 21.27 |

**Public Holidays:**

New Year's Day, 1 Jan
Epiphany, 6 Jan

| | |
|---|---|
| Day of the Americas, 14 April | Francisco Morazán Day, 3 Oct |
| Easter Thursday | Columbus Day, 12 Oct |
| Good Friday | Armed Forces Day, 21 Oct |
| Easter Saturday | All Saints' Day, 1 Nov |
| Labor Day, 1 May | Christmas Eve, 24 Dec |
| Independence Day, 15 Sept | Christmas Day, 25 Dec |

## HOW TO GET THERE

Fly Pan Am direct to San Pedro Sula, La Mesa Airport, from New York via Washington and Miami, and from Managua via San Salvador and Guatemala City. Flying time from New York, 6 hours; Washington, 4¾ hours; Miami, 2¼ hours; Managua, 2 hours; San Salvador, 1¼ hours; Guatemala City, ¾ hour.

## REQUIREMENTS FOR ENTRY AND CUSTOMS REGULATIONS

Passport, visa except for nationals of US, UK, Canada, Columbia, Denmark, Guatemala, and Panamá. Smallpox vaccination certificate not more than three years old. Advisable to have round trip ticket. No currency restrictions. Duty-free allowance: 200 cigarettes; two bottles spirits or wine; visitors should check in with Officina de Seguridad Pública within 48 hours of arrival and get exit permit from Foreign Affairs Office.

## AIRPORT INFORMATION

Toncontin Airport is three miles from Tegucigalpa; La Mesa Airport is 11 miles from San Pedro Sula; Colozón Airport is five miles from La Ceiba. Taxis available in all airports; 3-6 lempiras. Some buses, but as they are small, not recommended for travelers with a lot of luggage; 10 centavos for adults and children. No airport arrival tax; departure tax, 6 lempiras. Duty-free shops, but no nurseries and no accommodations bureau. Tip airport porters 50 centavos.

## ACCOMMODATIONS

There are good hotels in Tegucigalpa and other main towns but in the rest of the country are sparse. The **Instituto Hondureño de Turismo,** Casa Presidencial, Tegucigalpa, will help to find somewhere to stay. Hotels in Tegucigalpa:

**Boston** 6a Calle, 310 (single from US$5)
**Gran Hotel Lincoln** PO Box 175 (single from US$9)
**Honduras Maya** Colonía Palmira (single from US$14)
**Prado** Avenida Cervantes (single from US$9)

## USEFUL INFORMATION

**Banks:** Open 8-12 and 2-4 Mon-Fri; 8:30-12, Sat. Change currency and travelers' checks at hotels and some stores.

**Postage:** Stamps only at post offices.

**Telephone Tips:** No booths in streets, some in bars, hotels, restaurants and cinemas. Telephone communications are poor except in the main towns; telegrams widely used. Useful numbers: **Pan Am office,** Tegucigalpa, 20151; **Tourist Office,** Tegucigalpa, 228934.

**Newspapers:** No local English-language publications, but English-language newspapers and magazines from abroad on sale.

**Tipping:** Service charge not generally included in restaurant checks so tip 10%. Taxi drivers and chambermaids do not expect a tip; give porters 50 centavos.

**Electricity:** 110 or 220 volts, 60 cycles AC.

**Laundry:** Dry-cleaning available and not expensive (dry-cleaning a suit, 2-4 lempiras; laundering a shirt, 60 centavos—1 lempira).

**Hairdressing:** All first-class hotels have salons (shampoo and set, 3-6 lempiras; man's haircut, 1 lempira).

**Photography:** All types of film available. Black and white developed within a week; color takes longer, less reliable.

**Clubs:** Rotary and Lions.

**Babysitting:** None.

**Toilets:** No public toilets in streets; try hotels and restaurants. Ladies, *Servicio de Damas*; men, *Servicio de Caballeros.*

**Health:** Many doctors and dentists speak English. Hospital services satisfactory. Imported pharmaceuticals available but expensive. Wash raw fruit and vegetables. Take precautions against malaria in coastal areas. Water must be boiled before drinking.

## TRANSPORTATION

Mini-buses in Tegucigalpa, standard fare 10 centavos. San Pedro Sula has a bus service and there are long-distance services connecting principal cities. Taxis can be rented by phone, or sometimes flagged in streets. Tegucigalpa has cruising taxis, which are less expensive as they are shared. Rented cars can be had in the capital on payment of a deposit and production of driver's license. Apart from the Pan American Highway and a few routes connecting main cities, road conditions poor and, in rainy season, many routes impassable. Although 700 miles of railroad have been constructed in the north, these are used to carry banana freight. Passenger services few. Tegucigalpa is the only Central American capital without a railroad station. But it is the hub of Central American air services with daily flights to and from the other capitals and good services to the US. Internal air services excellent—flights from Tegucigalpa to 28 other airports within the country.

## FOOD AND RESTAURANTS

*Tortillas* are a popular native food and inside these pancakes can be anything from meat or cheese to red beans. *Tapado* is a stew of local vegetables and grated coconut; also try the unusual taste of *mondongo* soup—made from vegetables, bananas and yucca root. Snack meals include *currilles,* a seafood cocktail, and *yucca con chicharrón,* a salad of tomatoes and boiled yucca root. In the capital inexpensive restaurants can be found in the Avenida Centenario district.

Mealtimes are breakfast 6:30-8:30; lunch noon-2; dinner 5:30-7 or 8. International cuisine available in the major cities, especially Tegucigalpa where **La Ronda** is an expensive international restaurant, and **El Prado** is medium-priced. Good food is served at a number of Italian restaurants in the capital, notably **Roma** and **Dino's** and Spanish cooking can be tried at **El Chico Club. Boca**

**del Mar,** near the airport, specializes in seafood. In San Pedro Sula two hotels; **Hotel Sula** and **Hotel Bolívar,** have an international menu and **Hotel Vitanza, Touche, Vicente's** and **El Rincón Gaucho** are also recommended.

## DRINKING TIPS

No licensing restrictions and bars open all the time. Good spots for a leisurely drink in Tegucigalpa are **Jardin d'Italie,** the **Café Paris, Le Papillon** and **El Goyescas.** The **Honduras Maya Hotel** has a pleasant coffee shop and there are two drive-ins near the airport, the **Riviera** and **El Pinguino,** where drinks can be bought. Imported wines, spirits and beers available; a whisky and soda costs about 2 lempiras and a bottle of ordinary red wine, 4 lempiras.

## ENTERTAINMENT

Tegucigalpa is not a culturally oriented city. At the National Theater performances are few, concerts are rare and there is no opera or ballet. No national museum or art gallery. English and American movies are shown and Tegucigalpa has a discothèque, **Le Papillion.** There is dancing at **La Belle Epoque, Honduras Maya Hotel** and **La Ronda.** The native instrument is the marimba, a single or double keyboard using gourds or tubes of fine wood as resonators. The **Belén** area is the place to go for 'low' nightlife; it is exciting but it can also be dangerous.

## SHOPPING

Shops open 8:30-noon and 2-5, Mon-Fri; closed half-day Sat and all day Sun. Panama hats are among the best tourist buys. There are handbags made of straw and also some good pottery, leatherwork, woodcarvings and baskets. One of the best places in Tegucigalpa to go for these is **Los Dolores** market. Bargaining is customary. Better-class shops are to be found on **Avenida Paz Barahona** in Tegucigalpa and on **Calle Comercio** in San Pedro Sula.

## SPORTS

Football and basketball are the most popular spectator sports. There is also baseball and cockfighting. There are several golf clubs and facilities are available at the **Tegucigalpa Country Club** for golf, tennis, and swimming. It also has bowling alleys. **Bay Islands,** off the Caribbean coast, are excellent for swimming and fishing and **Lake Yojoa** is good for fresh water fishing. There is some horseback riding in the mountains and hunting is popular. You need a permit to import guns.

## WHAT TO SEE

Honduras is not sophisticated. The pace of life is easy-going, the people are friendly, the country is unspoiled and the towns not highly developed. Tropical plants and flowers, including orchids, which are the Honduran national flower, can be seen at the Pan American agricultural school near Tegucigalpa. The capital is built mainly in the Spanish colonial style and is on the side of **Mount El Picacho,** 3,200 feet above sea level. In the **Cathedral** are elaborate wood carvings and a pulpit covered in pure gold.

The **President's palace** faces the river like a fortress and the **Palace of the Congress** is on stilts. At the top of Mount Picacho is the **United Nations Park.**

The ruins of **Copán** cover 12 square miles and are an hour from Tegucigalpa by air. On each pyramid you see the steps leading up to a temple where the ritual of human sacrifice was carried out. There is a well-preserved ball-court where players had to shoot a solid rubber ball through a ring in the wall. The loser often had his head chopped off.

**Comayagua,** once the capital of the country, is a 16th-century town remaining almost as it was at the time of the Spanish conquest. Its beautiful **Cathedral** and churches have altars of solid gold and the **Padres Franciscanos Museum** at the Casa Cural is interesting. Here there is the hotel **Astoria** (1a Calle 3a, 4a Avenida 331).

There are frequent flights between the capital and **San Pedro Sula,** the country's biggest industrial town and port. The coastal area is hot and humid, but there are good accommodations here at the **Hotel Bolívar** (2a Avenida 8) single from US$6; and **Gran Hotel Sula** (4a Avenida 1a) single from US$13.50. Along the coast **Tela** and **La Ceiba** have fine beaches. From La Ceiba you can take a boat to **Bay Islands,** 30 miles into the Caribbean; at La Ceiba there is the **Paris Hotel** (Apartado 18), single from US$10.

**SOURCES OF FURTHER INFORMATION**

**Pan Am office,** Edificio Pan Am (6a Avenida, Calles 2 y 3), Tegucigalpa; Edificio Bolívar (San Pedro Sula) and from any **Pan Am** office round the world; **Instituto de Turismo,** Casa Presidencial, Tegucigalpa; **Honduran Consulate,** 290 Madison Avenue, New York, NY 10017; **Honduran Consulate,** 48 George Street, London W1.

## WHAT'S SPECIAL

Mexico is a good place to relax. A benign, almost continuously sunny climate helps. So do two long coastlines with deep blue, fish-filled seas, fishing villages and the high hotels of Acapulco. Twice in 400 years the state was destroyed and a new culture imposed. First, when Cortés conquered a huge, ancient empire with only 400 men, to impose the Spanish language and a Christian God. Then again, in the repeated revolutions of the last century. Each upheaval has left contrasts: great pyramids strangled by the jungle; Christian fiestas that would be as familiar to a pagan Aztec as to a modern Catholic; a capital city that used to float on a lake, and now has a subway system famous for its modern art. Mexico is made up of Indians, Latin Americans, Catholics and revolutionaries. So you'll meet strong conflicts and a strong identity. Without leaving the beaten track you can see a bullfight, watch cliff-divers, eat exotic meals and buy handicrafts at low prices.

Mexico can offer a holiday of long beaches, air-conditioned hotels, beautiful countryside and friendly people.

## COUNTRY BRIEFING

**Size:** 759,528 square miles **Population:** 48,377,363
**Capital:** Mexico City **Capital Population:** 8,541,070

**Climate:** Tropical in the south, coastal resorts temperate, mountains cool. Rainy season is from June to September.

**WEATHER IN MEXICO CITY**—Lat N19°24′—Alt 7,575 ft

| Temp | Jan | Feb | Mar | Apr | May | Jun | Jul | Aug | Sep | Oct | Nov | Dec |
|---|---|---|---|---|---|---|---|---|---|---|---|---|
| Ave Low | 42° | 43° | 47° | 51° | 54° | 55° | 53° | 54° | 53° | 50° | 46° | 43° |
| Ave High | 66° | 69° | 75° | 77° | 78° | 76° | 73° | 73° | 74° | 70° | 68° | 66° |
| Days of No Rain | 27 | 23 | 22 | 16 | 14 | 9 | 4 | 4 | 7 | 18 | 24 | 27 |

**Government:** A republic known as the United States of Mexico.

**Language:** Spanish. Some English spoken.

**Religion:** Roman Catholic.

**Currency:** The Peso; 100 centavos = 1 Peso.

| | 50c | 1 Peso | 5 Peso | 10 Peso | 20 Peso | 50 Peso | 100 Peso | 500 Peso |
|---|---|---|---|---|---|---|---|---|
| US (Dollars.Cents) | .04 | .08 | .40 | .80 | 1.60 | 4.00 | 8.00 | 40.00 |
| UK (Pounds.Pence) | .01 | .03 | .17 | .34 | .68 | 1.71 | 3.42 | 17.12 |

**Public Holidays:**

New Year's Day, 1 Jan
Day of the Kings, 6 Jan
Constitution Day, 5 Feb
Birthday of Benito Juárez, 21 Mar
Holy Week (optional)
Labor Day, 1 May
Battle of Puebla, 5 May
National Day, 1 Sept
Independence Day, 16 Sept
Columbus Day (optional), 12 Oct
Revolution Anniversary, 20 Nov
Guadalupe Day (optional), 12 Dec
Christmas Day, 25 Dec

## HOW TO GET THERE

Fly Pan Am direct to Mexico City, International Airport, from Houston and from San Juan via Miami and Tampa. Also direct flights from Caracas via Panamá City, San José and Guatemala City and from Managua and San Salvador (via Guatemala City). Flying time from Houston 2 hours, San Juan 6 hours, Miami 3½ hours, Tampa 2¾ hours, Caracas 6 hours, Panamá City 4 hours, San José 3 hours, Guatemala City 1¾ hours, Managua 2¾ hours and San Salvador 2¼ hours. Also direct Pan Am Flights to Mérida, International Airport, from New Orleans, and from Miami via Tampa. Flying time from New Orleans is 1½ hours, Miami 2½ hours and Tampa 1¾ hours.

## REQUIREMENTS FOR ENTRY AND CUSTOMS REGULATIONS

Passport, international certificate of vaccination against smallpox (except for passengers who have been resident in the US for 14 days immediately before arriving in Mexico), and tourist card in duplicate. This may be obtained (free) from a Mexican Consulate, Mexican Government Tourist Office, at the border, or from your Pan Am office.There are two kinds: single and multiple entry—both valid for 180 days. For the single entry card, citizens of the US and Canada need only present proof of citizenship. Radios and TV sets may be registered; permission needed for hunting guns. Duty-free allowances: up to 250 grammes of tobacco; (200 cigarettes or 50 cigars); quarter liter perfume; quarter liter spirits and one bottle of wine; 12 rolls of film. Gifts up to US$100. No currency restrictions. No gold or archeological antiquities may be exported.

## AIRPORT INFORMATION

Mexico International Airport is eight miles from the city center. Taxis are plentiful and cost 25 pesos, or only 10 if you share with others. A local bus runs from the airport to Aeropuentes subway station. The airport has its own hotel reservations counter. No airport tax. Crescencia Rejón airport is five miles from Mérida; the taxi fare is 25 pesos, or there is a local bus into town. Duty-free shop and hotel reservations counter.

## ACCOMMODATIONS

The range is from air-conditioned skyscrapers to inns and *haciendas,* and plenty of motels. You pay more in Acapulco and other resorts during the high season (March-November), and less in the country. Resort hotels will often give a 30 per cent discount in the off-season. Budget travelers should look for pensiones and *casas de huespedes,* where you can arrange bed and breakfast by the month for about 1,000 pesos. For help and information go to the **Tourism Department,** Avenida Juárez 94, Mexico City (tel: 585 30 60). Reserve well in advance at resorts in the high season, everywhere at Christmas and Easter.

**Single from US$19 (238 pesos); double from US$24 (300 pesos)**

**Alameda** Avenida Juárez 50
**Aristos** Paseo de la Reforma 276
**Camino Real** Mariano Escobedo 700
**Continental Hilton** Paseo de la Reforma 166
**El Presidente** Hamburgo 134
**Fiesta Palace** Paseo de la Reforma 80
**Maria Isabel-Sheriton** Paseo de la Reforma 325
**Tecpan Towers** 630 Paseo de la Reforma Norte

**Single from US$12 (150 pesos); double from US$15 (188 pesos)**

**Alffer** Revillagigedo 18
**Del Prado** Avenue Juárez 70
**Reforma** Paseo de la Reforma y París

**Single from US$6 (75 pesos); double from US$8 (100 pesos)**

**De Carlo** Plaza de la Republica 35
**Metropol** Luís Moya 39
**Ritz** Avenida Madero 30

## USEFUL INFORMATION

**Banks:** Open from 9-1pm, Mon-Fri. Big hotels and restaurants and some shops will change money and travelers' checks, but watch the rate.

**Postage:** Some shops sell stamps.

**Telephone Tips:** Phones in shops, restaurants and in all towns public booths. Useful numbers:

**Pan Am Office,** 566 26 00
**Airport,** 571 36 00
**Airport Reservations,** 571 32 90
**Tourist Board,** 585 30 60
**Directory,** 04
**International,** 09
**Long Distance,** 02

**Newspapers:** English-language papers are *The News, Mexico City Daily Bulletin* and *Mexico This Week.*

**Tipping:** Luggage porters 1 to 2 pesos per piece; taxi drivers no tip; hotel porter, 2 pesos for getting a taxi; chambermaid, 3 pesos a day; cloakroom attendants optional; waiter, 15% (service charge is rarely included); museum guides, 1 peso; sightseeing guides, 10 pesos per person per trip.

**Electricity:** 125 volts, 50 cycles AC in capital; 110-120 volts, 60 cycles AC elsewhere.

**Laundry:** Readily available and high standards (dry-cleaning a suit, 12 pesos; laundering a shirt, 6 pesos).

**Hairdressing:** Major hotels have salons (shampoo and set, 40 pesos; man's haircut, 12 pesos).

**Photography:** Film and equipment readily available in cities; it may take a week for processing. The cost of Instamatic black and white film, 20 pesos; color, 30 pesos.

**Clubs:** Lions, Rotary, Freemasons and Jaycees.

**Babysitting:** Arranged by good hotels, or Servicio Social Doméstico (tel: 514 99 04); Comercial Doméstica (tel: 543 95 47).

**Toilets:** In hotels, restaurants and big stores. Ladies, *Damas*; men, *Caballeros.*

**Health:** Doctors and dentists generally speak English. Drink bottled water and wash fruit. Imported pharmaceuticals available, but Mexican-made equivalents are good and less expensive. Remember the altitude and take it easy at first.

## TRANSPORTATION

In Mexico City, the metro (6am-midnight), is best outside the rush hour. Stations are decorative works of art. At Pino Suárez station there is a complete Aztec altar. Books of tickets at stations and some tobacco shops. Buses frequent and inexpensive. Shared cruising taxis cost 1 peso; ordinary taxi 6-8 pesos for rides in the center.

In the country buses are inexpensive and there is a first-class long-distance service to all major cities. Most cities can also be reached by railroad but air is the most convenient form of travel. Several internal airlines, including **Aero-Mexico** and **Mexicana.** Cars can be rented with or without driver, from about 100 pesos a day plus milage charge (25 pesos an hour chauffeur-driven; double for English-speaking driver).

## FOOD AND RESTAURANTS

Lunch is the heavy meal and can go on to 3pm; dinner is about 9pm. In all the big cities there is international cuisine, but Mexico has unique and unforgettable dishes including *mole de guajalote,* which is turkey in a chocolate, nut and spice sauce; *ceviche,* raw, finely-sliced fish marinated in lime juice with tomatoes and, of course, *tortillas,* thin, flat, corn pancakes in a hundred different guises—as *tacos,* filled with shredded meat, cheese, eggs or vegetables and fried; as *enchiladas,* cooked in tomato sauce with a filling of meat or cheese; as *tamales* with a filling that varies from state to state—or just as a sort of edible spoon to scoop up stews like *guisados.* They turn up again in *chalupas,* with chicken, tomatoes and lettuce and *guesadillas,* wrapped around cheese and green peppers or beans and under *huevos rancheros,* which are fried eggs covered with tomato and chili sauce. The sauces, too, are of a kind you're not likely to meet elsewhere—such as *mole pipián,* made of green tomatoes, chili and pumpkin seeds, and *mole verde,* a green vegetable sauce. Look for fish specialties: *pescado blanco*—delicate white lake fish and *huachinango*—red snappers. They have an imaginative way with vegetables as well. Try *chiles rellenos* (stuffed peppers) and *frijoles refritos* (fried mashed beans), or *guacamole* (avocado mashed with onion and tomato). Other dishes to look for are *cabrito* (kid) and all the tropical fruits—papaya, pineapples, limes, *higos rebanadas* (sliced fresh figs), mangos, pomegranates, guavas, and *zapote*. Wash fruit if you have any doubt about the restaurant. The price of a meal can be as low as 12 pesos (under US$1) but four courses in a medium-price restaurant costs about US$5 (63 pesos) or US$10 (125 pesos) in the best places.

For restaurants with Mexican atmosphere and food as well as international cuisine, there are two *haciendas;* **Los Morales** (Vásquez de Mella, 525) and **San Angel Inn** (Palmas 50) both expensive. In the same class are **Ambassadeurs** (Paseo de la Reforma 12); **Mirabel** (Reforma 509); **Da Vinci** (Reforma 195); **Carlos Anderson's** (Reforma 400); **del Lago** (Nuevo Bosque de Chapultepec); **Jena** (Morelos 110), à la carte only; **Rivoli** (Hamburgo 123); **Loredo** (Hamburgo 29) for regional Mexican dishes and **Passy** (Amberes 10). Specialty restaurants include: **La Lorraine** (San Luís Potosí 132); **Normandie** (Niza 5); **Fouquet's** (Camino Real) all French; **Picadilly** (Copenhague 23) English; **Párador** (Calle de Niza 17) Spanish; **Mauna Loa** (San Jeronimo 240) Polynesian; **Focolare** (Hamburgo 87) Italian; **Acapulco** (López 8) sea food; **Chalet Suizo** (Niza 37) German-Swiss, very popular with tourists; **Bellinghausen** (Londre 95) German; **La Mansion** (Insurgentes 778), and **La Troje** (Insurgentes and Millet) Argentinian; **Shirley's Restaurant** (Sullivan 166) US. Recommended moderately-priced places are **La Cava** (Insurgentes 37) French; **El 77** (Londres 77), and all the 13 branches of **Sanborn's** (one at Reforma 45 next to Pan Am) and the five branches of **VIP's.** Try too, the **Pago Pago** (Reforma 137) and **Woolworth's** blue-plate specials. Look for inexpensive meals in the Arizpe area, opposite Frontón.

## DRINKING TIPS

Mexico's own drinks are made from the cactus plant. Most famous is *tequila,* drunk as an apéritif or in cocktails like tequila sour, Margarita (with lime juice and Cointreau), or sunrise (grenadine and lime juice). Other cactus derivatives are *mescal* and *pulque*—less popular with the tourist. Imported drinks are expensive: a whisky costs about 20 pesos and even wine can be over 60 a bottle. But there are good cheap local wines, beers and liqueurs. Mexican men drink in *cantinas* or *salones de cerveza,* which are open from mid-day to 1 am but closed on Sundays and on the days before public holidays. Ladies never enter these places. Bars are for mixed drinking; but even here a woman should be escorted.

## ENTERTAINMENT

Most important center is the **Palacio de Bellas Artes,** where visiting companies appear and which is the home of the **Ballet Folklorico,** presented on Sundays at 9:30am, 5 and 8 and on Wednesdays at 9pm. Theater is in Spanish, but an English performance of *Sound and Light* at the pyramids of **Teotihuacan** takes place at 7pm. Movies are usually shown in their original language. There are frequent musical concerts both in halls and in the open air and you can choose from several musical comedies, vaudeville shows and a burlesque theater. Night life is plentiful and imaginative. Most big hotels have their own cabarets and discothèques including the **Barbarella** at the Hotel Fiesta Palace, the **Hotel María Isabel,** and the **Hotel Aristos,** Camino Real, Alameda. At the **Hotel Cortés** there is folk dancing in the patio of an old building. Other places with music until 4am include the **El Patio** (Atenas 5); **El Senorial** (Hamburgo and Florencia); **Gitanerías** (Oaxaca 15); **El Leon Rojo** (Insurgentes Sur) and restaurants and clubs around Garibaldi Square.

## SHOPPING

Shops usually close for a two-hour lunch at 12:30, but are open until 7 and 8 on Wednesdays and Saturdays. The best shops are in the **Niza** district, off Reforma. No bargaining there but do haggle in markets and small shops. The obvious bargain is silver, sometimes as a setting for amethysts and opals. But look for the official hallmark, a spread eagle. There is also basket work, pottery and tiles, carved onyx, tin and copper work, lacquerware and hand-blown glass. The blankets are thick and brilliantly colored, the blouses beautifully embroidered and the long-fringed shawls a specialty. For under US$10 you can also get hand-worked leather, dolls and full-size guitars. Good places to buy are the **Museum of Popular Arts and Crafts,** government run and housed in an old colonial church (Avenida Juárez 44); the **Monte de Piedad** (Zócalo), which is a pawn shop also run by the government, and the **Bazaar Sábado** in the San Angel suburb. This opens only on Saturdays. For basketwork go to the **San Juan Market** and on Sunday morning at 11 you can find the **Flea Market** at La Lagunilla. Also go to the **Handicraft Market** at Revillagigedo 29 and to branches of **Sanborn's.** Other markets: **Xochimilco, Teotihuacán, Chalco**—open every day. On Sunday only: **Amecameca, Cuernavaca.** And on Friday, the fabulous market at **Toluca,** an hour's drive from the city.

## SPORTS

The great spectacles are the bullfight and the *charreada*—a Mexican rodeo. The proper season for bullfights is from November to April, and they start at 4pm on Sundays. Tickets cost between 30 and 80 pesos. At 7:30 every night except Mondays and Fridays there is *jai-alai* at **Frontón Mexico,** and horse racing at the **Hipódromo de Las Américas** on Tuesday, Thursday, Saturday and Sunday afternoons. Admission is free to tourists with their tourist card, except for a small tax. There is also auto racing, soccer, golf, tennis, horseback riding, polo, bowling, swimming and water sports of all kinds. The island of **Cozumel** off the Yucatán coast, 35 minutes by air from **Mérida,** is one of the world's best places for fishing and skin-diving. For surfing you go to **Mazatlán.** The fisherman can choose from countless lakes and rivers and the hunter has every kind of terrain from mountains to jungle where animals still roam free. Fishing and hunting permits have to be obtained, as well as a license to bring a gun into the country.

## WHAT TO SEE

From the center of Mexico City, the Zócalo, you can see the

imposing **National Palace,** the **Cathedral,** the **Town Hall** and the **Supreme Courts,** the **Aztec Ruins,** the **Monte de Piedad** (official pawnshop) and the **Latin-American Tower.** Walk towards it to find the **House of Tiles,** the baroque church of **San Francisco** and the **Alameda Gardens.** Go to the top of the Tower for a superb view over the city and its site. Then down to the **Palace of the Bellas Artes** with exhibitions of Mexican art and glass Tiffany curtain. At **Chapultepec Park** you will find the whole of Mexico's history vividly set out. The **National Museum of Anthropology** (open Tuesday to Friday, 10-2 and 4-8; Saturday and Sunday 10-7), should be at the top of your list. Next go to **El Castillo,** Palace of Maximillian and now the

**National Museum of History** (open daily 9-6). In the same park are a zoo, botanical gardens, a fun fair, an elaborate playground for children, two further museums and an underwater mural by Diego Rivera. His collection of Aztec sculpture is to be seen at the **Anahuacalli Museum** (in the suburb of San Pablo Tepetlapa). You may also want to see the **Museum of Religious Art** (open 9-1 except Thursday and Sundays), for its vestments and altar furniture; the **San Carlos Museum** with its paintings by El Greco, Titian, Bosch, Van Dyck etc.; the **National Museum of Popular Arts** (open Wednesday, Saturday 11-8; other days 10-5, closed Sundays), where you can buy the crafts on display; the **Museum of Mexico City,** in a palace of pink stone at Pino

Suárez 30 (open Tuesday to Sunday, 9:30-7); the ex-convent **de la Merced,** 170 Calle de la Republica, famous for its cloisters; the **Square of the Three Cultures** at Insurgentes North and the **Plaza Domingo** where the Inquisition once sat, and where letter-writers still offer their services. In the suburb of Tlalpán is the oldest building on the American continent—the **Pyramid of Cuicuilco.**

Outside the city two trips are musts: to the **Floating Gardens of Xochimolco,** to be poled in bright boats (*trajineros*) through green canals to the sound of *mariachi* music, and to the great pyramids of Teotihuacán, from a civilization older than the Aztecs. A more ambitious day trip is to **Cuernavaca** and **Taxco.** The first has been a fashionable resort since Aztec times: see **Cortés' palace** with its Rivera murals, the **Cathedral, Teopanzolso double pyramid** and the beautiful **Borda Gardens.** Then on to **Taxco, Silver City,** a good place to buy sterling silver, to sit and listen to music, to see an outstanding baroque church **(Santa Prisca),** and to enjoy a fiesta. Dates are 18 January, Santa Prisca; 2 February, Candelaria; 4 March, Holy Week, when children dance; 3 May, Santa Cruz (fireworks); and 24 September. Hotels in Taxco are: **Posada de la Misión** (Cerro Cruz de la Misión 32) and **Victoria** (Soto las Marinas) both from US$20 single (American Plan). From Mexico City you can drive out to the **Toluca** district and explore Indian villages, drive into the crater of a volcano called the **Nevado,** bargain in **Toluca's** famous market and see the great ruins at **Calixtlahuaca** and **Malinalco,** one of the most beautiful of ancient buildings. To the east about 86 miles is **Puebla,** city of ceramics. Homes, fountains, churches are all covered with brilliant local tiles. You can buy the pottery in the market. Here there is the **Hotel Gilfer** (2 Oriente 11) single from US$13. From here go to visit the richly-decorated church of **San Francisco Acatepac,** five miles south-west and do not miss **Cholula,** holy city of the Aztecs with its vast pyramid. Fiestas here on 2 February, 25 July, 15 August, 6-9 September (Indian dances), 2 November. On your way find time to see the ancient frescoes at **Tizatlán.**

North lies **Tula,** long-lost city of the Toltecs, with its majestic stone figures and 16th-century church. On the same trip you can go to **Tepotztlán**—a village famous for its baroque seminary—and **Pachuca.** Beyond is the flower garden of Mexico where orchids are grown, and the towns of **Huachinango** and **Xocotopec de Juárez.**

**North, South and Acapulco:** To the northwest is the great seasport area. **La Paz, Guaymas** and **Mazatlán** are the famous resorts, where the hunting is also good. You can get to Mazatlán most easily by air from Mexico City or Los Angeles. Nearer the capital is Mexico's second city, **Guadalajara.** A gracious colonial town, it is famous for its mild, healthy climate and the paintings of Orozco. Hotels in Guadalajara: **Camino Real** (Avenida Vallarta 5005) single from US$12; **Guadalajara Hilton** (Avenida Niños Héroes) single from US$16; **Posada Guadalajara** (López Mateos 1280) single from US$8; and **Holiday Inn** (Avenida López Mateos) single from US$14. Near here is **Tequila** home of the drink, where a celebrated fiesta is held on 12 December. Also north of the capital are **Guanajuato** and **San Miguel Allende,** where there is the **Hotel Posadade San Francisco** (Plaza Principal) single from US$13.60 (MAP). And the enigmatic but strangely preserved city of **La Quemada.**

Southwest is the richest route for travelers. First, go south to **Oaxaca,** City of Jade, reached by freeway (eight hours), plane or train. This is the center for exploring the fabulous cities of **Monte Alban** and **Mitla,** holy ground of the Zapotecs and Mixtecs. Here have been found, beside the huge buildings and some sculptures, gold and jade jewelry and fine carvings in crystal

and alabaster—all in the museum of Oaxaca. There is a market worth waiting for on Saturday, and spectacular fiestas at the end of July. In Oaxaca there is the **Hotel Victoria** (Carretera Panamericana) single from US$8. **Villahermosa** is best approached via the lively city of **Vera Cruz,** famous for its Mardi Gras celebrations. Or you can fly the 500 miles direct. Here is the great **La Venta Museum** of Olmec carvings—old as Tyre. From here you should visit **Palenque,** 89 miles south. Trips are easily organized by car, train, or air taxi; you can stay in a small hotel next to the ruins. This is the center of a great complex of ancient ruins—palaces—extending over 20 square miles. Next site is

**Bonampak,** where the final leg must be done on horseback. Even more hidden by the jungle is **Yaxchilán,** reachable only by the determined. To discover the great Maya culture you must go to **Mérida** in the Yucatán, a thousand miles from Mexico City. Here you will be at the center of a vast area of deserted cities of the Mayans, most prolific of builders and sculptors. Many of the sites are choked by the jungle, still to be discovered or reachable only by long jeep rides. Hotels in Mérida include: **Casa del Balam** (488 Calle 60) single from US$14; **Maya Excelsior** (474 Calle 60) and **Panamericana** (455 Calle 59) both single from US$8; **Del Prado** (PO Box 784) and **Montejo** (507 Calle 57) both single from US$4. From the White City of Mérida you can go for a day to spectacular **Chichén Itzá.** In the shadow of the great pyramid lie the **Red Jaguar Throne,** the ball court, a round observatory and the complex **Temple of the Warriors.** Go first, though, to the Institute to learn about what has been found here. To the south is **Uxmal,** which has perhaps the finest of the Mayan buildings: the remarkable House of the Governor. Here graceful Mayan work is seen beside later grim Toltec carvings. By contrast, just off the coast are the holiday islands of **Cozumel** and **Isla Mujeres** where there is superb fishing, sailing and swimming.

Then there is the great Mexican resort of **Acapulco,** said to have the best sea, best beach, best hotels and nightclubs in the Americas. Hotels include: **Acapulco Hilton** (Costera M Alemán) single from US$43.50; **Las Brisas** (Carretera Escenica) single from US$28; **El Presidente** (Costera M Alemán) single from US$24; **Caleta** (Playa Caleta) single from US$15.60 and **Posado del Sol** (Costera M Alemán) single from US$9.60. Yet not far away along the coast are other beautiful spots such as **Puerta Vallarta** and **Zihuatenejo.** All around here the hunting is marvelous and you will have no difficulty renting horses or equipment for any sport you like.

## SOURCES OF FURTHER INFORMATION

**Pan Am offices,** Paseo de la Reforma 35, 3ero, Mexico City 1DF; (Edificio Condiminio Acero, Despacho 1105), Monterrey; Calle 61 no 496, Mérida; Avenida 16 de Septiembre 456-105, Guadalajara; Avenida de la Revolución 1232-2a, Tijuana; and from any **Pan Am** office around the world; **Mexican Government Tourism Department,** Juárez 94, Mexico City, Offices at 630 Fifth Avenue, New York, and in other major cities in the US; **The Mexican National Tourist Council,** 677 Fifth Avenue, New York, NY 10022 will mail you information; **Mexican Tourist Office,** 52 Grosvenor Gardens, London SW1.

# Nicaragua

## WHAT'S SPECIAL

Nicaragua has deep blue oceans on either side, winding tropical rivers, huge lakes with fresh water sharks and little tropical islands with coconut trees. Tigers stalk its jungle-covered mountains. There are ancient Spanish cities, even older Mayan ruins, an English pirate's settlement with houses on stilts, and even a gold mine or two. It has a long tradition of culture and learning, with a long-established university. The capital, Managua, was completely devastated by an earthquake in December 1972, the second time this century. No tourist facilities were available at the time of writing and food and hotel accommodations are likely to be in short supply in 1973; we cannot, therefore, advise tourists to visit Nicaragua this year. But in the future, this beautiful, historic and friendly country will still have much to offer in spite of the recent disaster.

## COUNTRY BRIEFING

**Size:** 50,193 square miles. **Capital:** Managua.

**Climate:** Tropical. Cooler in the northern mountainous regions. Year is divided into two seasons: dry, which is summer (December to July) and the best time to visit; and wet, winter.

**WEATHER IN MANAGUA**—Lat N12°8′—Alt 180 ft

| Temp | Jan | Feb | Mar | Apr | May | Jun | Jul | Aug | Sep | Oct | Nov | Dec |
|---|---|---|---|---|---|---|---|---|---|---|---|---|
| Ave Low | 69° | 70° | 72° | 73° | 74° | 73° | 73° | 73° | 73° | 72° | 71° | 70° |
| Ave High | 88° | 89° | 91° | 94° | 93° | 88° | 88° | 89° | 89° | 88° | 88° | 87° |
| Days of No Rain | 31 | 28 | 31 | 29 | 25 | 17 | 20 | 21 | 19 | 21 | 27 | 30 |

**Government:** The country is a Republic of 16 departments.

**Language:** Spanish. Some Indian dialects. English spoken in tourist centers.

**Religion:** 80%-90% are Roman Catholic. Other denominations are represented.

**Currency:** The Córdoba; 100 centavos = 1 Córdoba.

| | 50c | C1 | C5 | C10 | C20 | C50 | C100 | C400 |
|---|---|---|---|---|---|---|---|---|
| US (Dollars.Cents) | .07 | .14 | .71 | 1.42 | 2.85 | 7.14 | 14.28 | 57.14 |
| UK (Pounds.Pence) | .03 | .06 | .30 | .60 | 1.21 | 3.03 | 6.07 | 24.31 |

**Public Holidays:**
New Year's Day, 1 Jan
Fiesta de San Sebastian at Diriamba, 20-27 Jan
Holy Week
Labor Day, 1 May
Armed Forces Day, 27 May
Santo Domingo de Guzman, 1-10 Aug
Anniversary of Battle of San Jacinto, 14 Sept
Independence Day, 15 Sept
Día de la Griteria, 7 Dec
Christmas Day, 25 Dec

## REQUIREMENTS FOR ENTRY AND CUSTOMS REGULATIONS

Native-born American citizens may visit Nicaragua for a short stay on a tourist card issued by the airline offices. Others need valid passport, visa issued by the Nicaraguan Consulate, health certificate and smallpox vaccination certificates. Visas are issued free of charge and are valid for 30 days. A return ticket is required. Travelers may bring into the country duty-free: two bottles spirits or wine; 500 grams tobacco, two cartons cigarettes; gifts up to the value of US$100; camera and film. Archeological artifacts may not be taken from the country without a certificate from the Ministry of the Interior.

## HOW TO GET THERE

Fly Pan Am direct to Managua, Las Mercedes Airport, from New York via Miami and Guatemala City (some days also via Washington and San Pedro Sula). Also direct from Houston via Mexico City, Guatemala City and San Salvador. Flying time from New York, 6 hours; Miami, 1½ hours; Guatemala City, 1 hour; Washington, 6¼ hours; San Pedro Sula, 1¾ hours; Houston, 4¾ hours; Mexico City, 2¾ hours; San Salvador ¾ hour. Also direct flights from Panamá City via San José. Flying time from Panamá City, 1¾ hours; San José ¾ hour.

## AIRPORT INFORMATION

Nicaragua's airport is Las Mercedes, six miles east of Managua. It was fortunately not heavily damaged in the earthquake. There is an airport departure tax of C7 for all foreigners and an arrival tax for Mexicans and Panamanians.

## ACCOMMODATIONS

No accommodations in Managua. Hotels outside capital are not available for tourists at the present time.

## USEFUL INFORMATION

**Banks:** There are branches of main banks, including Bank of London and South America, Bank of America, First National City Bank, in large towns.

**Postage:** Mailboxes are American-style, red and blue; they can be found at post offices and Banco de America offices, where one can also buy stamps.

**Telephone Tips:** Pay-phones can be found in restaurants, bars and pharmacies. Local calls costs C25. Insert coin, wait for dial tone, dial call.

**Newspapers:** English-language newspapers available at some book stores and hotels.

**Tipping:** Service is generally not included in bills; about 10% is customary. It is not necessary to tip cab drivers, but C1 is appropriate for hairdressers, porters, 50c for shoeshine boys.

**Electricity:** 110 volts, 50 cycles AC.

**Laundry:** Dry-cleaning and laundry services are good in main towns (dry-cleaning a suit would cost about C6; laundering a shirt about 30c).

**Hairdressing:** Available at first-class hotels (shampoo and set about C17; man's haircut C5).

**Photography:** Good selection of films and camera equipment is available (Kodak, Agfa). Black and white costs C7.50, color C3.50. Processing takes under a week for color and a matter of a day or two for black and white.

**Toilets:** Toilets are provided in restaurants, hotels, large stores and theaters. They are marked *Caballeros* for men, *Damas* for women, and are free.

**Health:** Most doctors and some dentists are English-speaking. Pharmacies carry some imported products. Fruits and vegetables should be washed before being eaten and it may be advisable to drink bottled water and avoid eating food from street stalls.

## TRANSPORTATION

Although the tourist will probably prefer to drive, before the earthquake there was a train service to León, Chinandega, Masaya, Granada and Corinto. A bus service links the towns and cities as well. There are two internal air services: **Lanica** serves Bluefields, 1 hour; Corn Island, 1¼ hours; Puerto Cabeza, 1 hour 40 minutes. **Aero Taxis** also flies to Bluefields and Corn Island, and also to San Carlos, 45 minutes. However, transportation throughout the country will not be back to normal for some time. There are some boat services on the coast, lakes and rivers.

## SPORTS

Nicaragua's geography makes it ideal for the outdoor sportsman and those who enjoy the water. There is year-round swimming, and one has the choice of the beautiful sandy beaches of the Pacific, where there is surfing on the Atlantic **Corn Islands.** The yachtsman also has Atlantic and Pacific to choose from, and at **San Juan del Sur, Bluefields** and the Corn Islands, as well as the crystallike waters of **Xiloá** and **Apoyo Lagoons** and **Lake Nicaragua.** The great Lake Nicaragua and Rio San Juan also offer the fisherman the challenge of tarpon, saw fish and fresh water shark. Corn Island and San Juan del Sur have sea fishing. Lake fishing from September to April.

Hunting and horseback riding are to be found in the mountains around **Matagalpa** and **Jinotega.** There are wild boar, deer, birds and other game to shoot. Golf and tennis available in private clubs such as **La Cuesta Country Club** near Managua. You can see baseball, cockfighting and bull fighting.

## FOOD AND RESTAURANTS

You will not want to leave Nicaragua without acquiring at least a nodding acquaintance with the exotic local specialties. The staples of the native diet are rice and beans and those familiar with other Latin American foods will find many similarities. *Sopa de mondongo* is the national dish. It is a soup of tripe and vegetables, including yuca root. It is usually eaten with tortillas. A typical appetizer is *vigorón,* fried salt pork and boiled yuca root. But perhaps the native fare that will appeal most to the visitor is charcoal barbecued steak. For snacks and light meals try *gallo pinto,* (rice and beans), *enchiladas,* or *carne asada*—roast meat.

## DRINKING TIPS

The national soft drink of the country is **Tiste,** which is made from corn and cocoa; there are also various tropical fruit drinks. **Pozol** is made from corn and sugar and is drunk mid-morning. There are several native rums, including **Flor de Caña,** which when served with Coca Cola make a *Nica Libre*. **Santa Cecilia** is an apéritif like Tequila. **Victoria** is a good local beer. Imported wines and spirits are available: a whisky and soda would cost about C7 and a bottle of ordinary red wine about C40.

## ENTERTAINMENT

The folk dancing at local fiestas and religious holidays is not to be missed. The **Fiesta de San Sebastian** at Diriamba is 20-27 January. Also September in Masaya.

## SHOPPING

There are many lovely handmade articles available that would serve as souvenirs of your visit; wooden articles, shoes, leatherwork, embroidered shirts and dresses, and hammocks are good buys. Nicaragua is also famous for gold filigree work.

## WHAT TO SEE

**Masaya,** near Managua, has a large Indian population and thriving handicrafts, including hats and hammocks.

**Granada,** 30 miles from the capital on Lake Nicaragua, is the oldest 'European' city. Founded by the Conquistadors in 1524, it has fine examples of Spanish architecture and in the Lake, the beautiful **Isletas,** a miniature archipelago of 300 tiny islands. The **Condor** restaurant is a good place to eat.

**León** is another Spanish colonial city, with churches of quite remarkable beauty. Here is one of the oldest churches of the new world, superb religious artifacts and the tomb of one of its finest poets—Rubén Darío. Nearby is **León Viejo**, the ancient capital of Nicaragua, founded by Hernandez Córdoba in 1524 and destroyed by a volcanic eruption 85 years later. Excavations have revealed the main street and important buildings, including the **Cathedral.**

**Lake Nicaragua,** also known as Colcibolga, is one of the largest lakes in the world and one of the most fascinating. Rich in tropical vegetation, dotted with islands and marked by volcanoes, its sweet fresh water is stocked with voracious shark, saw fish and tarpon.

You can drive through León to the Pacific Coast and the resort of **Poneloya,** or you drive south from the capital via

**Diriamba,** through the cool, high-altitude coffee plantations to the more southerly Pacific resorts on the way to Costa Rica. Also cooler than the coastal plains is **Matagalpa,** two hours drive north of Managua, in an alpine setting of misty pine forest and wild orchids. The wildlife here includes the rare quetzal, jaguar and mountain lion. There is good fishing and of course good hunting.

While many Nicaraguans swear that the resorts of **Masachapa** and **Pochomil** on the Pacific cannot be beaten, many others say that the Caribbean Coast of Nicaragua is even better. A short flight from the capital is the old English colonial town and port of **Bluefields.** Its old houses, built on stilts, and surrounded by coconut palms, present a great contrast to the rest of Nicaragua. Fifty miles off shore and also linked by air to the mainland, are the fabulous **Corn Islands.** These are the essence of the Caribbean Island—crystal-clear waters, dazzling white sand, a few simple hotels and coconut palms. They are quite unspoiled, so far.

## SOURCES OF FURTHER INFORMATION

Any **Pan Am office** around the world; **Nicaraguan Consulate,** 1270 Avenue of the Americas, New York, NY 10019; **Nicaraguan Embassy,** 8 Gloucester Road, London SW7.

# Panama

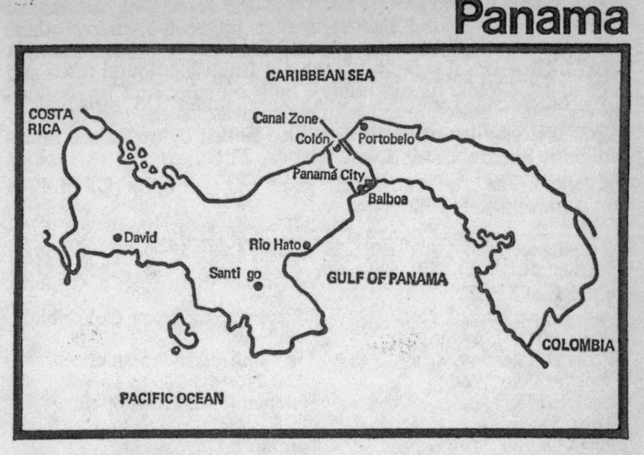


## WHAT'S SPECIAL

Panama's narrow land mass divides the oceans of the Pacific and Caribbean and for centuries it has been a natural short-cut between the two great oceans. It was from Panamá that the Spanish set out to explore South America and discovered the legendary treasure of the Incas. The gold was shipped up to Panamá City and carried across the isthmus on muleback to Portobelo. So much royal wealth attracted roving buccaneers and in 1671 the two towns were sacked by the English pirate, Henry Morgan—later governor of Jamaica. During the Californian Gold Rush, Panamá again came into its own as an inter-ocean route and proposals to build a canal were mooted. After delays and false starts a treaty was finally agreed between Panamá and the US, granting a narrow strip of land for the construction of a canal to be run as a US government corporation. The first ship passed through in August 1914. The country today has a prosperous business community and its economic stability relies heavily on the great 'ditch' that now forms part of its coat of arms. Panamá is an enviable trade crossroads and this is reflected in its low-duty shops where there are Siamese bronzes, Swedish crystal, fruitwood from Guatemala and Scottish cashmere. The population is a mingling of races. Over 60% are of mixed blood, owing their ancestry to Spanish, Indians, Jamaicans and other Latin Americans. In the jungles of Darien are long-haired Choco Indians living in river huts of woven reeds and lashed palm fronds. In the San Blas islands are the picturesque, closely-knit Cuna Indian tribes.

## COUNTRY BRIEFING

**Size:** 31,890 square miles
**Population:** 1,425,343
**Capital:** Panamá City
**Capital Population:** 418,000

**Climate:** Tropical, but trade winds keep the temperature down. The best time to visit is January—April, the dry season.

**WEATHER IN BALBOA HEIGHTS**—Lat N8°57′—Alt 118 ft

| Temp | Jan | Feb | Mar | Apr | May | Jun | Jul | Aug | Sep | Oct | Nov | Dec |
|---|---|---|---|---|---|---|---|---|---|---|---|---|
| Ave Low | 71° | 71° | 72° | 74° | 74° | 74° | 74° | 74° | 74° | 73° | 73° | 74° |
| Ave High | 88° | 89° | 90° | 90° | 87° | 83° | 87° | 87° | 86° | 85° | 85° | 87° |
| Days of No Rain | 26 | 26 | 30 | 24 | 16 | 14 | 16 | 16 | 14 | 13 | 13 | 19 |

**Government:** A republic. Canal Zone under US jurisdiction.

**Language:** Spanish. English widely spoken.

**Religion:** Roman Catholicism.

**Currency:** The Balboa, which is at par with the US dollar; 100 centesimos = 1 Balboa.

| | 5c | 10c | 25c | B/1 | B/5 | B/10 | B/20 | B/50 |
|---|---|---|---|---|---|---|---|---|
| US (Dollars.Cents) | .05 | .10 | .25 | 1.00 | 5.00 | 10.00 | 20.00 | 50.00 |
| UK (Pounds.Pence) | .02 | .04 | .10 | .42 | 2.12 | 4.25 | 8.50 | 21.27 |

**Public Holidays:**

New Year's Day, 1 Jan
Constitution Day, 1 Mar
Carnival Tuesday, (day before Ash Wed)
Good Friday
Easter Saturday
Labor Day, 1 May
Anniversary of the Revolution, 11 Oct
Independence from Colombia, 3 Nov
First call of Independence, 10 Nov
Independence from Spain, 28 Nov
Mother's Day, 8 Dec
Christmas Day, 25 Dec

## HOW TO GET THERE

Direct Pan Am flights to Panamá City, Tocumen Airport, from Houston via Mexico City, Guatemala City and San José (some days also via San Salvador and Managua). Also from San Francisco via Los Angeles and Guatemala City and from New York via Miami (some days also via Washington). Also flights from Buenos Aires, São Paulo via Rio de Janeiro and Brasília and from Caracas. Also from Chicago via Montego Bay and Kingston. Flying times: from Houston, 5¾ hours; San Francisco, 7¾ hours; New York, 5¼ hours; Washington, 5 hours; Buenos Aires, 6¾ hours; São Paulo, 7½ hours; Brasília, 5½ hours; Caracas, 2 hours; Chicago, 6 hours.

## REQUIREMENTS FOR ENTRY AND CUSTOMS REGULATIONS

Passport; tourist card or visa; valid smallpox vaccination certificate; cholera vaccination if arriving from infected area. No currency regulations. You may take out US$100 worth of goods. Duty-free allowance: three bottles wine or spirits; 200 cigarettes or 50 cigars or one pound of tobacco; reasonable amount of perfume.

## AIRPORT INFORMATION

Tocumen Airport is 17 miles from Panamá City. There is no airport bus but taxis (B5) are always available, and there is a limousine service (four passengers, B2.50 each). Airport departure tax, B2. Duty-free shop.

## ACCOMMODATIONS

The tourist season in Panamá is January to April and this is when prices are at their highest. Rooms are 10% less expensive out of season. Government tax is 5%. Pension and boarding house rates start at B3. Hotel apartments also available. Hotels include:

**Single from US$16; double from US$20**

**Ejecutivo** Calle Aquilino de la Guardia & Calle 52
**El Panamá** Vía España III at Augusto Poyd
**La Siesta** Panamá 5 (EP)

**Single from US$12; double from US$16**

**Caribe** Avenida Peru & Calle 28
**El Continental** Vía España & Calle Ricardo

**Single from US$5; double from US$8**

**Colón** 7-55 Transversal 1A
**Granada** Avenida Eusebio A Morales Elcangrejo
**Gran Lux** Calle 35 & Avenida Peru
**Internacional** Plaza 5 de Mayo
**Premier** PO Box 3096

## USEFUL INFORMATION

**Banks:** Open 8:30-12:30 and 2:30-3:30 or 4, Mon-Fri. Stores will change currency and travelers' checks.

**Postage:** Some drugstores and magazine stands sell stamps.

**Telephone Tips:** Phones in booths, restaurants, cafés and drugstores. Useful numbers:
**Pan Am Office,** 25-6500
**Tourist Office,** 64-5316
**Airport Information,** 66-5316
**Operator,** 02
**Directories,** 02

**Newspapers:** English-language newspapers and magazines available. Local publications are the *Star & Herald* and the *Panama American* (in the canal zone).

**Tipping:** Taxi drivers not usually tipped; restaurants do not have service charges, leave 10%-15% of the check; airport and hotel porters, 25 centesimos per case; hairdressers, 25-50 centesimos; chambermaid, B2-B5; cloakroom attendants, 25 centesimos.

**Electricity:** 110 volts, 60 cycles AC.

**Laundry:** First-class hotels have their own services (dry-cleaning a suit, B1-B1.50; laundering a shirt, 40-60 centesimos).

**Hairdressing:** First-class hotels have salons (shampoo and set B3; man's haircut, 75 centesimos-B1.50).

**Photography:** Low duty on German and Japanese cameras encourages the buying and selling equipment in the major cities. A black and white film costs B1 or more and usually takes one day to be developed. A color film costs from B2.25 and takes from three to five days for developing.

**Clubs:** Lions; Kiwanis; Rotary; Knights of Columbus.

**Toilets:** In hotels, cafés, restaurants. Ladies, *Damas*; men *Caballeros.*

**Health:** Doctors and dentists speak English. Imported pharmaceuticals at reasonable prices. Water safe to drink.

## TRANSPORTATION

Panamá City has an ample supply of buses. Taxis are easily called by phone and have a fixed tariff for distance (by city zone) and number of passengers. Micro-taxis charge 35 centesimos for the first zone and then 15 centesimos per additional zone; large taxis charge 50 centesimos for the first zone. Green taxis (limousines) have a meter and are slightly more expensive. Limousines with bi-lingual drivers can be rented by the hour for B3 (within city limit) and cost B40 per day.

Panamá City to Colón is the only railroad service (90 minutes) but it is comfortable. Buses link most cities, ranging from the open wooden-framed buses and small vans (holding eight to 10 passengers) to the air-conditioned **Tica Bus,** which serves all Central America. The island of Taboga has a regular launch connection with the mainland and on the Pacific coast boats are for rent from B60-B200 per day. Several airlines fly to David, San Blas, Chitré and Chiriquí.

## FOOD AND RESTAURANTS

Panamanians are very fond of small delicacies before a meal. *Carimañolas* are yuca puffs filled with meat or shrimp. *Patacones de plátano verde* are fried plantain. *Sancocho* is a tasty chicken and vegetable soup and *ceviche* is fish marinated in lime or lemon juice. Panamanian *tamales* are very good. Seafood is excellent and there are a variety of Spanish, French, Italian, Chinese and American restaurants. Breakfast is 7-9; lunch 12-3; dinner 6-11. A meal in an expensive restaurant costs about US$10; in a medium priced restaurant about US$5 and in a less expensive one, US$1. A Panamanian meal has four courses: hors d'oeuvres, soup, meat with rice or beans and vegetables or salad, and dessert.

Typical Panamanian food is served in **El Gallo de Oro** (Avenida 1, 24, El Carmen—tel: 23-8228); **Bohío Turístico** (Vía Cincuentenario—tel: 26-1304) which offers a view of the sea and Old Panamá from under a large thatched roof and **El Jorón** (Vía Fernando de Cordova—tel: 61-0005) with a bistro atmosphere. Restaurants specializing in seafood are **La Casa del Marisco** (Avenida Balboa—tel: 23-7755) and **Club Panamar** (Calle 50—tel: 26-0892). **La Pampa** on the waterfront (Avenida Balboa—tel: 23-6879) has good charcoal broiled steaks. A good Italian restaurant is **Sarti** (Calle Ricardo Arias 5—tel: 28-8275). The major hotels offer international cuisine, as do the **Chalet Suizo** (Calle Columbia—tel: 23-5141), the **Restaurante de las Américas** (Calle San Miguel Obarrio—tel: 23-7724) and **Panamá Señorial** (Calle Ricardo Arias—tel: 23-5733). The **Pana-China** (Avenida 7, España—tel: 23-9237) has good Chinese and international food. The Boulevard Balboa, Vía España and Avenida Perú, are all well supplied with restaurants of all classes. Snack food is popular and some hors d'oeuvres are sold in cafeterias or on the street as snacks. Both Colonel Sanders' **Kentucky Fried Chicken** and **MacDonald's Hamburgers** are to be found. **Rizzo's** in Vía España and Avenida Balboa sells good pizza and ice-cream.

## DRINKING TIPS

Many different types of rum are widely drunk and rum punch is popular, particularly in Taboga. There is no shortage of imported wines, spirits and beers and local brews are Balboa, Atlas, Panamá and Cristal beers and the spirit Seco Herrerano. Whisky and soda costs about US$1.40 and wine is very expensive—about US$7 in a restaurant. Liquor is usually sold until the early hours of the morning. Coffee or soft drinks (*Chica de Naranja* is a delicious fresh-fruit drink) can be enjoyed in boulevard cafés: two of the most popular are **Café Squirt** and **Café Boulevard Balboa** on Avenida Balboa.

## ENTERTAINMENT

The **Teatro Nacional** puts on opera, ballet, drama and music (concert season May to December). National folk music and dancing every Saturday (10am) in February and March in the ruins of Old Panamá. Movies are shown with their original soundtrack with Spanish sub-titles. Drive-in movies at **La Cocería** and **Avenida Balboa.** Major hotels have dancing and there are floor shows at the **Panamá** and **Continental** hotels. **La Siesta Hotel** has a supper club. The principal night clubs in Panamá City are **El Sombrero** (vía España) with three shows per night and **Maxim's** (Calle 55) with international cabaret. **Club Oricornio** (Calle 55) is an elegant discothèque; others are **Las Molas, Los Angeles** and **Club Windsor.** Dozens of small *boîtes* have music and dancing, and pop music is played at **Llave-Dorado** (Calle 1) by two American bands. Gambling has universal appeal in Panamá and if you forego the lottery (played Wednesday and Sunday at noon in Santa Anna Plaza), a big killing can still be made in the casinos at hotels **El Panamá, La Siesta, Granada** and **Continental** and at the **Oricornio.** Panamá is famous for its colorful festivals, spread liberally throughout the year. The biggest event of all is the **Panamá Carnival,** lasting for four days. *La Pollera,* 10 yards of embroidered flounced dress, is traditionally worn by the female revellers and troops of dancers close the streets to traffic. Decorated floats, fireworks and bands brighten the streets until dawn of Ash Wednesday when the mock solemn 'burial of the sardine' closes the festival.

## SHOPPING

Shops open 9-12 and 2-6, Mon-Sat. Best buys are low-duty luxury goods from all over the world—English bone china, Irish crystal, French perfumes, Swiss watches, German and Japanese cameras and radios, Indian silk, jade antiques, precious stones. *Molas* blouses of hand-stitched reversible appliqué made by Cuna Indians and *chaquiras,* necklaces of tiny beads, make good gifts for less than US$10. *Tembleques* are attractive hair ornaments worn with national costume. Where prices are not marked in stores, it is usual to bargain. Major stores will pack and ship purchases.

**Avenida Central** is the main shopping center with the two large department stores, **Dante** and **Felix B Maduro,** and the superb oriental store **Salomón** (branch at the Continental Hotel). The **Avenida Tivoli** in Suburban Panamá City has the best merchandise at good prices and **P Jhangimal** at 18-68, is clean and spacious with fine jewelry, inlaid furniture, carved ivory and other imports. **Shaw's** (Campo Alegre) specializes in china and old coins. **Avenida Ricardo Arias,** near the Continental and Panamá Hotels, is the chic shopping area. A good place for jewelry here is **Banchero Joyera. Artesanía Panammeña** (Calle 55), is good for handicrafts. **Ben Betesh** (137 Vía España) imports French couture and perfume, wool and cashmere from the US, silk and shoes from Italy and shirts from Australia. There is a duty-free branch at the Airport. **Salsipuedes** off Avenida Central is a colorful waterfront market area, selling anything from fresh fish to souvenirs, food, clothing, household and fancy goods.

## SPORTS

Fishing can go on all the year in Panamá, which holds 15 world records. Mackerel, kingfish, snook and tarpon are there for the catching in the blue waters of the Caribbean and marlin, dolphin, tuna, amberjack and others, in the ocean-next-door of the Pacific. Freshwater fishing in **Chagres** and **Chiriquí** rivers, and **Gatún** and **Gamboa** lakes. Horse racing is highly popular and there are meetings at the **Presidente Remón** racetrack Wednesday, Saturday and Sunday and holidays. Cockfights are held Sunday and Monday at the **Club Gallistico.** Boxing, soccer, basketball, baseball (Dec-Feb), car racing (Feb-Apr) and speedboat racing are all popular. Visitors are welcome to play at the **Country Club,** Panamá City and **Panamá Golf Club's** Open Tournament is held in February. Swimming is particularly good at the **Olímpico Pool** and the beaches 60 miles west of the city.

## WHAT TO SEE

**Panamá City** divides into three distinct areas: the downtown area of the 'new' city built by the Spanish in the 17th century with narrow streets and overhead balconies, the beautiful residential suburbs with gracious villas, modern hotels, gardens and pools, and Old Panamá destroyed by the notorious Henry Morgan. **King's Bridge** marks the boundary of the old city whose scattered ruins lie beneath the looming tower of the former cathedral. The **National Museum,** Avenida Cuba (9-12 and 2-5, closed Mon) has collections of pre-Columbian artifacts and natural history, and Colonial life sections. Spanish Colonial architecture at its best can be seen in the **Palace of Justice** facing the Promenade Las Bovedas with fascinating old dungeons. The **Cathedral** (mother of pearl towers) and the churches of **San José** with a golden altar saved from the original church in Old Panamá, and **Santa Domingo** (Calle 3a) with an unusual flat arch, are worth seeing. In the **Presidencia,** home of the president, plumed egrets wander freely through the patios.

**Panamá Canal:** The canal is an irresistible attraction to all visitors to Panamá and the Panamá Canal Administration provides a guide service at **Miraflores Locks** where there is also a canal theater showing historical and documentary films. The famous 'ditch' is about 50 miles long and dues are B6,650; this is still a tenfold saving to the alternative route around Cape Horn. Arrangements can be made to take a trip through a set of locks. The headquarters of the 10-mile wide zone is **Balboa** with beautiful orchid gardens. At the Atlantic end of the Canal the port of **Cristóbal** is one of the busiest in Latin America. **Colón,** a few hundred yards away in the Republic, is a free zone area and this typical town is alive with tourists and sailors, in bazaars and bars. The most impressive building is the ornate **Hotel Washington,** which has a casino and salt-water pool (single rooms from US $7.25). The **Sotelo Hotel** has single rooms from US$8. Restaurants are **Alhambra, VIP Club** and **El Trópico.** The **Club 61** and **Club Florida** have floor shows and poker machines. Twenty miles from Colón are the extensive ruins of the Spanish gold city of **Portobelo,** captured by Morgan, who forced the nuns to place ladders against the walls of the fort for his men to enter.

**El Valle:** Behind the Pacific coastal resorts of Playa Coronada San Carlos, Rio Hato and Santa Clara, lie the **El Valle** mountains (two hours from Panamá City). The **Hotel Club de Golf Turístico** (single from US$20 MAP) with golden frogs, for which the resort is famous, in its pool, provides transport down to the beaches (30 minutes), horses for riding the mountain trails, golf and swimming pools.

**Taboga:** The clear sea and the silvery beaches are the main attractions of the Island of Flowers. Scuba-diving, glass-bottomed boats, fishing, water skiing and parasailing (parachutes drawn by speedboat) are all popular. There are no cars on the island and even taxis take to the water (*pangas*). The only other means of transport are the electric trolley-trains and bicycles. During the July Saints' Day festival, there is a marine procession. **Taboga Hotel** has single from US$12.50.

The San Blas Archipelago Islands in the Caribbean are the homes of Cuna Indians who live in bamboo huts among the coconut palms. The lives of these shy, happy people have changed little since pre-Columbian days and, although Panamanians, they still live by their own tribal laws. The women wear ear disks, arm and leg bands and nose rings and have beaten gold round their necks. Experts have identified some of the designs of the traditional cloth *molas* sewn by the Cuna women as curiously similar to those on coins minted thousands of years before Christ, in the Euphrates Valley. **Pidertupo Village** (thatched cottage accommodation) costs US$34 single including meals, trips and snorkeling equipment. Rates at the **Islandia** are US$40 single (AP), and include boat trips and guided tours. The **Kuna Inn** charges US $31.80 per person (AP), which includes round trip by air and sightseeing by boat.

**The Chiriquí Province:** The mountains in the province bordering on Costa Rica are famous for their Easter lilies, blue jacaranda and wild strawberries. The coffee-growing areas of **Boquete** and **El Hato del Volcán** are excellent centers for all-year-round wild game hunting and rainbow trout fishing in the mountain streams. The **Fundador Hotel** in Boquete has single rooms from US$5. **David,** the capital of the province is a pleasant, quiet city, with an airport. The biggest hotel is the **Nacional** with swimming pool and air-conditioning (single from US$6). **Bocas del Toro** on the

Caribbean coast, can be reached only by air or boat from Colón. Some beaches in this area, although underdeveloped, are among the most beautiful in the Caribbean.

## SOURCES OF FURTHER INFORMATION

**Pan Am office,** Edificio Hatillo, Avenida Justo Arosemana, Panamá City, and from any **Pan Am** office round the world; **Instituto Panameño de Turismo** (Tourist Office), El Panamá Hotel Grounds, Vía España, Panamá City; 630 Fifth Avenue, New York, NY 10020; **Panamanian Embassy,** 16 The Boltons, London SW10.

# Paraguay

## WHAT'S SPECIAL

In 1865 Paraguay's third dictator plunged his people into a cat astrophic war against Argentina, Brazil and Uruguay (the Triple Alliance), and Paraguay never really recovered. At the end of the war, out of a population of nearly 500,000, only 30,000 males were alive. Today the country is still sparsely populated, the economy largely agricultural, almost feudal, and, except for the privileged few, the standard of living is very low.

The country is cut in half by the Paraguay River, which is also its only access to the ocean, 900 miles away. To the west lies the forbidding Gran Chaco—95,300 square miles of cattle country and scrub forest. To the east of the river is Paraguay proper, with wooded hills and flat plains stretching towards the rich lands and forests of the Paraná Plateau.

## COUNTRY BRIEFING

**Size:** 157,047 square miles
**Capital:** Asunción
**Population:** 2,400,000
**Capital Population:** 440,000

**Climate:** Sub-tropical. Summer (December-March) can be oppressively hot; winters are much cooler, with occasional frosts at night. Best time to go: between May and September.

**WEATHER IN ASUNCION**—Lat S25°17′—Alt 456 ft

| Temp | Jan | Feb | Mar | Apr | May | Jun | Jul | Aug | Sep | Oct | Nov | Dec |
|---|---|---|---|---|---|---|---|---|---|---|---|---|
| Ave Low | 71° | 71° | 69° | 65° | 58° | 53° | 53° | 57° | 60° | 62° | 65° | 70° |
| Ave High | 95° | 94° | 92° | 84° | 77° | 72° | 74° | 78° | 83° | 86° | 90° | 94° |
| Days of No Rain | 23 | 22 | 25 | 23 | 25 | 24 | 26 | 27 | 23 | 23 | 22 | 24 |

**Government:** A republic.

**Language:** Spanish, but Guaraní more popular.

**Religion:** Roman Catholicism.

**Currency:** The Guaraní; 100 centimos = 1 Guaraní.

| | 5G | 10G | 50G | 100G | 500G | 1,000G | 2,000G | 5,000G |
|---|---|---|---|---|---|---|---|---|
| US(Dollars.Cents) | .04 | .08 | .40 | .81 | 4.05 | 8.10 | 16.20 | 40.50 |
| UK(Pounds.Pence) | .01 | .03 | .17 | .34 | 1.70 | 3.41 | 6.82 | 17.06 |

**Public Holidays:**
New Year's Day, 1 Jan
San Blas, 3 Feb
Heroes' Day, 1 Mar
Maundy Thursday
Good Friday
Labor Day, 1 May
National Independence Day, 14 and 15 May
Chaco Peace Day, 12 Jun
Corpus Christi
Foundation of Asunsión Day, 15 Aug
Constitution Day, 25 Aug
Battle of Boquerón, 29 Sep
Día de la Raza (Columbus Day), 12 Oct
All Saints' Day, 1 Nov
Immaculate Conception, 8 Dec
Christmas Day, 25 Dec

## HOW TO GET THERE

Fly Pan Am to São Paulo and Buenos Aires, then by connecting flight to Asunción, Presidente General Stroessner Airport. Flying time from São Paulo is 1¼ hours; Buenos Aires, 1½ hours.

## REQUIREMENTS FOR ENTRY AND CUSTOMS REGULATIONS

A passport and a tourist card, which you can buy for US$1 from your airline or on arrival in the country. You must also have smallpox vaccination certificate. It is advisable to be inoculated against typhoid and paratyphoid. No restrictions on amount of currency you can take in or out. Duty-free allowance: one bottle spirits; one bottle wine; 200 cigarettes; a small quantity of perfume for personal use; a portable typewriter, for personal use. Visitors will be asked to open their suitcases. Colonial antiques may not be taken out of the country.

## AIRPORT INFORMATION

The international airport for Paraguay is Presidente General Stroessner, eight miles from Asunción. Bus No 30 runs every 10 minutes from the city (fare 10G). Taxis available at all times (fare to city center, 500G). No airport arrival tax but departure tax of 150G to 300G depending on destination. No duty-free shop at the airport. Tip porters 30G per suitcase.

## ACCOMMODATIONS

A *pensión* or *residencia* has rooms for US$4.50, all meals included. For help in finding accommodations go to the **Dirección de Turismo,** Alberdi esquina Oliva—tel: 47865. Hotels in Asunsión:

**Asunción** Estrella & Colón (single from US$8)
**El Presidente** Independencia Nacional & Azara (single from US$11)
**Gran Paraguay** De las Residentas & Triunvirato (single from US$12)
**Guarani** Independencia Nacional & Azara (single from US$13)
**Plaza** Eligio Ayala 469 (single from US$12 CP)
**International** Brasil & Pettirossi (single from US$8 CP)

## USEFUL INFORMATION

**Banks:** Open only 7:30-10:30am. Only banks are authorized to deal in foreign exchange, but several semi-legal dealers operate openly.

**Postage:** Stamps at post offices only. No mailboxes in use.

**Telephone Tips:** Phone booths in public places and in cafés and restaurants. Useful numbers:

**Pan Am agents,** 4.4171
**Airport Information,** 2.2012/3
**Tourist Office and Information,** 41 530
**Operator and Directories,** 12
**Long Distance Operator,** 00
**Time,** 15
**Weather,** 19
**First Aid,** 21 000
**Police,** 49 116

**Newspapers:** *The Buenos Aires Herald* and other English-language magazines are regularly flown into Asunción.

**Tipping:** Customary. In restaurants, leave 10% (no service charge); porters, 50G; taxi drivers, 10G or 5 per cent; hairdressers, about 12 per cent.

**Electricity:** 220 volts, 50 cycles AC.

**Laundry:** Dry-cleaning and laundry services good and inexpensive (dry-cleaning a suit, 150G; laundering a shirt, 30G).

**Hairdressing:** Some better hotels have salons (shampoo and set, 300G; man's haircut, 120G).

**Photography:** Equipment and films available in Asunsión only. Black and white film costs about 165G and a color film 330G. Developing services not reliable.

**Clubs:** Lions; Rotary.

**Babysitting:** Not available.

**Toilets:** In cafés and restaurants. Ladies, *Damas*; men, *Caballeros.*

**Health:** Many doctors and dentists speak English. Fees high. Pharmaceuticals expensive. Tap water safe only in Asunción. Peel all fruit and vegetables.

## TRANSPORTATION

Asunción has a streetcar service, except on Sundays, and buses and micro-buses. Fares inexpensive. Metered taxis readily available. Minimum fare 20G—the average run will cost 100G. You may find it less expensive to rent a taxi by the hour: rates are about 300G plus a 10% tip. Self-drive rates average from 926G to 2,593G, depending on the size of the car. Asunción has no traffic lights and conditions can be chaotic. If you want a chauffeur, add another 1,605G to the bill.

Railroad services outside Asunción are limited and not recommended—except for the train to Encarnación—but go first-class unless you really want to rough it. The journey is very dusty. Long-distance bus services are better. There is a quite new paved highway between Asunción and Puerto Presidente Stroessner, near Iguazú Falls (227 miles) and fairly good roads to Encarnación, Villarica, through the Chaco to Filadelfia, etc. There are also ferry and boat services from Asunción: northwards towards Rosario and Concepción (in the Chaco) and southwards towards Pílar and Buenos Aires. Boats leave for Buenos Aires every 10 days (journey takes 2½ days) except during heavy rains. Scheduled air services to most parts of the country by **TAM** (Transportes Aéreos Miltares) and **LATN** (Líneas Aéreas de Transporte Nacional)—planes can also be chartered. Flying times from Asunción: Concepción (335 miles), 1 hour; Pilar (229 miles) 50 minutes; Filadelfia (285 miles), 1 hour 40 minutes; Encarnación (222 miles), 1 hour.

## FOOD AND RESTAURANTS

The basic meal is *soyo sopy,* a meat soup made from soya beans and ground beef. *Sopa Paraguaya,* is a stiff soufflé of mashed corn, cheese, milk, eggs and onions. If you like meat try *asados,* beef charred over an open spit. The *surubí* fish, served in a number of ways, is a great delicacy. International cuisine is readily available in the **Hotel Guaraní** and in the **Gran Hotel Paraguay. La Pérgola del Bolsi** (Estrella y Alberdi); **Hermitage** (15 de Agosto y 3a); **La Preferida** (Estados Unidos 443); **Tripudio** (14 de Mayo y Jesui)—also serve good local dishes. *Parrilladas* are restaurants specializing in Paraguayan charcoal beef; perhaps the best are **La Calandria** (Avenida General Santos y Teniente Fariña); **Jardín de la Cerveza** (Avenida San Martín) and **Restaurante Paraguai** (Chóferes del Chaco y Cerro Cora). **El Dragón de Oro** (Independencia Nacional y Azara) is good for Chinese food and the **Caballito Blanco** (Alberdi y General Díaz) for inexpensive German cooking.

Breakfast is usually taken from 6:30-8:30; lunch 11:30-1:30; dinner 8:30-10:30. A meal for one in an expensive restaurant will cost about US$4.20; medium priced restaurant, US$3-4; and you will have to pay from about US$2-2.50 in an inexpensive restaurant. You can also get a snack meal for about US 80 cents in a cafeteria.

## DRINKING TIPS

The national drink is *Caña,* a potent Paraguayan rum made from the sugar cane or from honey. Imported wines and spirits are available: a large whisky and soda, or a bottle of wine, will cost about US$1. No liquor restrictions; some bars stay open until 3am.

## ENTERTAINMENT

There are some pleasant night spots in Asunción. Have a drink in one of the sidewalk *whiskerías* (bars) at the Main Plaza, in front of the river. **Capri** (Palmas 5 15 de Agosto) and **San Marino** (Palmas y Independencia Nacional) are also very popular with young people, especially after dinner. Concerts and recitals are held in the Auditorium at the **Centro Cultural Paraguayo-Americano** (Avenida España c/Brasil). Movies are very popular too. For nightclubs, the **Hotel Guaraní** has a roof-top club at weekends and **Boite 648** (Chile y General Díaz) is also pleasant —but take someone of the opposite sex with you or you will not be let in. You can also try **Africa** (Villa Morra); **Zafari** (Avenida San Martín y General Genes); **Hermitage** (Yegros 850) and **Elite** (22 de Setiembre). If you are a single man you might like **Playboy** (14 de Mayo y Oliva) where there is a strip show

Good gambling casinos at **Quinta Avenida** (Avenida Quinta y Antequera) or the **Gran Hotel Casion Acaray,** in Puerto Presidente Stroessner.

## SHOPPING

Shops open 7:30-11:30 and 3-7, Mon-Fri (the siesta at lunchtime is observed, especially in summer); 7:30-noon, Sat. Government offices open only 6:30-11:30am summer and 7:30 to noon winter. Most items will cost under US$10. Best buys include dresses or shirts of *aho-poi* cloth (linen woven by the people of Yataity) or tablecloths, mantillas, quilts, or pleated capes tied at the waist by a wide sash. **La Recova del Puerto** is a good shopping street and **Casa Arnaldo** (Calle Palina 640) a good store. For local crafts, including carvings made from the rare Paraguayan wood *lapacho,* go to the shop formerly run by the Society of Brothers in Calle Independencia Nacional, behind the Hotel Guaraní. You can also get leather goods, basketry, bright ceramics and woven rugs, silver *bobillas* (straws for drinking *yerba maté*) and *maté* gourds, handmade guitars and harps. Gifts include puzzle rings or multi-looped bracelets that uncoil to great lengths. No bargaining in larger stores, but do your best in street markets (**Petirossi Avenue** is the largest one in the city).

Football (soccer) is the national sport. In Asunción alone there are 30 clubs. Golf at the nine-hole course at the **Botanical Gardens** (Artigas y Primer Presidente); tennis at the **Paraguay Lawn Tennis Club;** boxing at the **Comuñeros Stadium.** Basketball, volleyball, horseback riding, polo and horse racing facilities are available. There are two rowing and swimming clubs, a motor boat club and the **Paraguayan Aviation Club.** For hunting and fishing go out on safari after jaguar, puma, tapir, armadillos, large barking *cururu chini* toads, alligator, the 150-pound *surubi* and the lungfish. Book a safari through **Tiger Hill** (Independicia Nacional 225, PO Box 934, Asunción) or **Hugo Pesce** (Finantur), at 14 de Mayo y Presidente France, PO Box 762A.

## WHAT TO SEE

**Asunción:** Guaraní women in colorful dresses and smoking big cigars sell local merchandise. Interesting buildings are the **Government Palace** (El Paraguayo Indpendente); the **Cathedral** (Plaze Constitución); the **Pantheon of Heroes,** a replica of Les Invalides, which contains the body of Francisco Solano López; the **Congressional Palace** (Plaza Constitución) and the **Casa de la Independencia** (14 de Mayo y Presidente Franco). Museums are open from 8:30-11:30 and 1:30-6:30, closed Saturday afternoon and Sundays. The **Museum of Natural Sciences** of the Colegio Internacional (Mayor Fleitas y Río de Janeiro) is probably the best; the museum in La Casa de la Independencia has recently been modernized. Children will enjoy the very pleasant parks in Asunción: **Parque Carlos Antonio López** (not very well maintained), **Parque Caballero** (which has a swimming pool and waterfalls) and **Parque Gaspar Rodríguez de Francia.** The **Botanical Gardens** with a **Zoo** and the **Museum of Natural History** is four miles out of town: microbus No 23 or a taxi will get you there. From here you can go by open motorboat across the Paraguay River to the wild **Chaco,** where a group of 600 former-warrior Maka Indians live. A popular tour is to the resort of **San Bernardino** on the shore of Lake Ypacaraí, 35 miles from Asunción.

Other places of interest: Along the paved highway to Puerto Presidente Stroessner you will pass **Capiatá,** where there is a fine cathedral and a 16th-century carving made by Indians under the tutelage of the Jesuit Fathers; **Itauguá,** where you can watch women weaving the ñandutí lace and **Caacupé,** with the beautiful church of the Blue Virgin of the Miracles.

The other main road out of Asunción goes towards **Encarnación,** a port on the Alto Paraná River. On the way pass **Yaguarón,** which has one of the most exciting churches in South America, completed in 1729. The altars, pulpits and images were worked by native Guaraní Indians under supervision of the Franciscan Friars. The paints, made from local plants, are as vivid now as they were three centuries ago.

## SOURCES OF FURTHER INFORMATION

**Pan Am agents,** A y C Abente Haedo, Calle Independencia Nacional, Asunción, and from any other **Pan Am** office around the world; the **Dirección Nacional de Turismo,** Alberdi y Oliva, Asunción; **Paraguayan Embassy,** 211 East 43rd Street, Room 1104, New York, NY 10017; the **Paraguayan Embassy,** Braemar Lodge, Cornwall Gardens, London SW7.

# Peru

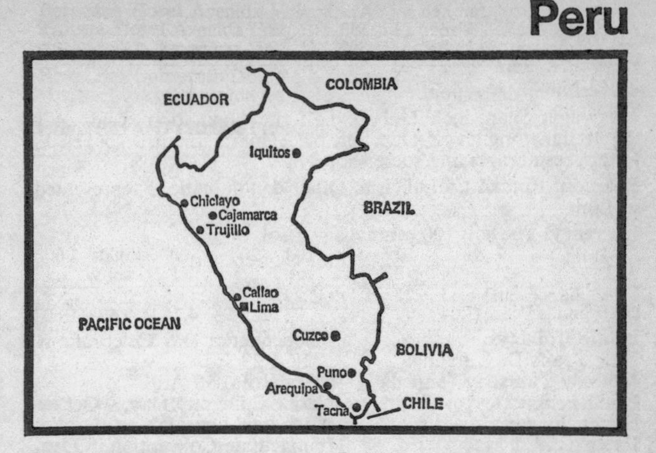


## WHAT'S SPECIAL

Peru is an archeologist's dream: the coastal desert is littered with shell-mounds dating back to 3,000 BC. Near the present-day city of Trujillo are the ruins of Chan Chan, believed to have been the capital of the great pre-Inca Chimu civilization, builders of the Great Wall of Peru across the desert plains and deep into the Western Andes. Cuzco, center of an empire that dominated the central Andes for nearly three centuries, and Machu Picchu, built by the Incas fleeing from the Spanish conquerors, are awe inspiring. Scarcely a month goes by without some archeological discovery and legends about lost cities and undiscovered treasures are still plentiful. But modern Peru is also one of the most sophisticated and conservative countries in South America, proud of its traditions and customs.

## COUNTRY BRIEFING

**Size:** 496,223 square miles
**Population:** 13,586,300
**Capital:** Lima
**Capital Population:** 2,500,000

**Climate:** Temperatures along the coast are cooled by the Humboldt Current—the thermometer rarely rises above 80° or falls below 50°. Lima sits under a massive low cloudbank most of the time, but it hardly ever rains. There is considerable mist and damp during the winter (June-September). Summer lasts from December-April. The jungle region is humid and warm; the mountain areas are generally cooler than the coast with a rainy season lasting throughout the summer. Best time to visit Lima is January-April; the mountain and jungle regions are at their best from June-October. Lima lies in an earthquake zone; the last major tremor was 31 May, 1970.

**WEATHER IN LIMA**—Lat S12°05′—Alt 394 ft

| Temp | Jan | Feb | Mar | Apr | May | Jun | Jul | Aug | Sep | Oct | Nov | Dec |
|---|---|---|---|---|---|---|---|---|---|---|---|---|
| Ave Low | 66° | 67° | 66° | 63° | 60° | 58° | 57° | 56° | 57° | 58° | 60° | 62° |
| Ave High | 82° | 83° | 82° | 80° | 74° | 68° | 67° | 66° | 68° | 71° | 74° | 78° |
| Days of No Rain | 30 | 27 | 31 | 29 | 30 | 29 | 30 | 29 | 29 | 31 | 30 | 31 |

**Government:** A republic.

**Language:** Spanish, but about half the population speak only the Indian tongues of Quechua or Aymara. English spoken in hotels, restaurants and some shops.

**Religion:** Roman Catholicism. Other denominations represented in Lima.

**Currency:** The sol; 100 centavos = 1 sol

| | 5 sol | 10 sol | 50 sol | 100 sol | 200 sol | 500 sol | 1,000 sol | 2,000 sol |
|---|---|---|---|---|---|---|---|---|
| US(Dollars.Cents) | .11 | .22 | 1.14 | 2.29 | 4.58 | 11.46 | 22.93 | 45.87 |
| UK(Pounds.Pence) | .04 | .09 | .47 | .97 | 1.90 | 4.76 | 9.52 | 19.04 |

**Public Holidays:**
New Year's Day, 1 Jan
Maundy Thursday (half day)
Good Friday
Easter Sunday
Labor Day, 1 May
St Peter and St Paul, 29 Jun
Independence Day Celebrations, 28 & 29 Jul
Santa Rosa, 30 Aug
National Dignity Day, 9 Oct
All Saints' Day, 1 Nov
Immaculate Conception, 8 Dec
December 24 (half day)
Christmas Day, 25 Dec

## HOW TO GET THERE

Fly Pan Am to Panamá City, Caracas or New York, then by connecting flight to Lima; Jorge Chavez International Airport. Flying times from Panamá City, 3 hours; Caracas, 4 hours; New York, 7½ hours.

## REQUIREMENTS FOR ENTRY AND CUSTOMS REGULATIONS

Passport, onward or round-trip ticket and tourist card, obtained for US$2 from carriers or on arrival. International certificate of vaccination against smallpox. Immunization against yellow fever, typhoid tetanus, Polio-myelitis and typhus also recommended. Visitors are asked to declare the currency they bring in. Duty-free allowances: two quarts liquor; 200 cigarettes or 25 cigars or half-pound tobacco; reasonable amount of camera film.

## AIRPORT INFORMATION

The international airport for Lima is Jorge Chavez, about eight miles from the city center. There is a public bus service into the city, fare 12 centavos and an extra charge of 12 centavos per suitcase. Large hotels have buses waiting at the airport. Taxis also available; fare to the heart of town (maximum five passengers), about 130 sol (US$3). Tip porters 15-20 centavos per suitcase. Duty-free shop, information and hotel reservation counters at airport.

## ACCOMMODATIONS

There are many excellent hotels in Lima with high standards of service. In most towns there are government-controlled hotels called *Turista;* for information about these contact the Corporación de Turismo del Peru, (Jirón Lima 298—tel: 76-176). All reservations must be made through head office.

**Hotels in Lima:**

**Single from US$15 (654 sol); double from US$18 (785 sol)**

**Gran Bolívar** Union 91-58
**Granja Azul Inn** PO Box 2585
**Country Club** PO Box 1875

**Single from US$10 (436 sol); double from US$14 (610 sol)**

**Columbus** Avenida Arequipa 1421
**Crillón** Nicolas de Piérola 589
**Riviera** Avenida Garcilaso de la Vega 981
**Savoy** PO Box 3567

**Single from US$4.50 (196 sol); double from US$6.75 (294 sol)**

**Alcázar** Camana 564
**Claridge** Jirón Cailloma 427
**Continental** PO Box 3950
**Maury** PO Box 1385
**Wilson** Jirón Chancay 639

## USEFUL INFORMATION

**Banks:** Open 9:30-12:30 and 4-7 or 8, Mon-Fri. Change currency and travelers' checks at hotels, travel agencies and exchange bureau.

**Telephone Tips:** Booths available and phones in restaurants and cafés. Useful numbers:

**Pan Am office,** 28-9999
**Airport Information,** 29-2090
**Tourist Office,** 83732/81606
**Tourist Information,** 38-440
**Operator,** 08
**Directories,** 03
**British American Hospital,** 23-000

**Newspapers:** *The Peruvian Times* is the local English-language weekly. *The New York Times* (a day or so after publication), the *Miami Herald* (on day of issue), as well as *Time, Newsweek* and other American magazines available.

**Tipping:** A 15% service charge usually added to checks in restaurants and hotels, but you should leave the waiter an extra 5%, and give the hotel porter 15-20 centavos per bag. Tip porters 10-15 centavos per bag; taxi drivers are not tipped.

**Electricity:** 220 volts, 60 cycles AC.

**Laundry:** Services in first-class hotels are good and fast.

**Hairdressing:** Salons available in first-class hotels.

**Photography:** All main brands of film and camera equipment available in Lima, but generally expensive. Take your films home for developing.

**Clubs:** Lions, Rotary, Jaycees.

**Babysitting:** Large hotels may be able to arrange.

**Toilets:** In restaurants, bars and hotels. Ladies *Damas*; men *Caballeros*.

**Health:** English-speaking doctors and dentists available. The Anglo-American Hospital is in the San Isidro residential suburb; some of the staff of the Clínica Loyaza speak English. Imported pharmaceuticals on sale in Lima; toiletries can be expensive. In the Andes, you may suffer from altitude sickness (symptoms very much like sea-sickness) but hotels have oxygen bottles. There is a man in white overalls on board trains crossing the mountains whose duty is to resuscitate passengers. Drink only bottled water, except in top hotels. Fruit and raw vegetables should be washed thoroughly.

## TRANSPORTATION

Lima has a local bus service as well as a fleet of *colectivos* (shared taxis), which travel along fixed routes. Normal taxis are also easily available—there are stands in the main plazas or you can flag one down in the street—wave your arm up and down and hiss loudly! Meters are being installed. Fares average from 10 to 15 sol in the city, double at night. Car rental rates average about US$15 (645 sol) a day plus 4 sol per kilometer—weekly rates US$60 to US$70 (2,600 sol to 3,050 sol) Hertz is at Colmena 757 (tel: 71-197); U-Drive Autos at Los Mogaburu 179; Turamérica at Jirón Ocoña 164. Lima has four traffic jams a day: as well as normal morning and evening rush hours, there is also chaos before and after the siesta period at about noon and 1:30. You must leave your left window open as signaling has to be done by hand. Receptour at Rufino Torrico 889 (tel: 31-2022) will arrange excursions with chauffeur, bilingual guides, etc.

Railroad services to all major cities are comfortable and inexpensive. The journey along the highest normal gauge railroad in the world, from Lima to Huancayo, across the Andes, will take you from sea level to 15,688 feet in four hours and 48 minutes. Trains leave daily, Monday-Saturday, from the station at Desamparados. If you are going by train from Cuzco to Machu Picchu, you would be well advised to take the tourist train as the local service seems interminable. Food is usually available on trains and there is a sleeping car service between Arequipa and Puno. There are regular bus and *colectivo* services from Lima to most important centers on the coast and the sierras. *Colectivos* carry up to five passengers and charge higher fares than buses. There are several internal airlines including Faucett, which has daily jet services to key cities such as Cuzco, Arequipa, Tacna, Chiclayo and Piuna; SATCO and LANSA, with prop-jets from Lima to Iquitos, Trujillo, Cuzco, Arequipa and others. Take advantage of Lansa's *Know Peru Fare:* for US$99 (4,317 sol) you have unlimited travel on their routes. You can also travel by lake steamers across Lake Titicaca, and then by train to La Paz, in Bolivia, and there are speedboat trips to Yanamono Island.

## FOOD AND RESTAURANTS

Peruvian cuisine is imaginative and rich, but unless you like your food very hot, make sure you say *"No muy picante, por favor"* to the waiter: *ají* (pepper) seems to be used with almost reckless abandon. Try *ceviche de corvina,* uncooked sea bass marinated in lemon juice, hot peppers, onions, corn and sweet potatoes. Or you might prefer *chupe de camarones,* a soup made of potatoes, milk, shrimps, eggs and pepper. *Anticuchos* are a must: beef hearts, beef, fish or chicken livers, skewered and broiled and dipped in a piquant sauce. If you feel like a feast, order a *pachamanca,* which consists of chicken, pork, sweet potatoes and yuca cooked in a pit over hot stones. **Las Trece Monedas** (536 Ancash) is one of the loveliest restaurants on the Continent; a charming, well-furnished colonial mansion with a cobblestoned courtyard, where you will find some of the city's smartest shops: the service is excellent. Have a drink in the sitting room before going in to enjoy the cuisine. **Tambo de Oro** (Belén 1066) is the fanciest restaurant in town: there are five elegant dining rooms and a cocktail lounge; very expensive. The moderately priced **Chalet Suisse** (Colmena 560) across from the **Hotel Crillón,** is casual and good fun: Swiss specialties and first-class Peruvian dishes. **Le Pavillon** (Colmena 620) has French food at luxury prices. Opposite the **Hotel Gran Bolivar,** on Plaza San Martin, you will find **El Cortijo,** which is highly recommended for steaks and chicken while **Todo Fresco** (Petit Thousars 3251) in the San Isidro district, specializes in seafood. Also in San Isidro, the **Acquarium Room** of the Country Club has excellent cuisine and a dance orchestra. Downstairs at **Gianino** (R Torrico 899) there is a café-style restaurant where a meal for four, including wine, will not cost more than 654 sol (US$15). Start off with the *fondo alcachofas con camarones*—artichoke hearts stuffed with fresh shrimps and covered in tomato sauce. Upstairs, the menu is far more expansive and the prices higher. **Karamanduku** (Arenales 182) specializes in Peruvian food and gay folk music—or you might like **Raymondi** (Avenida Miro Quesada 110). **Club 91** (11th floor, 911 Avenida Wilson) has a Continental menu. Expensive too is the **Ebony 56** at the Todos Shopping Center (Arequipa 3,000) in San Isidro. **La Granja Azul,** 10 miles from the center of town along the Central Highway, is the most famous restaurant in Peru: make sure that you rent a taxi for the round trip or you may find yourself stranded: fix an hourly rate before starting off. There are also many good Chinese restaurants in Lima—all prefaced by the word *Chifa:* the **Chifa Lin-Nam** (Jirón Carabaya 651) is a nice place to have lunch: you can sit in booths closed in by curtains and enjoy Cantonese food at very reasonable prices. **Chifa Lung Fung** (Avenida Panamericana, San Isidro) is a Chinese pagoda complete with quiet gardens and ponds.

Dinner for one in an expensive restaurant will cost about US$10 (436 sol); in a medium-priced one, US$5 (218 sol); and in an inexpensive one, about US$2-US$3 (87 sol-130 sol). If you fancy a snack, very popular are the **Goyesca,** a café-confitería on Plaza San Martín; **Rucaray,** a sandwich and soda-fountain-type restaurant on Jirón de la Unión; the **Café Continental, Café Europa** and **Willy's Soda Fountain,** all on Unión and the **Tudos** snack bar, in the San Isidro Shopping Center. But if you are in a more sophisticated mood, go to the tea rooms under the stained-glass dome at the **Hotel Gran Bolívar.**

## DRINKING TIPS

The pisco sour looks innocent, but is potent. Made from the local grape brandy with the white of an egg, lemon juice and crushed ice, and served with a sprinkling of cinnamon, it will take you by surprise! Other *pisco* concoctions are the *chilcano* (*pisco* and ginger ale), *capitán* (*pisco* and Vermouth), and *algarrobina* (*pisco* and algarrobina syrup). Peruvian wines with *ocucaje* will remind you of a very ordinary French table wine, about US$2 (87 sol) a bottle. Imported wines and spirits are also available. *Chicha morada* is a soft drink made from purple corn, whereas *chicha de jora* is a kind of beer made from fermented but not distilled corn. Ladies should keep to hotel bars and cocktail lounges; they are not usually welcome in street bars.

## ENTERTAINMENT

Movie-going is by far the most popular form of evening entertainment in Lima: there are many excellent movie houses, including the Tacna, Metro, City Hall, Le Paris, Teatro Central, Ey Pacífico, Alcázar and Roma, where international movies are shown with original soundtracks. **The National Symphony Orchestra** gives concerts with visiting conductors and soloists at the Teatro Municipal (Jirón Ica 323) and during the summer there are open-air concerts at the *Campo de Marte,* with free seats for 10,000 people. Open-air concerts also on **Plaza Jorge Chávez.** Opera at the **Opera House** (Ica 355); drama and ballet at the **Teatro Municipal** and the **Teatro Segura,** (Plazuela del Teatro). There are several groups of amateurs in the city, including the Good Companions (British), Lima Theater Workshop (American), and the *Alliance Française* (French).

Although many Limeños prefer to entertain lavishly at home, there are several night spots. The **Tambo de Oro** has several orchestras, a floor show, dinner and dancing and both the **Grill Room** at the Hotel Grand Bolívar, and the **Sky Room** of the Hotel Crillón are attractive and expensive society haunts. Dinner and dancing also at the Country Club Acquarium. The **Unicorn** (Paseo de la República 3030) is the best discothèque in Lima, but many young people also go to the **Sunset Club** in San Isidro, which is dark, romantic and usually crowded. Also popular is the intimate **Le Popol** (Avenida Canabal 198, San Isidro). **Negro-Negro** on Nicolás de Piérola 955, is small and intimate and there are Peruvian floorshows at the **Embassy Club** (Carabaya 815) and at **El Chalón** (Avenida Liniatambo).

## SHOPPING

Shops open 9-12:30 and 2:30-7, Mon-Fri. Best buys are alpaca fluffy hats, slippers, mufflers and stoles in natural brown and beige—beautifully soft and for under US$10 (436 sol) handwoven wool fabrics, heavy wool ponchos in oranges and deep reds—they look marvelous in midi length; fur rugs and heavy handloomed wool rugs in brilliant colors, which can be used as bed covers or wall hangings (from US$10 to US$100—436 sol and 4,360 sol depending on size and quality). You will find many tourist shops along Dirón Unión, between Plaza de Armas and Plaza San Martín, but you must go to **Casa Tahuantinsuyo** (Colmena 661), just down the street from the Pan Am office, and to **Casa Inca** (Colmena 714). There are high-quality cottons and linen goods with Inca and pre-Inca designs at **Silvana Prints**

(Colmena 727); objets d'art of Indian inspiration at **Graciela Laffi** (Plaza Mexico); leather goods at **Pedro P Diaz** (Unión 415). If you enjoy browsing around for antiques and reproductions, **Galeria Pitta** (Miraflores, Pasaje Porvenir) and Casa Paracas (Jirón Unión 713) are the places to go. For handicrafts, the best shop in Lima is **Huamanqaqa** (Jirón Union 1041) just off Plaza San Martín—expensive but worth it for its quality and taste. Or you might try the **Artesanías del Perú** (Avenida Guillermo Marconi 378A), a handicraft marketing co-operative that has a branch in San Isidro at Orantia 610—or the **Art Center** (Avenida Ricardo Parma 246) in the suburb of Miraflores. The best markets in the capital are the **Lima Market** (Avenida de la Marina), and the **Mercado Central** (Huallaga 650)—but remember: bargain hard; even in shops with fixed prices bargaining is expected and the price will almost always be dropped by at least 10%—and you may get as much as 30% off the original asking price.

## SPORT

Horse races are held at the Hipódromo de Monterrico on Saturday and Sunday afternoons, and on Thursday and Friday evenings. Bullfights at the **Acho Bull Ring** on Sunday afternoons from January to March, but during the October Fair, from 15 October to 30 November, there are bullfights on both Saturdays and Sundays with top Spanish and Mexican toreros. **Cockfighting** at the Coliseo de Gallos Sandia (Sandia 150). **Soccer** at the Estadio Naciónal; **polo** at the Club Villa and the Lima Polo and Hunt Club. **Boxing** at Luna Park. There are facilities for **tennis and golf:** the finest courses in Lima are at the Lima Golf Course and the Los Incas Club—you must obtain a guest card from a member. Lima, Miraflores and San Isidro have **bowling clubs.** There are pools at the mountain resort of Chosica (25 miles east of Lima) where you can swim during the winter, while during the summer the Pacific Ocean is inviting. Little *cabañas* can be rented by the hour at beach resorts like Lobo de Mar and Herradura, among others. **Surfing** on the beaches of Lima ranks alongside the best in Hawaii—boards are on hire from the Waikiki Club (invitation necessary). The International Surfing Championships are held every February. **Deep-sea fishing** is incomparable off Chorrillos, Pucasana, Ancón and especially off Cabo Blanco (Talara)—the Cabo Blanco Fishing Club has offices in Lima: write for reservations to Enrique Pardo, Pardo PO Box 595, Lima: rates are about US$35 (1,526 sol) per day, including meals, plus US$175 (7,630 sol) for use of boat and US$15 (654 sol) for tackle. Lake Titicaca and the rivers flowing into it abound with salmon and trout but facilities are limited and information should be obtained in advance of a trip. Partridge, wild duck, pigeons, small deer and hares are to be found in regions not too far from Lima. If you are a keen mountaineer, you will find the Andean Cordilleras irresistable: there are several clubs for enthusiasts including the Club Andino Peruano, Club Andinista Cordillera Blanca, and the Club Peruano de Alta Montaña.

## WHAT TO SEE

As with many other countries in South America, the main points of interest lie outside the capital, but there are sights in Lima which you should not miss. In the heart of the old town lies the **Plaza de Armas:** although most of the buildings surrounding this historic sight are of modern construction, their façades have kept the intricately carved wooden balconies and arcades of Spanish colonial architecture. On one side of the Plaza is the impressive, white **Palacio de Gobierno,** the official residence and office of the President. Every day at 12:45 and about 6pm you can see the **Changing of the Guard**—red and black uniformed guards with gleaming Roman-style helmets, doing a slow, unaccompanied goose-step around the Palace courtyard. In a glass coffin within the Cathedral lie the remains of Francisco Pizarro, the great Conquistador, who founded the city in 1535 and was murdered in 1541. Next to the Cathedral you will see the **Archbishop's Palace,** with its lattice-work balcony. You must also visit the **Torre Tagle Palace,** a beautiful colonial mansion built in 1735 which now houses the Ministry of Foreign Affairs; nearby is the building where the Court of Inquisition sat until 1820; **San Marcos,** the oldest university in the Americas, founded in 1551; the **Puente de Piedra** (Bridge of Stone), 530 feet long, built in the early 17th century and the churches of Santo Domingo and San Pedro. But the most beautiful church in Lima is the baroque **San Francisco Church,** on Jirón Lampa, with its handcarved ceilings, gold-leaf altar and its mysterious catacombs; the adjoining monastery, which admits male visitors only, is famous for its tilework and paneled ceiling. Then take a stroll through **Chinatown** on Avenida Abancay.

Also worth a visit are the **Museum of Anthropology and Archeology,** where you can see mummies and over 80,000 other archeological finds; the **National Museum of Art** (Paseo Colón) covering 5,000 years of Peruvian culture; the **Peruvian Gold Collection;** the **Museum of the Republic** and the **Institute of Contemporary Art.**

The October Fair is a colorful traditional holiday lasting well into November. There are fiestas, street processions, the largest of which is that of **El Señor de los Milagros,** on 18, 19 and 20 October, and after nightfall, thousands of candles flicker in the darkness. During the Fiesta, street stalls sell a specialty known as the *Turrón de Doña Pepa,* an almond nougat candy.

**Pachacámac** lies 20 miles south of Lima in the Lurín Valley. Here you will see the ruins of a sacred city dating back to almost 900 BC; the immense **Temple of the Sun,** built by the Inca Pachacutec in the 14th century; the reconstructed **Temple of the Virgins** and the remains of the extraordinary Inca irrigation works and reservoirs. Puruchuco, five miles east, is where an authentically reconstructed village depicts early Peruvian life: not to be missed. And if you want to take a photo of a llama, here is your chance—there is a special corral for llamas. During the summer, **Indian dance festivals** are held after nightfall. **Huallamarca;** right in the heart of the exclusive San Isidro residential suburb stands a remarkable pyramid nearly 100 feet high and dating back to 100 BC. **Cajamarquilla,** 10 miles east of the capital, is a mysterious fortified city, abandoned even before the Incas' arrival. **Chosica,** 25 miles east of Lima, is a delightful summer resort where the Fiesta de la Cruz is held in May. **Ancón** is now an elegant beach resort, half-an-hour's drive from Lima. **Callao,** the port of Lima, lies seven miles from the city. Here you must see the star-shaped masonry stronghold of **Real Felipe,** built between 1747 and 1772 as a defense against the English and Dutch pirates. Early in the morning or late afternoon the pier is busy with fishing boats and you must have at least one meal in a dockside fish restaurant there.

## SOUTH AND EAST OF LIMA

**Huancayo** lies at an altitude of 10,690 feet. No planes fly here, but the rail journey over the Andes is really exciting—round trip about US$9 (392 sol). If you go over the weekend, which you should, you will see the **Sunday Fair:** at dawn the Indians come in from the surrounding countryside, laden with alpaca rugs, hats and slippers, food, pottery, woven baskets, gourds and jewelry. A tremendous amount of serious bargaining goes on, most of it almost in silence. Other local points of interest are the Convent of Santa Rosa de Ocopa and the Lagoon of Paca.

**Cuzco** is one of the prettiest and most fascinating cities of South America: a self-contained little place with an air of friendliness. This was the capital of Tahuantinsuyo the Inca Empire, when the Spaniards arrived and is now one of Peru's leading tourist attractions and the center of an important archeological region.

The city is a mixture of Spanish and Inca civilizations: many of its streets and buildings are constructed over old Inca stone walls of remarkable craftsmanship—the large stones are so finely hewn together that not even the thinnest object can be slipped in between them—and no mortar was used. The **Church of Santo Domingo,** of Spanish construction, was built over the walls of Coricancha, the great Inca Temple of the Sun, while the **Cathedral** on the **Plaza de Armas,** with its exquisite altar of silver, rests over the Palace of Inca Viracocha. The Great Monstrance of the Cathedral is a jeweled masterpiece of pearls and emeralds. You must also see the church of **La Merced,** built in 1534; the **Archeological Museum,** with its Inca and pre-Inca metal work, pottery, weaving, mummies and successfully trepanned skulls; the new **Museum of Art** at the Archbishop's Palace and the curious and imposing fortress amphitheater of Saqsayhuaman, standing guard over the city. Cuzco is 332 miles and only 50 minutes by air from Lima. The **Hotel Cuzco Turista** and the **Hotel Virrey** (Plaza de Armas) have single rooms from US$9; the modern and warm **Savoy Hotel** has single rooms from US$13.80. You can also stay at a number of smaller pensions. But make sure you reserve well in advance—and take things easy when you first arrive: Cuzco lies at an altitude of 11,444 feet.

**Machu Picchu,** the "Lost City of the Incas" and 70 miles from Cuzco by narrow gauge railroad, was built by the Incas who fled the Spaniards in Cuzco. It was so ingeniously located on a narrow saddle of almost inaccessible mountains that it remained virtually invisible from the valley floor. In the middle of a semi-tropical jungle and at an altitude of 8,200 feet, there are more than 200 buildings, including baths, temples, altars and houses, all intact except for the straw roofs which have rotted, and all connected by endless stairways carved out of solid rock. For centuries it was hidden under fern and bush until it was "discovered" in 1911 by Hiram Bingham, one-time Senator from Connecticut. If you want to see Machu Picchu at its finest, get off the train at the first hydro-electric dam and walk up the steep hillside to the ruins of **Huini-Huaynu,** and camp the night there. Very early next morning, walk along the old Inca road which will bring you to the military look-out over the city; the ruins of Machu Picchu, in the dawn mists, surrounded by the beautiful Urubamba gorge and the snowcapped mountains in the distance, have an almost mystical effect which is never to be forgotten. The **Machu Picchu Hotel** has single rooms from US$8.50; reservations should be made well in advance. Visits to Cuzco and Machu Picchu are in themselves worth a trip to Peru.

Southeast of Cuzco by road or rail (journey time about 12 hours) through the Andes, will bring you to the Peruvian *altiplano* and **Puno,** on Lake Titicaca, the highest navigable lake in the world. The streets of Puno are full of colorful Indian people—the women wear long skirts and bowler hats. During fiesta time (4 November to 2 February), the town is alive with music and dancing. From here you can visit the pre-Inca stone **tower-tombs of Sillustani;** the beautiful churches of Juli and

Pomata; the floating reed islands of Los Uros. The famous steamer trip across the lake, at an elevation of 12,664 feet, is made only at night, but there are daytime trips by hydrofoil (US$45—1,962 sol) across the lake to Huatajata in Bolivia, via the Island of the Sun. In Puno stay at the Government **Tourista Hotel,** single from US$5.75 (make sure you have reservations before leaving Lima) and the new **Tambo Titicaca** on the shores of the Lake.

**Arequipa** is the second city of Peru, in the shadow of the perfectly shaped El Misti volcano (19,200 feet). This picturesque city of white volcanic stone buildings lies in the most beautiful countryside. The air is clean and dry. Llamas wander the streets. The many churches, with their exceptionally fine carvings in baroque style, will delight you; San Augustín Santo Domingo, San Francisco, the Compañía and the Monastery of Santa Teresa. The **Convent of Santa Clara** and its lovely church, is one of the Arequipa's main tourist attractions: a miniature city inhabited only by cloistered nuns and their attendants for 400 years, it is now open to the public. The Convent's museum houses one of the finest collections of religious art on the Continent. You must also see the **mineral springs** of Jesús, Yura and Socosani and the Museum of Arequipa. This city is only 2½ hours by air south of Lima, but if you want to see the barren coastal desert and its green valley oasis, then you should take the 12-16-hour journey by road along the Panamerican Highway. Hotels: **Turista Arequipa,** single from US$5, and the new **El Presidente.**

## NORTH AND EAST OF LIMA

**Huaraz** is the chief town in the valley of Callejón de Huaylas, one of the beautyspots of Peru—it will take you 10 hours to reach the valley by car, but as most of the area was severely damaged by the 1970 earthquake and recuperation has been slow, you should check in Lima before visiting the area. From here you can visit the pre-Columbian ruins of **Chavin** and **Paramonga,** and the springs of **Monterrey** and **Chancos.**

**Trujillo,** the third city of Peru, lies 343 miles from Lima: a quiet, dignified Spanish colonial town, its main attraction is the nearby ruins of the Chimú city of **Chan Chan,** covering an area of 14 square miles and once the center of a great pre-Incan civilization. While in Trujillo, you must go to the Archeological Museum of the University, and for a swim at the **Huanchaco Beach.** Hotel: **Turista,** single from US$7. Cajamarca is the town where Pizarro waited to meet Atahualpa: when the Inca refused to swear allegiance to the King of Spain, many of his followers were slaughtered and he was captured alive and imprisoned. See the **Cuarto del Rescate,** a room said to have been filled with gold from floor to ceiling for Atahualpa's ransom and where he was traitorously garotted under orders from the Spaniards. See also the **Plaza** where the Incas were massacred. Other sights include the **Temples of Belén,** the ruins of Otuzco and the Inca baths.

**Iquitos** is a thriving commercial city and a busy river port in the heart of the Amazonian jungle. The great Amazon itself is formed nearby, by the merging of the Marañon and Ucayali Rivers. Expeditions are organized daily into the tropical jungle (contact the Pan Am Office in Lima for tour operators): **Yagua tribesmen** still use curare-tipped darts, blown through a long *cerbatana*, to capture wild monkeys, which taste like delicately smoked turkey. Hunting expeditions can be arranged

through local agencies and you can go on a launch trip to the tributaries of the Amazon, visiting Indian villages and orchid farms, or take a ship down the Amazon, home to Europe or the USA. It will take you about 1½ hours to fly from Lima to Iquitos. Hotels in Iquitos: **Amazon Lodge** (Jungle Location) from US$6 (AP) single; the **Iquitos,** single from US$9; **Posada Explorama** (PO Box 446), US$85 per person for all-inclusive three-day tour.

## SOURCES OF FURTHER INFORMATION

**Pan Am** office, Colmena 607, Lima, or from any **Pan Am** office around the world; **Empresa de Turismo del Peru,** Conde de Superunda 298, Lima; **The Peruvian General,** 10 Rockefeller Plaza, New York, NY 10020; 52 Sloane Street, London SW1.

# Surinam

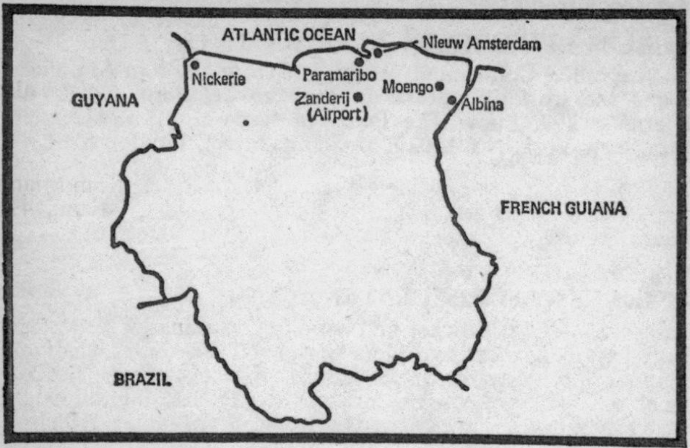


## WHAT'S SPECIAL

Surinam, the official name of Dutch Guiana, became autonomous from the Hague in 1948, but remains part of the Netherlands under the Charter for the Kingdom of 1954. The Governor of Surinam, elected by the people, is the official representative of Queen Juliana. It is a peaceful and easy-going country where the widely different ethnic groups live together in a workable and harmonious society. Here you will see Javanese birthday parties, Hindu weddings and creole processions, or Bush Negro fire dances. It is the only country outside Africa with typical African tribal communities.

## COUNTRY BRIEFING

**Size:** 63,000 square miles
**Capital:** Paramaribo
**Population:** 385,000
**Capital Population:** 150,000

**Climate:** Tropical and moist, but cooled by the trade winds. Average temperature about 81°.

**WEATHER IN PARAMARIBO**—Lat N5°49′—Alt 12 ft

| Temp | Jan | Feb | Mar | Apr | May | Jun | Jul | Aug | Sep | Oct | Nov | Dec |
|---|---|---|---|---|---|---|---|---|---|---|---|---|
| Ave Low | 72° | 71° | 72° | 73° | 73° | 73° | 73° | 73° | 73° | 73° | 73° | 72° |
| Ave High | 85° | 85° | 85° | 86° | 86° | 86° | 87° | 89° | 91° | 91° | 89° | 86° |
| Days of No Rain | 13 | 15 | 17 | 14 | 18 | 17 | 11 | 17 | 21 | 22 | 18 | 12 |

**Government:** Self-governing member of the Kingdom of the Netherlands.

**Language:** Dutch. English, Javanese and Hindu widely understood.

**Religion:** Mixed: 27% Hindus; 20% Muslims; 22% Roman Catholic. Also Moravians, Lutherans and others.

**Currency:** Surinam Guilder (or florin); 100 cents = 1 Guilder.

| | 10c | 25c | SF1 | SF5 | SF10 | SF25 | SF50 | SF100 |
|---|---|---|---|---|---|---|---|---|
| US (Dollars.Cents) | .04 | .12 | .48 | 2.40 | 4.80 | 12.01 | 24.03 | 48.07 |
| UK (Pounds.Pence) | .02 | .05 | .23 | 1.16 | 2.32 | 5.81 | 11.62 | 23.25 |

**Public Holidays:**

New Year's Day, 1 Jan
Pre-Lenten Carnival
Good Friday
Queen Juliana's Birthday, 30 April
Labor Day, 1 May
Freedoms Day, 1 Jul
Konfrieajarie, end Aug-beginning Sept
Surinam Trade Fair, Sept-Oct
St Nicholas Day, 6 Dec
Christmas, 25/26 Dec
Hindu and Moslim holidays also observed

## HOW TO GET THERE

Fly Pan Am direct to Paramaribo, Zanderij Airport, from Miami via San Juan and from Belem. Flying time from Miami, 4¾ hours; San Juan, 2½ hours; Belem, 1½ hours.

## REQUIREMENTS FOR ENTRY AND CUSTOMS REGULATIONS

Passport, round-trip ticket and smallpox vaccination certificate. Duty-free allowance: two liters spirits and four liters wine; 400 cigarettes or 100 cigars or 500 grams tobacco; perfume for personal use, and a reasonable amount in gifts. No limitations on the amount of foreign currency taken into the country. A permit is required for taking out certain antiques.

## AIRPORT INFORMATION

The International airport for Paramaribo is **Zanderij,** 30 miles from the city center. Buses available (fare SF4.50) but you may have difficulty in finding a taxi. To the city center the taxi fare is SF15-SF20. Porters are tipped S50c per piece of baggage. There is a departure tax of SF5. Airport has duty-free shop.

## ACCOMMODATIONS

Surinam has the most luxurious hotel in the Guianas, the Surinam Torarica Hotel in Paramaribo. All rooms are fully air-conditioned and the hotel has a nightclub, an international restaurant, swimming pool and one of the most modern gambling casinos on the continent. Hotel bills include a 10% service charge. If you need help in finding accommodations, get in touch with the **Tourist Information Office** (Kerkplein 10—tel: 73733).
Hotels in Paramaribo:

**Kersten** 27 Steenbakkerij Street; single from US$13 (AP)
**Iwan** Downtown, business center; single from US$8
**Lashley** Downtown, old city; single from US$7 (AP)
**Surinam Palace** Oranjeplein 6; single from US$11
**Surinam Torarica** Rietbergplein 1; single from US$18

## USEFUL INFORMATION:

**Banks:** Open from 7:30-1, Mon-Fri; 7:30-11, Sat.

**Postage:** Stamps available from post offices, hotel porters.

**Telephone Tips:** Few public telephones.

Useful numbers:

**Pan Am Office,** 72718, 72719, 72552
**Tourist Information,** 73733
**Operator,** 000
**Directories,** 008
**Police,** 77777
**Fire Department,** 99999
**Accidents,** 99933

**Newspapers:** English-language magazines and newspapers available.

**Tipping:** In restaurants it is customary to leave a tip of 10% unless a service charge of 10% has already been included in the check. Porters are tipped SF50c per suitcase. No need to tip taxi drivers, hotel porters or chambermaids.

**Electricity** 127-220 volts, 60 cycles AC.

**Laundry:** Dry-cleaning is poor; 24-hour service at Torarica Hotel.

**Hairdressing:** There are salons in Paramaribo.

**Photography:** Equipment and films are available in major towns. A black and white film will cost SF2.40 (20 exposures) and will take three days to develop. A color film, SF4.95 (20 exposures) and 10 days to process.

**Clubs:** Rotary, Lions, Round Table, Jaycees.

**Babysitting:** Can be arranged in first-class hotels.

**Toilets:** Not easy to find and can be rather sub-standard. Ladies, *Dames*; men, *Urinoir*.

**Health:** English-speaking doctors are plentiful. Good selection of pharmaceutical goods in drugstores, but these and toiletries expensive. Water safe to drink.

## TRANSPORTATION

There is a bus service in the city and its suburbs, and unmetered taxis are readily available, but agree the fare in advance. For a rental car, go to **Curaçao Trading Co** (agents for Hertz) or to **Success Tourist Service** in Hotel Torarica. The daily rate for a small car is SF20.80 plus 25c for every kilometer above 100. You will also be asked to leave a deposit of SF120.65. Traffic drives on the left and conditions are chaotic: beware of mopeds and dogs. Daily rates for a chauffeur-driven car from SF104-SF125, but an English-speaking driver will not cost extra.

Only railroad enthusiasts will enjoy the old-fashioned service, but there is a good long-distance bus service along the east-west highway from Paramaribo to Moengo, Albina and Nickerie. **Surinam Airways (SLM)** is the domestic airline. Ferries are used to cross main rivers and you might enjoy traveling upstream across the rapids in a canoe with an outboard motor.

## FOOD AND RESTAURANTS

International cuisine is available in large hotels, but there are many specialties you must certainly try, including *pom* (a kind of chicken pie) and *pindasoep met Tom-Tom* (peanut soup with pounded plantain). There are many Chinese, Indonesian, and creole restaurants but the best of these in Paramaribo are the **Deli,** the **Njoeksang,** the **Bali** and the less expensive **Roline's, Waron Mauris** and the **YWCA Cafeteria.**

Breakfast is from 6:30-9; lunch from 12-3; and dinner 7-11. A meal in an expensive restaurant will cost from US$4.80-7.20; in a medium-priced restaurant about US$3.80 and in an inexpensive restaurant from US96¢-$1.90.

## DRINKING TIPS

There are a number of refreshing soft drinks including tamarind syrup, *orgeade* (extract from almonds) and cool rootbeer called *gemberbier*. Your whisky and soda will cost SF1. Popular drinking spots, especially with young people, are the **Spanhock Cafeteria, Jolly Fountain** and **Orlando's Coffee Shop.**

## ENTERTAINMENT

Evening entertainment revolves around the main hotels, where there is music and dancing; **Torarica, Surinam Palace** and at week-ends the **River Club Hotel.** There are also several amateur theater groups, including the **Thalia,** which is 135 years old. Movies are popular. **Club Numero Uno** has a discothèque on Sunday evenings and there is entertainment at the **Paradise Disco Bar. Club 77** is about three miles from the city.

## SHOPPING

Shops in Paramaribo are open from 7-1 and 4-6 on weekdays; 7-1 and 4-7 Sat. Best buys are dress fabrics (you can have a custom-made suit delivered within 48 hours or even less)—go to **Het Manufakturen Poleio** on Sivaplein or **Brokespondo** on Zwartenhovenburgstraat; gold and silver jewelry and wood carvings made by the Bush Negroes—you can get delightful small wood carvings with seeds of fish stones. Other souvenirs are balsa figurines, Amerindian seed necklaces, weapons, hammocks, trays: you can browse for these at the **Bush-Negro Woodcarving Association** in the Hotel Torarica Arcade; **Boutique Rosita; Sjiem Fol** on Dominiestraat and many others. For Javanese-style bamboo and wickerwork, go to **Surindo** on Landesmostraat. Large department stores are **Kesters, Kirpaloni,** and on Maagdenstraat, **J. Nassief & Co.** Bargaining not customary in stores but a must in markets.

## SPORTS

Soccer and basketball are the most popular sports, but there are also facilities for cricket, volleyball, tennis and cycling. Golf at the **Paramaribo Golf Club.** All sports clubs welcome visitors when introduced by a member.

## WHAT TO SEE

Twelve miles from the mouth of the Suriname River, **Paramaribo** is one of the most fascinating cities in South America. A little bit of Holland on the edge of the jungle, where the Indians still hunt with poisoned arrows, the city is vibrant with color; Muslims, Hindus, creoles, Amerindians, Europeans and Chinese throng the market on Konkantriestraat and the Central Market on Waterkaut, the waterfront, where dug-out canoes weave their way among ocean-going steamers and river boats. The center of activity is **Oranje Square,** with the Governor's House and other Government buildings nearby. Be sure to see the **Palm Gardens,** the **Botanical Gardens** behind the Governor's Palace and the **Surinam Museum,** in the suburb of Zorgenhoop.

There are excursions to the new open-air museum in **Nieuw Amsterdam,** half-an-hour from Paramaribo; to the ruins of the

**Berachaahve Salon Synagogue** and its cemetery at **Joden Savannam**; to Bush Negro and Amerindian villages: a must is a trip up the **Saramacca River,** where you can fish for the piranha or alternatively pan for gold, to the bush village of **Santigron.** One hundred miles east of Paramaribo lies the bauxite mines and the port of **Moengo:** in the neighboring settlements you can see Bush Negroes working their beautiful carvings (they charge 50c for each photo you take of them) and in the village of **Neger Creek** the residents perform a voodoo fire dance at the height of which the dancers are immersed in a bed of hot coals. Exciting, too, is the two-day trip in a dug-out canoe with an outboard motor up the rapids of the Marowijne River to the island of **Tamara.**

Eighty per cent of Surinam is jungle and tour operators can arrange hunting and fishing safaris when you stay overnight at simple but very comfortable guest houses like those at Raleigh Falls Nature Reservation, Brownsberg National Park and Mamadam on the Saramacca River.

## SOURCES OF FURTHER INFORMATION

**Pan Am office,** Cabell Building, Malibatrumstraat 5, Paramaribo, and from any **Pan Am** office round the world; **Surinam Tourist Development Board,** Kerkplein 10, Paramaribo; **Surinam Tourist Bureau,** 1 Rockefeller Plaza, New York, NY 10020.

# Uruguay

## WHAT'S SPECIAL

Uruguay is remarkable for its delightful capital and for its 200 miles of coastal resorts: holiday makers from all over the continent, even from far off Rio de Janeiro, flock to the 'Riviera of South America,' with its luxurious hotels and casinos and dazzling sandy beaches where you can go yachting, surfing, water skiing and swimming—or simply mingle with movie stars and celebrities at the Punta del Este Film Festival. In the *estancias* in the interior of the country, the romantic and legendary Gauchos roam the countryside, rounding up cattle, or gallop after ostriches with their *bolaedoras*—heavy metal balls wrapped in leather—or relax against the *estancia* bar sipping the potent *grappa* or drinking *yerba mate* through a silver straw. Uruguay is remarkable too, in that it is the only 'welfare state' in South America. And although the social system is far from perfect, this is one of the most enlightened and advanced nations on the Continent, and the most European in outlook.

## COUNTRY BRIEFING

**Size:** 72,172 square miles **Population:** 2,750,000
**Capital:** Montevideo **Capital Population:** 1,260,000

**Climate:** Ideal. Summer days (from December to March) are beautifully warm, with cooling breezes from the sea. Temperatures hover around 80 degrees. Nights are mild and pleasant, with temperatures between 60° and 65°. Winters (June to September) are cool, but rarely does the thermometer fall below 40° and there is never any snow.

Best time to go—springtime, October and November, or January-February at the seaside.

**WEATHER IN MONTEVIDEO**—Lat S34°33′—Alt 30 ft

| Temp | Jan | Feb | Mar | Apr | May | Jun | Jul | Aug | Sep | Oct | Nov | Dec |
|---|---|---|---|---|---|---|---|---|---|---|---|---|
| Ave Low | 62° | 61° | 59° | 53° | 48° | 43° | 43° | 43° | 46° | 49° | 54° | 59° |
| Ave High | 83° | 82° | 78° | 71° | 64° | 59° | 58° | 59° | 63° | 68° | 74° | 79° |
| Days of No Rain | 25 | 23 | 26 | 24 | 25 | 25 | 25 | 24 | 24 | 25 | 24 | 24 |

**Government:** Presidential democracy.

**Language:** Spanish. Some English, French and German.

**Religion:** Roman Catholic. Other denominations represented.

**Currency:** Pesos and Centesimos; 100 centismos = 1URP.

| | 5 URP | 10 URP | 50 URP | 100 URP | 500 URP | 1,000 URP | 5,000 URP | 10,000 URP |
|---|---|---|---|---|---|---|---|---|
| US (Dollars.Cents) | — | .01 | .06 | .12 | .60 | 1.20 | 6.00 | 12.00 |
| UK (Pounds.Pence) | — | — | .03 | .06 | .31 | .63 | 3.15 | 6.30 |

**Public Holidays:**

Landing of the 33 Orientales, 1 Jan, 6 Jan and 19 Apr
Battle of Las Piedras, 18 May
Birth of the hero Don José Gervacio Antigas, 19 Jun
Signing of the 1st Constitution, 18 Jul
Independence Day, 25 Aug
Discovery of America, 12 Oct
All Souls' Day, 2 Nov
Immaculate Conception, 8 Dec
Christmas Day, 25 Dec

## HOW TO GET THERE

Fly Pan Am direct to Montevideo, Carrasco Airport, from New York via Buenos Aires (some days also via Rio de Janeiro). Flying time from New York is 11½ hours, Buenos Aires ¾ hour and Rio de Janeiro 3¾ hour.

## REQUIREMENTS FOR ENTRY AND CUSTOMS REGULATIONS

Passport and international vaccination certificate against smallpox. Visa is not required from citizens of the US, the UK, Canada and many European countries for stays of less than three months. If coming from an infected area, a vaccination certificate against cholera is required. Duty-free allowance: one bottle of wine, 200 cigarettes or 50 cigars. No restrictions on the amount of currency which may be brought in or taken out.

## AIRPORT INFORMATION

The International Airport for Montevideo is Carrasco, 13 miles from the city center. Only the airlines flying between Montevideo and Buenos Aires have buses to downtown—buses run all day and the fare is 400 pesos. Taxis are regularly available up to 11pm—the fare to the heart of town is 3,000 pesos. Airport departure tax of 200 pesos to another Latin American country; 400 pesos to any other country. There is also a tax of 3% on all tickets issued and paid for in Uruguay. No duty-free shop, nor hotel reservation counter. Airport porters are tipped 150 pesos per piece of luggage.

## ACCOMMODATIONS

Hotel rates in Uruguay are very reasonable, though higher in the summer months. Some hotels close down after 1 April. Hotels in Punta del Este charge 40% more than those in the capital, especially during the Carnival Week (bginning on the Monday preceding Ash Wednesday) and the Semana de Turismo (which coincides with Holy Week). Advance reservation is advisable throughout the year but absolutely essential for the summer months. Hotels in Montevideo.

**Single: US$13 (10,833 pesos); double: US$17 (14,166 pesos)**

**Crillón Hotel** Andes 1318 (CP)
**Victoria Plaza** Plaza Independencia 759

**Single: US$9 (7,500 pesos); double: US$12 (10,000 pesos)**

**Columbia Palace Hotel** Rambla Republica de Francia 473 (CP)
**Lancaster Hotel** Plaza Libertad 1334 (CP)
**Carrasco Casino** Montevideo Beach (AP)

**Single from US$7 (5,833 pesos); double from US$9 (7,500 pesos)**

**California** San José 1237/99 (CP)
**Gran Hotel Americo** Rio Negro 1330
**London Palace Hotel** Rio Negro 1278
**Oxford Hotel** 1286 Paraguay
**Presidente Hotel** Avenida 18 de Julio

## USEFUL INFORMATION

**Banks:** Are open on weekdays Mon-Fri only from 1:30 to 5:30 during summer; 1-5 in winter. The best exchange rates are obtainable at the authorized exchange offices: Exprinter is at Sarandi 700; Wagon-Lits Cook is at Rio Negro 1356.

**Postage:** Stamps obtainable only in post offices or from *conciérges*. No mailboxes in Montevideo but you can mail letters at the Pan Am office to avoid delays. For cables, go to Western Telegraph Co (Mercury House, Calle Cerrito 449) or All American Cables & Radio (Calle Zabala 1451).

**Telephone Tips:** Phones available in restaurants and cafés.

Useful numbers:

**Pan Am Offices,** 89787, 80697 914312 in Montevideo, 502289 at Carrasco Airport
**Airport Information,** 502261 extension 247
**Tourist offices,** 916773 and 80509
**Tourist Information,** 85216 and 917394
**Directory Inquiries,** 212
**Special Information** (weather communications, etc) 214
**Police,** 890
**First Aid,** 401111
**British Hospital,** 409011
**Long Distance (International) Operator,** 218
**Time,** 6

**Newspapers:** English-language newspapers are available.

**Tipping:** A tax and service charge of 15-25% is generally included in restaurant bills, but a tip of 10% is still expected. Tip porters, 150 pesos for each piece of luggage; taxi drivers, 10% of the fare or a minimum of 50 pesos; hairdressers, 10% of the bill or a minimum of 100 pesos; hotel porters, 150 pesos per suitcase; chambermaids, 200 pesos for each day spent at the hotel; museum guides 200 pesos (except at Parliament House, where a tip will not be accepted). In cafés, leave a tip of about 15% of the bill. Movie ushers get a small tip.

**Electricity:** 220 volts, 50 cycles, AC throughout the country.

**Laundry:** Dry-cleaning and laundry services are readily available and in Montevideo you can count on a 24-hour service (dry-cleaning a suit, 1,000 pesos; laundering a shirt, 150 pesos).

**Hairdressing:** The Victoria Plaza Hotel has a very good salon and you will not have any difficulty in finding a salon in Montevideo and Punta del Este (shampoo and set, 1,000 pesos; man's haircut, about 650 pesos).

**Photography:** Equipment and films will be found only in Montevideo, Punta del Este, Salto, Paysandu and Rivera. Black and white film takes 24 hours to be developed; color, 3-5 days. Prices are moderate.

**Clubs:** Lions, Rotary, Junior Chamber of Commerce. The Golf Club, Automobile Club and Yacht Club are open to visitors.

**Babysitting:** Services can be arranged through your hotel.

**Toilets:** Can be difficult to find, but tea rooms (*confiterías*), bars and petrol stations have conveniences. Ladies, *Ellas* or *Dames*; men, *Ellos* or *Cabelleros*. There is no charge.

**Health:** Medical services are of a very high standard and many doctors speak English. The British Hospital at Avenida Italia 2402 has a British matron and nursing sisters. Most pharmaceutical goods are produced locally; neither these nor toiletries are expensive. Water and milk are safe in Montevideo and you enjoy fresh fruit and salads without fear. Outside the capital it is advisable to drink mineral waters: Salus and Matutina are excellent. If you do not want it carbonated, ask for *Agua singas*. For night duty pharmacist call **214.**

## TRANSPORTATION

Bus and trolley-bus services cover the city and suburbs. Buses number 116; 117; 121 and 122 will get you to the beaches. Taxis are also readily available—flag one in the street—they have meters and there is an extra charge depending on the number of passengers. Night fares are 30% higher. You can rent a car from **Sudamcar** at Cerro Largo 885, for 6,000 pesos a day plus 35 pesos per kilometer (plus petrol)—but you will probably find traffic conditions in Montevideo absolutely hair-raising—vehicles will not stop and there is no right of way at uncontrolled crossroads and intersections. But if you would rather play it safe, the average daily rate (8 hour period) for a chauffeur-driven car is 28,000 pesos—and you will have to pay for the '*chofer's*' lunch or supper as well! English-speaking drivers are not easily available—best thing is to take a bilingual guide with you—at an extra cost of 4,500 pesos a day. Long distance travel by rail is not recommended. Bus services, on the other hand, are first-class: **Onda** (Plaza Libertad—tel: 92333), **Cot, Cora** are reliable companies with a fleet of comfortable air-conditioned buses, operating to most Uruguayan cities. **Tamu** (Transportes Aeroes Militaires) **Causa** and **Pluna** (on Colonia, near Agraciada—tel: 96591) are domestic airlines with flights to most major cities. There are 775 miles of navigable waterways: a delightful way to travel to Buenos Aires is by ferry, which leaves from the dock near Plaza Constitución—the boat leaves at 9pm and arrives in Buenos Aires next morning at 8 (sailing times are 1½ hours later in winter). There are also ferries connecting Montevideo to Mercedes, Fray Bentos, Salto. Boats leave from Paysandu to Concepción and Colón in Argentina and from Salto to Concordia, in Argentina.

## FOOD AND RESTAURANTS

Uruguay is one of the largest consumers of beef in the world: the man in the street will not usually consider that he has had a full meal without a steak *churrasco*. Uruguayans are, therefore, experts at providing a wide variety of delicious grills, barbecues and stew, each more succulent than the next—and at astonishingly low prices. *Parrilada* is a mixed grill fit for a king: steak, beef chunks, chicken and sausages grilled over a *parrilla*. *Puchero* is a delicious beef stew, with vegetables, bacon, beans, and sausages. *Carbonada,* another superb meat stew, is made with rice, peaches, raisins and pears. Try *asados* (meat roasted on a spit) and *Churrasco* (a juicy barbecued steak); For dessert, *Dulce de Leche* is a great favorite: it is made with boiled milk and sugar; or try a *Torta* (pastry) with whipped cream. And though an average meal will have three courses, you'll find that your check, even in an expensive restaurant, will rarely exceed US$2.00. In a medium-priced restaurant you can expect to pay about US$1.20 and in an inexpensive one, as little as US$0.75. Good snack foods are pizzas and delicious beef sandwiches called *chivitos*. As dinner is served late, from 9-11, you will probably enjoy an afternoon tea at a *confitería*—there are many of these attractive tea rooms around the Avenida 18 de Julio, where you can have a *mate* and really light pastry or a strawberry tart. In Punta del Este, by the way, meals are served even later: lunch is from 2-4pm.

There are some splendid restaurants in Montevideo: **El Águila** (Plaza Independencia, near the Solis Theater) where you should try the house specialty, rich with shrimps, followed by *gâteau águila*; **Victoria Palace Hotel,** has international and local food; **Morini** (Ciudadela 1229) does a gorgeous entrecote steak; **La Brasas** (San José 909); **El Fogón** (San José 1080); **Tahiti** (Boulevard Antigas); **Mio Tio** (Rivera 2697), where the *parrilladas* and other typical dishes will certainly not diasppoint you. For chicken and fish, **El Galeón** (Leyenda Patria 3096, in Playa Pocitos) is unbeatable. If you fancy fondue and pork chops, go to **El Bungalow Suizo** (Sol 150, in Playa Carraso) and you must try the *smörgåsbord* at the **Bristol Hotel** (Rambla R de Mexico 6995). **Club Alemán** (Paysandu 935) for good German and local food; **Hong Kong Restaurant** (8 de Octubre 2691) for a Chinese meal; **Catari** (Colonia 971); **Cicillo** (Acevedo Diaz 1161) and **Anacapri** (Mercedes 871) are good Italian Restaurants. A very elegant place for a business lunch is the **Golf Club** where you must try *perdices en escabeche* (partridge boiled in oil and spices)—the view from here is superb.

## DRINKING TIPS

Uruguayan light beers are called *rubia,* darker beers are called *negra.* Made of barley, they have plenty of body and a delicious flavor. Local wines are very good and very inexpensive: you will not be let down by a bottle of *Cabernet* or *Santa Rosa* with your

Chateaubriand steak; or by a bottle of *Chablis* or *Mil Botellas* with your fillet of sole. Local champagnes worthy of respect are *Faraut* and *Fond de Cave*. *Grappa,* a delicious and very potent brandy made from the residue of grapes, is excellent as an apértif, but you should also try *Caña*, an equally potent brandy made from the sugar cane. *Mate,* a stronge tea made of yerba leaves, is very popular, specially between meals; the gaucho seems to carry his silver-edged gourd and silver straw for *mate* drinking wherever he goes. Ladies are welcome in bars (except in the harbor area) but here's a tip: locals are usually rather shocked if they see American wives paying their own bills, when traveling with their husbands. You can enjoy a good drink at the bar of the **Hotel Columbia Palace** overlooking the River Plate, or the sophisticated **Carnival Room** at the Victoria Palace Hotel.

## ENTERTAINMENT

The Government of Uruguay not only runs its own ballet, opera and theater companies and subsidizes individual artists and theaters, but it also engages international touring companies while in Uruguay, on a non-profit making basis. The result is that tickets are surprisingly inexpensive and there is a lively interest in the performing arts. **Solís Theater** (at the Plaza Independencia) houses most visiting international companies: it is also the home of the excellent **Comedia Nacional.** There are also experimental and exciting theater groups in Montevideo, performing in Spanish, of course, and if you are a lover of the theater, you should certainly not miss a performance at the **Teatro del Centro** or at the **Teatro Circular,** both theaters-in-the-round. There is an imaginative children's theater at the Hotel Victoria Plaza on Saturday and Sunday afternoons. The **Sodre Theater** (Mercedes and Andes) is the city's main concert hall for ballet and music—there are two state symphony orchestras. The opera season here is in August and September. During the summer, you can enjoy a fine open-air concert at the **Rodó Theater** in Parque Rodó and in the Parque Rivera, where the *pericón,* a stately and lovely old Uruguayan dance can be enjoyed by the public. Movie going is a great favorite with Uruguayans. There are splendid movie houses and movies are shown with original soundtracks. Tickets are available three days before the performance at the movie box office, so there is no need to line up. Matinees at 3, evening performances at 6 and 9pm—for current programs, look up *The Montevidian*. For late night entertainment, go to the **Parador del Cerro,** at El Cerro, for dinner, music and floorshows. **Lancelot, Scrum 5** and **Tom-Tom** are pleasant nightclubs. **Anacapri** (Mercedes 871), where the waiters and customers sing along with the show, is great fun. **Zum Zum** (Edificio Panamericano) is a lively disco always packed at weekends while **Baiuca** (Benito Blanco and Juan Maria Perez) is deliciously dark and intimate—but the music is wild! If you like tango or gaucho songs, you must go to **La Cumparsita** (Carlos Gardel and Cuareim) or the **Teluria** (Cuareim), which are very popular with young people. Open from midnight to 5am, the small **S640** (Sarandí 640) has flamenco music and strip tease. If you want to try your luck at baccarat or roulette before going to Punta del Este, there are casinos at the **Hotel Parque Casino** (Playa Ramirez) and the **Hotel Carrasco,** near the Airport.

## SHOPPING

The main shopping area in Montevideo is around the **Avenida 18 de Julio** and the **Plaza Independencia.** Shops are open from 9-7 from Monday to Friday, but on Saturdays they close at 12:30 pm. Best buys are leather goods and furs. Antelope, sealskin, pony, nutria (the best in the world, with thicker, longer, softer fur and better color), *nonato* (the soft skin of unborn calf), sea-wolf, leather and suede jackets, handbags, gloves, stoles, even ostrich bags are all incredibly good value. The best furriers in town are **Victoria Pieles** (at the Victoria Plaza Hotel); **Paris-New York** (Avenida 18 de Julio 1114); **Los Renos** (Avenida 18 de Julio 915). At **King's** (Plaza Independencia 729) or at the **Montevideo Leather Factory** (Plaza Independencia 832) you can pick a ready-made suede or leather jacket off the rack, or have one made to order. For leather handbags, alligator wallets, belts, cigarette cases and other goods, go to **Expres** (Plaza Independencia 1327) or **Faborelli,** in Madrilene. Also very good values are jewelry and precious stones: topazes, tourmalines; the locally mined amethysts are said to be the darkest in the world. **H. Stern** has a shop at the Victoria Plaza Hotel; **Brela** (Avenida 18 de Julio 928) and **Freccero** (25 de Mayo 561) are strongly recommended. Sweaters made from a cashmere-like wool called burma (from US$8), woollen skirts, ponchos are also good buys: look for these goods in the large department stores like **Angenscheidt** (Avenida 18 de Julio 985); **Soler** (Avenida 18 de Julio 958) and **La Opera** (Calle Sarandi). There are a large number of shops selling handicrafts and souvenirs like gaucho dolls (about US$3) silver *mate* gourds and *bombillas,* gaucho knives and *bolaedoras,* the stone or metal balls wrapped in leather used by the gauchos to catch ostriches, and many others: **Schiavo** (Avenida Uruguay 1050) and **Manos del Uruguay** (Reconquista 599) are the best. There are branches of top Montevideo stores in Punta del Este.

Two very interesting markets are the **Mercado del Puerto** (in front of the harbor) and the **Feria de Tristan Navaja**, held in the open air on Sundays—ask about this flea market at the Government Tourist Office. Major stores will pack and ship purchases for you, but bargaining is definitely not a custom in Uruguay.

## SPORTS

**Soccer** and **basketball** are very popular: the Estadio Centenário, in Parque Batlle y Ordoñez is an 80,000 seat stadium where important soccer matches are played. There are also a bicycle race track and grounds for athletic sports in this park. **Polo** at Carrasco Polo Club. **Golf** at the Club del Uruguay and the Cerro Golf Club. Hotel guests of the Victoria Plaza, Lancaster, Carrasco and Parque Hotels are granted guest cards for the Montevideo Golf Club. Punta del Este has the Golf Club of Cantegril. There are several **tennis** clubs in Montevideo and beach resorts and there is a yearly rugby football championship. Montevideo has a Cricket

Club. **Water sports** are very popular in summer and there are year round swimming clubs in Montevideo, the best of which is the Neptuno. **Surfing** in Montevideo, Punta del Este, Maldonado and Rocha from November to April; **yachting** in Montevideo and Punta del Este from October to May (Uruguayo, Nautilus and Punta del Este Yacht Clubs). **Deep sea fishing** is excellent throughout the year and there is superb fishing for the fresh water dorado at Salto and Paysandú. You can hunt the wild boar from December to March. An exciting event during the Easter holidays is the Domas **rodeo.**

## WHAT TO SEE

**Montevideo:** One of the first things that will strike you about Monte (as the English colony affectionately call the capital) is a marvelous feeling of openness. There are many wide avenues and tree-lined streets, parks, gardens and plazas surrounded by pleasant flat roofed houses and attractive skyscrapers. The city is not particularly notable for its public buildings and once you have seen the pink granite pillars, mosaic floors and historical murals in the **Palacio Legislativo:** the obligatory **Cathedral,** in the oldest square in the city, **Plaza Constitución;** the **Teatro Solís** and the **Museum of Natural History** (open Tues, Thur, Sun—2-5pm) in the Plaza Independencia; and once you have inspected the few really interesting monuments such as the obelisk to the 1810 Constitutional Assembly (18 de Julio and Boulevard Antigas) and the statue of the Gaucho by Zorilla de San Martin, in the Avenida 18 de Julio, you can really start enjoying Montevideo. First of all there are the beautifully kept parks: **Parque Batlle y Ordoñez,** at the end of Avenida 18 de Julio, is a delightful spot for a picnic. Here you will find **La Carreta** (The Oxcart), a monument by the sculptor Bellini in honor of the early Uruguayan settlers; three yokes of oxen pulling a covered wagon. Not far from this park is the zoo and the modern **Planetarium,** one of the best in South America. Then go to **El Prado,** a really glorious park along the Avenida Agraciada: there are lakes, grottoes, impeccable lawns and a rose garden that would do an Englishman proud: there are no less than 850 varieties! During the **Semana del Turista** (Tourist Week), horse-breaking competitions are held in El Prado. Most beautiful of them all is **Parque Rodó,** on Rambla Presidente Wilson, with its beautiful lake where you can go canoeing around delightful little islands—if you're feeling particularly romantic you can hire a gondola! Take a stroll around the open air theater while the kids enjoy themselves in the children's playground. Take them to the amusement center, too. In Parque Rodó you will find the National Museum of Fine Arts (open every day from 1-5pm, except Mondays) where you can see paintings by Juan Manuel Blanes, Pedro Figari and other Uruguayan artists.

Half an hour from the center of town is the **Tablada,** which is a must: very early in the morning Gauchos on horseback bring their cattle to market. In his baggy trousers, tight fitting shirt and hand-embroidered jacket, with the traditional black broad-brimmed hat and black boots, and carrying a silver handled rawhide whip, the legendary gaucho is held in great respect—he is also the back-bone of the country's economy. Make sure you see him by arriving at the Tablada before 8am.

Before going to the beaches, there is something else you really must do: at the western end of Horseshoe Bay and rising 388 feet above Montevideo is the **Cerro:** legend has it that during Magellan's historic voyage around South America, the lookout on board his ship sighted this isolated hill and shouted to his comrades *'Monte videu!"* (meaning 'I saw a hill,' in Portuguese)—hence the name of the city. At the top of the Cerro stands the **oldest lighthouse** in the country (1804) and from the fort, which is a Military Museum, you'll get an unforgettable view of the **River Plate Estuary** and the surrounding countryside.

Tours of Montevideo can be arranged through Cot (Sarandí 699); Tudet (Julio Herrara y Obes 1338, tel: 987921); Viajes Cynsa (18 de Julio 1120) and Onda. There are also half-day tours to nearby *estancias,* working ranches, where you can see the gaucho on his own ground, rounding up steers, drinking grappa at the *estancia* bar or just riding through the plains.

## EASTWARD ALONG THE COAST

Uruguay is famous for its 'Riviera'—over 200 miles of glorious beaches, with their clear sands and unpolluted waters, a major attraction for the 3,000,000 tourists who visit the country every year. Montevideo itself boasts eight delightful beaches along the **Rambla Naciones Unidas.** Among them **Playa Ramirez,** the nearest to the city center and the most crowded; the more fashionable **Playa Pocitos,** with smart apartment houses and restaurants; and the **Hermitage Hotel,** single from US$6.50; **Puerto Bucéo,** where there is a Yacht Club and the Oceanographic Museum; **Playa de Los Ingleses,** beneath the pleasant Virgilio Park and the most beautiful of them all, **Playa Carrasco,** which is backed by a thick forest, now a national park. Here you will find the imposing **Hotel Carrasco.**

Further east, along the 'Interbalnearia' road, lie the pretty resorts of **Atlantida, La Floresta, Solís,** where the fishing is superb **(Hotel Solís Golf)** and **Piriápolis,** a very popular resort with a yacht club and a country club, a golf course, an auto racing track and many fine hotels **(Argentino,** with a casino, **Embassy, Rex** are recommended). Behind the town, volcanic hills rise 1000 feet above the sea —there are mineral springs and on top of Cerro San Antonio there's a very nice restaurant and tea room; **Maldonado,** which has some very interesting colonial remains.

**Punta del Este,** 90 miles from Montevideo, is the most famous and dazzling of Uruguayan beach resorts. Laguna del Sauce is the airport for this international pleasure spot where every two years the **Punta del Este Film Festival** is held: there are flights from Montevideo and direct from Buenos Aires. **Onda** (Plaza Libertad—tel: 92333) has several buses a day from the capital: return fare is under US$2. Situated on a peninsula, it has miles of stunning beaches, including the calm **Playa Mansa,** facing the bay and the **Playa Brava,** on the other side of the peninsula, with large breakers absolutely ideal for surfing.There is a yacht club, and the many sports facilities include excellent fishing in three nearby lakes and on the river Maldonado. **Lobos Island,** within sight of the town, is home for nearly 400,000 seals. Night life revolves around the casinos but there are also some very pleasant nightclubs: **Mau Mau, El Carousel, My Drink, Club de las Grutas.** First-class restaurants are the **Marisconéa, Catari** (Gorlero Avenida), **Bungalow Suizo** (Avenida Roosevelt) and the restaurant at the **San Rafael Hotel** (Rambla Lorenzo Battle —tel: 82161). An ideal place to stay is the **Cantegril Country Club,** which is beautifully situated in wooded grounds. You can rent a bungalow complete with kitchen, living room with fireplace, bedrooms and bath for about US$10 per person. You can also rent apartments at the **Edificio Santos Dumont** and the **Edificio Lafayette;** or you can stay at the luxurious Tudor-style **San Rafael Hotel** the less expensive **Playa, La Cigale, London**

and **Marbela Hotels.** The season is from December to March and advance booking is essential.

Further east lie **Rocha,** near the colonial fort of **Santa Teresa, La Paloma,** another popular beach resort, **La Caronilla,** where ocean fishing is superb (shark, skate, black corvina) and **Chuy** through the middle of which runs the border with Brazil.

Other places of interest in Uruguay are **Colonia,** on the River Plate, a pleasure resort with appealing colonial buildings **(Hotel Esperanza)**; the beautiful **Colonia Suiza,** a Swiss settlement ideal for autumn holidays. In nearby Nueva Helvecia, you can buy real Swiss musical boxes—made locally. Perhaps the prettiest town in Uruguay is **Mercedes,** 170 miles from Montevideo, a livestock center and holiday resort. **Salto** (population 60,000) is a center for oranges and citrus fruit and mines, set in a most delightful countryside with wooded hills which supply the granite and marble used to construct the Legislative Palace in Montevideo (**Hotel Parador Salus,** eight miles out of town; **Garibaldi, Verdun**).

## SOURCES OF FURTHER INFORMATION

**Pan Am Office.** Avenida 18 de Julio 945, Montevideo, and any **Pan Am** Office around the world; **The National Tourist Commission Information Bureau** is at 18 de Julio 845, Montevideo; The **Uruguayan Consulate,** 17 Battery Place, New York, NY 10004; and The **Embassy of Uruguay,** 48 Lennox Gardens, London SW1.

# Venezuela

## WHAT'S SPECIAL

After a sneak preview by Columbus, the Spaniards came to Venezuela in 1499. One hundred years later, Sir Walter Raleigh, who traveled more than 400 miles up the River Orinoco in search of his golden city of El Dorado, said he had "never seen a more beautiful country, nor more lively prospect" and begged his Queen to possess it. Venezuela, however, remained firmly in the hands of Spain until the War of Independence, when Simon Bolívar and his revolutionaries (including a contingent of veterans from the Peninsular War, recruited in London) defeated the Spanish at the battle of Carabobo, in 1821. But Venezuela, now an independent republic, had her "lively prospects" still unfulfilled. The miracle happened in 1917: oil was discovered on Lake Maracaibo.

The country is now the third largest producer of oil in the world and the richest country in South America. Venezuelans enjoy the highest standard of living, the highest income per capita and the finest highway system on the Continent. They also enjoy a country with superb beaches backed by lovely mountains and forests that hide gold, great game hunting, and the world's highest waterfall, among other delights. Caracas, the capital, is a modern cosmopolitan city comparable to New York, Paris or London, with superb hotels and restaurants, excellent, if somewhat expensive shopping centers, and lively nightclubs. Visitors are welcomed not only by the people themselves, who are friendly and *simpático*, but also by the government, which publishes maximum excursion and transportation rates and solicits complaints in case of non-compliance. Perhaps Sir Walter Raleigh in searching for El Dorado, was going in the right direction.

## COUNTRY BRIEFING

**Size:** 352,150 square miles
**Population:** 10,200,000
**Capital:** Caracas
**Capital Population:** 2,600,000

**Climate:** Venezuela is a tropical country but climate is largely a matter of altitude. Caracas, 3,418 feet above sea level, has summer temperatures in the 80's, but evenings are cool. In winter when temperatures can fall to about 48°, the weather is mild and pleasant. In Maracaibo, on the coast, the average temperature is 83°. The rainy season is June-November and the dry season December through March.

**WEATHER IN CARACAS**—Lat N10°30′—Alt 3,418 ft

| Temp | Jan | Feb | Mar | Apr | May | Jun | Jul | Aug | Sep | Oct | Nov | Dec |
|---|---|---|---|---|---|---|---|---|---|---|---|---|
| Ave Low | 56° | 56° | 58° | 60° | 62° | 62° | 61° | 61° | 61° | 61° | 60° | 58° |
| Ave High | 75° | 77° | 79° | 81° | 80° | 78° | 78° | 79° | 80° | 79° | 77° | 78° |
| Days of No Rain | 24 | 26 | 28 | 26 | 22 | 16 | 16 | 16 | 17 | 19 | 17 | 21 |

**Government:** A constitutional republic.

**Language:** The official language is Spanish, but many people can speak English, especially in Caracas and Maracaibo.

**Religion:** 90% of the population is Roman Catholic. The Caracas American Church is at Avenida La Arboleda 54, El Bosque; the Anglican Church is in the San Roman section of La Mercedes. There are also Lutheran and Baptist churches. The main synagogue is the Union Israelita (Avenida Marqués del Toro, San Bernadino); B'nai Brith has a chapel on Transversal 9 and Avenida 7, Altamira.

**Currency:** The Bolivar; 100 centimos = 1 Bolivar

| | 50c | Bs1 | Bs10 | Bs20 | Bs50 | Bs100 | Bs200 | Bs300 |
|---|---|---|---|---|---|---|---|---|
| US(Dollars.Cents) | .11 | .22 | 2.28 | 4.57 | 11.44 | 22.88 | 45.76 | 68.64 |
| UK(Pounds.Pence) | .04 | .09 | .97 | 1.94 | 4.85 | 9.70 | 19.41 | 29.12 |

**Public Holidays:**

New Year's Day, 1 Jan
40 Days before Easter
St Joseph's Day, 9 Mar
Easter Thursday
Good Friday
Easter Saturday
Declaration of National Independence, 19 Apr
Labor Day, 1 May
Battle of Carabobo, 24 Jun
Independence Day, 5 Jul
Birth of Simon Bolívar, 24 Jul
Discovery of America, 12 Oct
Anniversary of the Death of the Liberator, 17 Dec
Christmas Day, 25 Dec

## HOW TO GET THERE

Fly Pan Am direct to Caracas, Maiquetia Airport, from Philadelphia via Baltimore and San Juan; Port au Prince via Santo Domingo and San Juan; San Francisco via Los Angeles, Guatemala City and Panama City; Houston via Mexico City, Guatemala City, San José and Panama City; Barranquilla via Maracaibo; Rio de Janeiro via São Paulo; direct flights from Miami, New York and Buenos Aires. Flying time from Philadelphia is 5½ hours; Baltimore, 4¾ hours; San Juan, 1½ hours; Port au Prince, 3 hours; Santo Domingo, 2¼ hours; San Francisco, 9¾ hours; Los Angeles, 8½ hours; Guatemala City, 4 hours; Panamá City, 2 hours; Houston, 7¾ hours; Mexico City, 5¾ hours; San José, 3 hours; Rio de Janeiro, 6½ hours; São Paulo, 5½ hours; Barranquilla, 1¾ hours; Maracaibo, 1 hour; Miami, 3 hours; New York, 4½ hours; Buenos Aires, 6½ hours.

## REQUIREMENTS FOR ENTRY AND CUSTOMS REGULATIONS

Citizens of Belgium, Canada, Denmark, German Federal Republic, Netherlands, Sweden, Switzerland, UK and USA, need only a smallpox vaccination certificate and a tourist card, obtainable free of charge from Pan Am or a Venezuelan Consulate on production of proof of citizenship, two small photos (1½" x 1½") and a ticket to leave Venezuela again. The tourist card is valid for eight days and can be extended up to 30 days. If you want to stay longer you will need a tourist letter, issued by Venezuelan Consulates. Other nationals require passport and visa.

Visitors may bring, duty-free: two quarts liquor; 400 cigarettes; 50 cigars; personal belongings including camera, typewriter etc., and a reasonable number of personal gifts. If you want to take your car, notify the Venezuelan Consul, who will register details about it. Firearms are not allowed into the country. There are no restrictions as to the amount of foreign currency that may be brought in or taken out of the country.

## AIRPORT INFORMATION

The International Airport for Caracas is Maiquetia, 12 miles from the city center, on the coast. Though there is no bus service to a downtown terminal, taxis are plentiful. The fare to Caracas is Bs35 (about US$8), but you can also travel in *Por Puesto* (collective taxis) which are much less expensive: Bs5 (about US$1) per person. But remember that these five-passenger taxis leave only when they are full and that they travel along fixed routes, picking up and dropping off passengers on the way. You will find a hotel reservation counter at the airport; tip the porter Bs2 per piece of luggage. There is no arrival tax but you will be charged Bs8 departure tax.

## ACCOMMODATIONS

There are a number of international hotels in many Venezuelan cities, with luxurious accommodations and many extra facilities—air conditioning (a blessing on the coast), a panoramic view of the city, tropical gardens, a swimming pool or other sports facilities, an international restaurant or a nightclub on the premises. TV or piped music in your room. But even the less expensive guest houses have comfortable clean rooms. At most hotels a 10% service charge will be added to your bill, but a tip is still expected. If you need help finding accommodations, ring the **Hotel Reservation Center** at the airport (tel: 0313605). Hotels in Caracas:

**Single from US$19 (Bs 83); double from US$23 (Bs 101)**

**Avila Hotel** Avenida Washington
**Caracas Hilton Hotel** Avenida Libertador/Sur 25—Apartado 6380
**Humboldt** Sabana Grande
**HOTEL TAMANACO** Avenida Las Mercedes

**Single from US$11 (Bs 48); double from US$15 (Bs 66)**

**Las Americas Hotel** Calle Los Cerritos, Bello Monte

**Macuto-Sheraton Hotel** Apartado 65, La Guaira
**Potomac Hotel** Avenida Vollmer (AP)
**Tampa Hotel** Avenida Francisco Solano López 9, Sabana Grande
**Single from US$5 (Bs 22); double from US$7.25 (Bs 32)**

**Hotel del Comercio** Dolores A Puente Soublette
**Waldorf Hotel** Avenida La Industria, San Bernardino

## USEFUL INFORMATION

**Banks:** Open 8:30-11:30 and 2:30-5:30. There are branches in major cities and many towns. You can also change foreign currency at *Casas de Cambio* and hotels; restaurants and shops will take travelers' checks. The First National Bank of New York has a branch in the Edificio Torre del Este (Avenida Francisco de Miranda).

**Postage:** Stamps obtainable from post offices (*Estación de Correos*); the main one is on Avenida Urdaneta, corner of Carmelitas; stamps also from the desk in some hotels. Mailboxes are blue and have an inscription of *Correos.*

**Telephone Tips:** Phones in restaurants and cafés as well as public booths; coin operated; lift the receiver, wait for dialing tone, deposit a *medio* (25 centimos coin) then make call. Useful numbers:

**Pan Am office,** 54 70 46/7
55 81 01/11
**Airport Information,** 031 50 84
**Directories,** 103
**Time,** 19
**Weather,** 41 02 79
**Police,** 111/115 or 116
**Fire Department,** 113
**Overseas Operator,** 122
**Tourist Office,** 72 40 71 or
72 38 81

**Newspapers:** The English-language newspaper is the *Daily Journal,* the best in Latin America and a must for the visitor. You can also get the *Wall Street Journal* and *New York Times* (a day after publication). *Time* magazine and other English-language publications are also available, while *Radio Liberator* broadcasts in English for several hours a day.

**Tipping:** At restaurants 10% service charge will be added to your bill (as well as an extra Bs1 to Bs5 for the *cubierto*—bread, rolls, butter etc.—so you may as well enjoy them) but another 10% tip is expected. Give porters Bs2; hairdressers, 10% or more of check. Taxi drivers are not tipped, neither are museum guides.

**Electricity:** 110 volts, 60 cycles AC, throughout the country.

**Laundry:** Dry-cleaning and laundry services are excellent and very reliable: good 24-hour service in hotels *lavanderías* (laundries) in major cities. Hotels also have good express services (dry-cleaning a suit, about Bs5; laundering a shirt, 50 centimos).

**Hairdressing:** Most first-class hotels have excellent salons (shampoo and set about Bs22, man's haircut about Bs5).

**Photography:** Equipment and films are readily available throughout the country and prices are reasonable. Black and white film costs about Bs3.50 and you can have it developed in 24 hours. A color film costs Bs8 and will take 36 hours process time.

**Clubs:** Lions, Rotary, and Junior Chamber of Commerce.

**Babysitting:** Most hotels have services. US baby foods and disposable diapers available in Caracas.

**Toilets:** Can be found in hotels, restaurants and nightclubs. Ladies, *Damas*; men, *Caballeros.*

**Health:** Many Venezuelan doctors have trained abroad and speak English—you will find some advertise on page 2 of *The Daily Journal*—but fees are high. Private hospital rooms cost at least Bs109 (US$25) a day, if not more. Toiletries, pharmaceuticals and medicines are easily available. On Sundays there is always one chemist open in each district of Caracas. Water in all main towns is chlorinated and safe to drink, but in rural areas drink only bottled water. If you are going to the Orinoco Valley, you should be inoculated against typhoid and yellow fever.

## TRANSPORTATION

Although there is a bus service with very reasonable fares (25 centimos) the most popular form of city transport is *Por Puesto* (collective taxis). These sedans have fixed routes that cover the main parts of the city; you will see a printed sign on the windshield of the car, telling you its final stop. The fare is usually Bs1. Simply raise your arm when you see one and it will stop for you. Taxis are also readily available: you can flag one down in the street or phone a taxi stand. As there are no meters, ask the driver for the price of the journey before setting off. The average fare in Caracas is Bs5 but after midnight will cost more. If you wish to rent a car, go to Hertz (tel: 727255/329439) or Avis (tel: 325062) who have branches at the airport as well as in Caracas: you can use the drivers license from your own country. The average daily rate is Bs66 plus 43 centimos per kilometer—gas included. Venezuela has fine highways and international road signs are in operation, so a rented car is worth it here. But remember: rush hours at noon and 2pm (siesta time) as well as in the mornings and evenings. Hourly rates for a chauffeur-driven car are Bs22, but an English-speaking driver will cost no extra.

There is no railroad service as such, but long-distance buses are air-conditioned and very comfortable. Buses leave for all the main towns in Venezuela from a terminal in the center of Caracas. **AVENSA** (Esquina El Chorro, Edificio 29—tel: 419161) is the largest domestic airline, with regular flights to all parts of the country, and all-in tickets and excursions. Ask about the 17-day unlimited air travel ticket under the Conozca Venezuela plan for US$80, before arriving in the country. This worthwhile service is not available from within Venezuela. Aerotaxis are also available. Flying times from Caracas: Mérida, ¾ hour; Maracaibo, 45 minutes (by jet); Isla Margarita, 1 hour. There are ferry services from La Guaira harbor (Caracas) to Isla Margarita and from Puerto la Cruz and Cumana to Isla Margarita.

## FOOD AND RESTAURANTS

Dining in Caracas is an unforgettable experience, even if you do not consider yourself a gourmet. There are splendid and highly atmospheric international restaurants, but if you do not sample Venezuelan cooking you will miss out. For starters, try real turtle soup or avocados stuffed with shrimps, and then order the *hallacas*—small pieces of chicken, pork, beef, seasoned with olives, raisins and onions, rolled into a layer of corn dough, wrapped in plantain leaves and boiled for several hours (plantain is a banana-like fruit). Or try the *sancocho,* a thick chicken, beef or fish soup with vegetables; or the *pabellon*—black beans, white rice, fried plantain and shredded meat. *Mondongo* will make you change your mind about tripe; it is made of cowheel and tripe, plus lots of vegetables. If you like steak, order a *punta trasera,* served very tender, with hot red pepper and cool green pepper relishes. And if you enjoy seafood, you will not forget the *cazuela de mariscos*; baked clams, mussels, lobster, shrimp and squid served with hot creole sauce. For dessert, try *huevos chimbos,* egg yolk boiled and bottled in sugar syrup, or *cascos de guayaba con queso crema*—guavas in syrup with cream cheese. With your meal, instead of bread have *arepa,* a round corn cake, also sold as a snack with ham, pork, cheese or fish filling at *areperas* all over town.

For specialists in Venezuelan cooking go to **La Casa Grande** (El Rosal); **Los Porches** (Avenida La Castellana—tel: 33 43 27); **El Porton** (Avenida Pichincha, El Rosal—tel: 71 60 71); and **Tarzilandia** (Avenida San Juan Boscol—tel: 33 28 80). **Le Gourmet** at the Hotel Tamanaco is wholly international, while **Henry IV** (Avenida Los Jabillos 35—tel: 74 32 42), **Hector's** (Avenida Casanova—tel: 71 70 30), **El Sibarita** (Avenida Principal La Castellana—tel: 33 42 60), and **Bagatelle** (Edificio La Hacienda—tel: 91 41 40), are all excellent for French cuisine. Go to **Franco's** (Avenida los Jabillos, La Florida—tel: 72 09 96) and **Casa Italia** (San Bernadino, near the Pan Am office—tel: 54 64 34) for Italian dishes, and **Kamon** (Avenida Casanova, Bello Monte—tel: 76 96 71) for Japanese food. **Dragon Verde** (Avenida Maturin, Los Cedros—tel: 71 84 04) and **El Palmar** (Plaza Lincoln—tel: 76 12 20) for Chinese meals and **Lili Marlene** (Avenida Tamanaco, El Rosal—tel: 31 09 59) is a good German restaurant. **Lee Hamilton's** famous Steak House (Avenida San Felipe, La Castellana—tel: 32 52 27) for steaks, and **Shorton Grill** (Avenida Liberator—tel: 71 10 52) for Argentine barbecues.

An average meal will be made up of three courses. Breakfast is served from 7-9; lunch 12-2; dinner any time after 8. A meal for one in an expensive restaurant will cost around US$15 (Bs66); in a medium priced restaurant US$7 (Bs31); and in an inexpensive restaurant, about US$3 (Bs13). But if you want a snack or a light meal you can get hamburgers and hot-dogs, soups and sandwiches, in a variety of places—**Le Drugstore,** Centro Comercial. **Chacaito** and **Tropiburger,** all over town, are very popular during lunchtime. Kentucky Fried Chicken, translated into **Pollo Kentucky,** is doing a great business, but do not forget the local *areperas. Efe* and *Tio Rico* are makes of excellent ice cream, but if you are on the beach, oysters and clams sprinkled with lemon juice are a must.

## DRINKING TIPS

Cardenal and Solera are probably the best Venezuelan beers, but Polar and Caracas are more popular. Local rums and gin are also excellent and inexpensive. Try a *poncha crema* (made with milk, eggs, sugar and rum), or a rum punch before your dinner. You might also sample an assortment of non-alcoholic brews like the *chicha* (made from milk and rice), or the *chicha andina* (made from fermented rice), or *guarapos* of cane, or pineapple and other fermented tropical fruit. Your whisky and soda will cost at least US$1.48 (Bs6.50) (much more in a nightclub), and a bottle of ordinary red wine will cost about US$6.86 (Bs30). Bars and cafes are open from 10am to the small hours of the morning and ladies are welcome, but young people under 18 cannot be served alcoholic drinks. Popular drinking spots are the **automercados,** in all the big cities, the open air cafés and the **cervecerias,** where you can also dance. **El Papagayo** (Centro Comercial Chacaito) and the **Café Piccolo** (calle Real de Sabana Grande) are very popular.

## ENTERTAINMENT

Like any large cosmopolitan city, Caracas comes to life after dark. There are concerts, recitals and ballets at the **Teatro Municipal,** where international stars often appear. The opera season is in June. Concerts too at the **Sala Metropolitan de Conciertos.** Exciting live (Spanish-speaking) theater at the **Teatro Municipal,** the **Ateneo de Caracas,** the **Teatro Alberto dePaz y Mateo** and the **Aula Magna,** in the Ciudad Universitaria. An excellent non-professional theater group playing in English is the **Caracas Theater Club** (Calle Chiracoa in San Roman, La Mercedes district).

If you would rather go to a movie house, recent movies are shown with their original soundtracks, all over town; programs start at 5:30, 7:30 and 10. For a complete guide to the social and cultural life of the city, current programs and reviews, look in the *Daily Journal.*

Late at night your choice of entertainment is vast. A safe starting point is the **Hipocamp** (Centro Commercial Chacaito 25—tel: 75 50 96) for the best dance orchestra in Caracas; or the **Cota 880** on the 15th floor of the Hilton Hotel, overlooking the city; **Teorema** (Centro Capriles Plaza Venezuela—tel: 72 08 97) and **Mon Petit** (Edificio Autocomercial, Plaza Sur Altamira—tel: 33 00 06) are dark and intimate; **Mi Vaca y Yo**—My Cow and I—(Antigua Carretera de Baruta—tel: 91 86 51) is a French spot with an outdoor farm setting; Emilia the cow parades across the dance floor at midnight. **La Cueva de Monterrey** (Avenida Humboldt) is a flamenco club while **Blow Up** (Avenida Avila Sur Altamira) is a lively disco, packed at weekends. The **Salon Naiquata** (at the Hotel Tamanaco) has a good floor show. Most places will let you in only if you are accompanied by one of the opposite sex, and men should wear a jacket and tie. But **L'Insolite** (Avenida Tamanaco) is very trendy and full of young people and you can wear your levis. Another student spot with good folk music during the week, is **Underground**

(Centro Comercial del Este). A note of warning: at some of these nightclubs drinks are very expensive and your check could be quite staggering. Gentlemen: if you are on your own, you need not be for long at **Todo Paris** (Gran Avenida Sabana Grande).

**SHOPPING**

The main shopping areas in Caracas are the **Sabana Grande,** along the Avenida Lincoln, the **Centro Comercial Chacaito,** Sabana Grande, and the **Centro Comercial Beco,** near the Tamanaco Hotel. Shopping in Caracas is on a par with the major cities of the world: you will find international boutiques, large department stores, almacenas and supermarkets, excellent shoe shops and first-class jewelers—but prices are quite high. Shops open 8:30-12 and 2:30-6:30 or 7, Mon-Sat. Good buys are shoes and clothing—you can have a suit made to order and it will be ready in a few days. Handcraft items and souvenirs are plentiful, some of them exquisite: rugs, ceramics, Indian masks, bead necklaces. Chocano gold is used to make delightful trinkets for charm bracelets. A beautiful gift is the Hand of Fatima, in ebony and gold or silver; it is said to ward off evil spirits. Or the Cacique coins, honoring the Indians who fought the Conquistadors. Best buys, however, are pearls from Isla Margarita, sold in every jewelry shop in the city: you can get an 18 carat gold pin set with a pearl for as little as Bs22.

The best handicraft stores in Caracas are the **Palacio de Las Industrias** (Calle Real, Sabana Grande) and **Arte Folklórico** (Conde and Principal). There are street markets in all Venezuelan cities and good shopping centers in Maracaibo, Valencia, Maracay, Ciudad Bolívar, Mérida etc.

**SPORTS**

Baseball is a year-round sport in this country and during the winter months major league stars from the US play with Venezuelan teams in the Stadium of the **Ciudad Universitaria.** There are bullfights every Sunday during the winter—you will find bull rings all over the country. **La Rinconada** is the most lavish racetrack in South America: races on Saturdays and Sundays. On weekdays visitors with tourist cards need to pay only for their caddies at the **Valle Arriba Club** in Caracas and at the **El Junko** and the **Lagunita Golf Clubs,** just outside the city. Special arrangements will also be made for visitors to use club facilities at the **Altamiro** and **Tamanaco** clubs (tennis and swimming) and at the luxurious **Country Club,** which has an 18-hole golf course. There is swimming, surfing, yachting, all year round on the Caribbean and marvelous water skiing and snorkeling off **Margarita Island.** You can arrange to go deep sea fishing at one of the coastal boating clubs or at the **Macuto Sheraton Hotel:** cabin cruisers with a captain and *marinero* can be hired for Bs595 (about US$136), for a full day at sea, Bs398 (US$91) for half a day. Rates include tackle, bait, ice and soft drinks. For fishing along the coast you can hire a boat with inboard motor (including tackle and guide) for Bs60 (US$13.65) per hour. Maximum of two persons. There is splendid mountaineering, game hunting and fresh-water fishing inland (season from

March 17 to 30 September) and skiing from May to October. The cockfighting tournament of San Juan de los Moros, 70 miles from Caracas, is well worth the trip.

## WHAT TO SEE

**Caracas:** Known as the "City of Eternal Spring," Caracas has wide avenues and highways and modern architecture. The finest examples are the **Centro Simon Bolívar,** the **Military Academy** and the **Ciudad Universitaria,** with its 174-acre Botanical Gardens (open daily from 8-12 and 2-6) right in the heart of town. But the city also harbors treasures from the colonial past: it was here that Simon Bolívar was born—you can see the **Casa Natal** in Calle Traposos (open 9-12 and 3-5, Tues-Fri; 9-1 Sat and Sun). The **Cathedral,** with its beautiful facade, was built in 1595 and contains paintings by Rubens, among others. It is on the east side of the peaceful and spotless **Plaza Bolívar,** which has its stone walks scrubbed every day. Beautiful churches are the **Iglesia de San Francisco,** where Bolivar was given the title of Liberator in 1813 and **La Basílica de Santa Teresa** containing a miraculous image of the Nazareno de San Pueblo. Museums are usually open 9-12 and 3-5:30 weekdays; 10-2 on Sunday. A must for the visitor is the **Museo Bolívar** (San Jacinto & Traposos) where fascinating relics of the revolution against Spain are kept. The **Museo del Arte Colonial** is a delightful replica of an 18th-century villa, while the **Museo de Bellas Artes** (Avenida Mexico) has works by important international and Venezuelan artists. Opposite the Bellas Artes is the **Museo de Ciencias Naturales,** which has among its many precious items, fine specimens of pre-Columbian ceramics. When you are tired of sightseeing in town, go to the **Parque del Este,** with its beautifully landscaped acres of exotic plants and an artificial lake where you will see a replica of Columbus' ship, the *Santa Maria*. This is a beautiful spot for picnics and the children will love boating on the lake. Here too is the modern **Humboldt Planetarium. Parque El Pinar** is famous for its zoo. Children will also enjoy letting off steam at the **Patinata** rollerskating on top of the Centro Comercial Chacaito.

Take a trip by *Teleférico* (cable car) from Mariperez near the center of the city, to the top of **Mount Avila,** which lies between Caracas and the sea: the view is breathtaking. From here you can go down the 1,267-foot drop to **El Litoral**—the Riviera of Venezuela. Have a swim on one of the many beach resorts: **Macuto, Naiguatá, Catia La Mar** or the exclusive **Carabadella Beach** (closed on Monday).

**Maracay:** An important agricultural and military center, Maracay was first put on the map by the dictator Juan Vincente Gomez (1909-1935), who built **Las Delicias**, a beautiful estate, now a public park with an adjoining zoo. Gomez also built the magnificent **Maestranza Bull Ring**, an exact replica of the one in Seville. Just outside the city is the idyllic **Lake Valencia,** the second largest in Venezuela. With its 22 islands, this lake is superb for boating—but swimming here is not recommended. Twelve miles from Maracay is the **Henri Pittier National Park,** a lush tropical forest where Pittier and C W Beebee spent many

years studying the fauna and flora of the country. The **Hotel Maracay** has an 18-hole golf course, an enormous swimming pool and horseback riding stables.

**Valencia** is an old colonial city, 31 miles from Maracay. It is now the fourth largest city in Venezuela and an important industrial and commercial center; 1,600 feet above sea level, the climate is ideal (average temperature 76°) and many Europeans and Americans live there. Worth seeing are the 18th-century **Cathedral,** the **Capitol** and **Cellis House,** an architectural jewel from colonial days. Eighteen miles from Valencia, on the site of the decisive battle for independence, is the bronze **Monumento de Carabobo,** in honor of Bolivar. Hotels in Valencia: **INTER•CONTINENTAL VALENCIA** (Calle Juan Uslar) with single from US$15.90.

---

**Mérida:** the capital of Merida State, known as *el techo de Venezuela* (Venezuela's rooftop): 76 mountain peaks are crowded into this state, not one of them under 13,000 feet. The city which is 45 minutes by plane from Caracas, lies at an altitude of 5,397 feet and has a mean temperature of 66°. There are tree-lined streets, quiet plazas and colonial buildings. High point of your visit will be an awe-inspiring ride on the cable car to **Pico Espejo** (15,640 feet)—the highest and longest cable car in the world which goes up in four stages. Best time to go is from October-June; cars run from 7-12noon Thursday to Sunday and the round trip, which takes three hours, costs Bs22. But you need not come down straight away—one hour's walk from the last station you can see a magnificent ice cave with crystal ice stalactites and, if you like mountaineering, you can make your way to the **Glacier of Timoncito,** with its dazzling ice caves and steaming springs. Electric storms in the mountains are not uncommon. And from one of the intermediate stations on the cable car you can walk to **Los Nevados,** a village which is higher than Lhasa in Tibet. For further information write to the **Club Andino** (PO Box 66). Hotels in Mérida: **Moruco Hotel,** Santo Domingo, single from US$9.10; **Prado Rio Hotel** from US$10 single.

**Maracaibo:** When early Spanish navigators found the Indian lake dwellings of Maracaibo, they named the country "little Venice": Venezuela. On the shores of the lake, 45 minutes by jet from Caracas, now lies the oil city of Maracaibo enriched by two million barrels of "black gold" taken daily from the wells on the lake. The mean temperature here is 83° and the average humidity is 78%—but you will find air conditioning everywhere, except in the old part of town near the docks, which has changed hardly at all for 100 years, in spite of the prosperity. The city has a completely international population, fine theaters, first-class restaurants (**Mi Vaquita, Rancho Grande** and **El Pescadito,** are recommended). The **Hotel Del Lago** of the Inter•Continental Hotel group, has a fine restaurant, pleasant bar and outstanding nightclub and swimming pool; single room from US$13. Other hotels in Maracaibo are the **Kristof** (Rita, Maracaibo) from US$9 single and **Venecia** (Calle 3, No. 80-23) from US$4.50. Take a trip across the lake through the oil derricks: it is something you will never forget. Or take a sightseeing trip to **Rio Limón** where you can rent a boat and see Indians living in houses made of woven red mats built on stilts.

## EAST OF CARACAS

**Isla Margarita:** In just over one hour's flying time from Caracas you can get to the "pearl island"—a Caribbean paradise of magnificent unspoiled beaches, sheltered bays and peaceful lagoons, where pearl fishing has been carried out for centuries. Apart from enjoying the swimming and sunbathing on the vast sandy beaches, superb underwater fishing, snorkeling and scuba diving and seeing the many sights of the island, you should rent a craft and go sailing on **La Arestinga Lagoon.** This is one of the few places in the world where the ibis escarlata (a heron with red plumage) can be found. Or rent a launch to see the ruins of **New Cadiz,** on Cubagua Island, which was destroyed by a tidal wave in 1541. Best time to visit is from December to March, when the pearling fleet is fishing. **Porlamar,** on the east coast is the island's major resort. On Margarita Island stay at **Bella Vista Hotel,** Porlamar, with single from US$12.

## THE ORINOCO

**Ciudad Bolívar:** This romantic city lies 400 miles from Caracas and 250 miles from the sprawling delta of the Orinoco. This town has an average temperature of 85° and it is the best place to buy anything made of gold: handmade charms and earrings, and the exquisite Venezuelan orchid made of red, yellow and green chocano gold. From here you can go into the jungle to see diamond prospectors and Indian villages or on an excursion to the **Caroni Falls,** one of the tourist treasures of the country. There are also excursions to the magnificent **Angel Falls,** the highest in the world: the waters cascade down 3,212 feet from **Auyantepuy** (Devil Mountain) whose flat top was Conan Doyle's *Lost World* and W H Hudson's *Green Mansions.* **Canaima** is a tourist camp where you can spend the night in a thatched *cabaña,* on the edge of a pink lagoon surrounded by orchid-filled jungles, then go in a dugout canoe to the **Hacha Falls.** In Ciudad Bolívar stay at the **Gran Hotel** (Paseo Orinoco 88), single from US$6. **Avensa Airlines** have inclusive tours to Angel Falls and Canaima from Maiquetia Airport in Caracas, and **Aerotaxis Tanca** have day trips from Ciudad Bolívar. There is big game hunting, superb fishing and water skiing.

**Ciudad Guayana** (Puerto Ordaz): Sixty-seven miles downstream from Ciudad Bolívar, is the "Pittsburgh" of Venezuela, an entirely new metropolis of more than 80,000. One thousand people a month are pouring into this town: here you will find the famous **Cerro Bolívar** open cast-iron mine, the government steel works of Matanzas and the **Guri Dam,** site of the world's largest hydro electric plant. From here you can hire a dug-out canoe and go down river to **Los Castillos**; there are two old forts where children will sell you cannon balls and old Spanish coins which they find in the river. It was here probably that Sir Walter Raleigh's son was killed in the disastrous expedition in 1618. In Ciudad Guayana, stay at **GUAYANA•INTERCONTINENTAL** (Apartado Postal 293, Puerto Ordaz) single from US$15.90.

## SOURCES OF FURTHER INFORMATION

**Pan Am offices:** Edificio Pan American, Puente Urapal, Candelaria, Caracas; Hotel Tamanaco, Las Mercedes, Caracas; Edificio Tropical Avenida 5 de Julio, Maracaibo, and any Pan Am office around the world; **Venezuela National Tourist Board,** Centro Capriles, 7th Floor, Plaza Venezuela, Caracas; **Venezuelan Tourist Office,** 485 Madison Avenue, New York, NY 10022; **Venezuelan Consulate-General,** 71A Park Mansions, Knightsbridge, London SW1.

# Index